WELLESLEY STUDIES IN CRITICAL THEORY,
LITERARY HISTORY, AND CULTURE
VOL. 3

THE CANON IN
THE CLASSROOM

GARLAND REFERENCE LIBRARY
OF THE HUMANITIES
VOL. 1762

WELLESLEY STUDIES IN CRITICAL THEORY, LITERARY HISTORY, AND CULTURE

WILLIAM E. CAIN
General Editor

THE CANON IN THE CLASSROOM

The Pedagogical
Implications of Canon
Revision in American
Literature

edited by

John Alberti

GARLAND PUBLISHING, Inc.
New York & London / 1995

94-394

Library of Congress Cataloging-in-Publication Data

The canon in the classroom : the pedagogical implications of canon revision in American literature /
edited by John Alberti.
   p.   cm. — (Garland reference library of the humanities ; vol. 1762. Wellesley studies in critical
theory, literary history, and culture ; vol. 3)
   Includes bibliographical references and index.
   ISBN 0–8153–1416–7
   1. American literature—Study and teaching.
2. American literature—History and criticism—
Theory, etc.   3. Canon (Literature)   I. Alberti, John.
II. Series: Garland reference library of the humanities ; vol. 1762.   III. Series: Garland reference
library of the humanities.   Wellesley studies in critical
theory, literary history, and culture ; vol. 3.
PS41.C36   1995
810'.7—dc20   94–19101
                                                    CIP

Printed on acid-free, 250-year-life paper
Manufactured in the United States of America

Contents

v

SECTION THREE
The Teacher as Text: Rethinking Authority in the Classroom

Acknowledgments

An essay collection is by its nature a collaborative activity and thus reflects the talents and hard work of many people. Above all I would like to thank the contributors to this volume; whatever merits this work possesses have come from their imaginative and thoughtful writing on canon revision and pedagogy. I would particularly like to express my gratitude to Paul Lauter, who agreed to read the entire manuscript and write a response essay.

This project also owes its existence to William Cain, who spotted my call for papers on this topic in the Modern Language Association newsletter and asked me to consider putting a collection together as part of Garland Publishing's Wellesley Studies in Critical Theory, Literary History, and Culture series. As a first-time editor of an essay collection, I am especially grateful for his encouragement and sponsorship of the project. I would also like to thank Phyllis Korper, Adrienne Makowski, Chuck Bartelt, and Lynn Zelem at Garland for their help and advice.

Grateful thanks are due the following publishers who gave permission to reprint from the following:

"The End of 'American' Literature," by Gregory S. Jay, first appeared in *College English* 3 (1991). Copyright 1991 by the National Council of Teachers of English. Reprinted with permission.

An early version of "Teaching Native American Literature from *The Heath Anthology of American Literature*," by Jeanne Holland, first appeared in the Fall, 1992 issue of *CEA Critic*. Reprinted with permission.

Excerpt from "We the Dangerous" by Janice Mirikitani is reprinted by permission of the author.

Excerpt from "Legal Alien" by Pat Mora is reprinted with permission from the publisher of *Chants* (Houston: Arte Publico Press-University of Houston, 1984).

Excerpt from "Theme for English B" by Langston Hughes, from *Selected Poems of Langston Hughes* (Knopf and Vintage Books, New York), is reprinted by permission of Harold Ober Associates, 425 Madison Avenue, New York, NY 10017.

Excerpt from "Concentration Constellation" by Lawson Fusao Inada, from *Before the War* (copyright 1971 by Lawson Fusao Inada), is reprinted by permission of William Morrow and Company, Inc.

Brief excerpt from *One Hundred Years of Solitude* by Gabriel Garcia Marquez, English translation copyright (c) 1970 by Harper and Row Publishers, Inc., is reprinted by permission of HarperCollins Publishers, Inc.

Many colleagues lent their support and friendship, particularly Kevin Dettmar, who gave me the benefit of his experience in assembling an essay collection, and my fellow teachers and scholars at Northern Kentucky University, including the members of the faculty writing group who read a draft of the introduction and took time that I know they didn't have to write thoughtful and extensive comments.

I owe my biggest debts to my partner Kristin, for her love, tolerance, and keen editorial eye, and our daughter, Martha, also for her love and for the corrective perspective of a child's point of view.

Finally, I would like to thank all the students involved in this project, both my own at University of California, Los Angeles and Northern Kentucky University and those of my contributors, and also the students we all were and are. If there is a recurrent theme to these essays, it is that "teacher" and "student" describe strategic roles we all alternately play in the classroom, not essential and therefore separate states of being. This collection, then, is for all the members of the class.

General Editor's Introduction

The volumes in this series, Wellesley Studies in Critical Theory, Literary History, and Culture, are designed to reflect, develop, and extend important trends and tendencies in contemporary criticism. The careful scrutiny of literary texts in their own right remains today a crucial part of the work that critics and teachers perform: this traditional task has not been devalued or neglected. But other types of interdisciplinary and contextual work are now being done, in large measure as a result of the emphasis on "theory" that began in the late 1960s and early 1970s and that has accelerated since that time. Critics and teachers now examine texts of all sorts—literary and non-literary alike—and, more generally, have taken the entire complex, multi-faceted field of culture as the object for their analytical attention. The discipline of literary studies has radically changed, and the scale and scope of this series is intended to illustrate this challenging fact.

Theory has signified many things, but one of the most crucial has been the insistent questioning of familiar categories and distinctions. As theory has grown in its scope and intensified in importance, it has reoriented the idea of the literary canon: there is no longer a single canon, but many canons. It has also opened up and complicated the meanings of history, and the materials and forms that constitute it. Literary history continues to be vigorously written, but now as a kind of history that intersects with other histories that involve politics, economics, race relations, the role of women in society, and many more. And the breadth of this historical inquiry has impelled many in literary studies to view themselves more as cultural critics and general intellectuals than as literary scholars.

Theory, history, culture: these are the formidable terms around which the volumes in this series have been organized. A number of these volumes will be the product of a single author or editor. But perhaps even more of them will be collaborative ventures, emerging from the joint enterprise of editors, essayists, and respondents or commentators. In each volume, and as a whole, the series will aim to highlight both distinctive contributions to knowledge and a process of exchange, discussion, and debate. It will make available new kinds of work, as well as fresh approaches to criticism's traditional tasks, and indicate new ways through which such work can be done.

William E. Cain
Wellesley College

Reconstructing the Pedagogical Canon

The last twenty years have seen a revolution in the definition of "American literature." A radical critique—now broadly known as "multiculturalism"—has developed which questions the theoretical and political assumptions undergirding the discipline of American literary studies. A focal point for this critique has been the embodiment of those assumptions in the traditional "canon" of American literature: the list of supposed masterpieces that has come to be enshrined in college catalog course descriptions and the tables of contents of literature anthologies. Both poststructuralist literary theory and revisionist historical work have challenged the myth of the "timeless classic" by showing how the canon has functioned as part of a larger cultural effort to justify and reflect the values of the dominant culture in the United States. Along with this critique of the canon has come efforts to reclaim the "noncanonical" texts left off of syllabi and missing from the bibliographies of mainstream scholarship, texts often written or created by women, people of color, working-class and poor people. These texts represent a variety of cultural expression often rooted in aesthetic and cultural values that directly challenge those represented in the traditional canon. The perseverance of the scholars involved in this critique can be measured in the success with which they have moved their work from single articles and monographs to the creation of programs like African American Studies and Women's Studies and in the appearance of anthologies, textbooks and even hysterically written reactions against the movement by members of the traditional school.[1]

But while much has been written about changing the texts we bring to class, not enough work has been done about what happens *inside* the class with those texts, on what the connections are between theories of aesthetic merit, cultural analysis and scholarly purpose and theories about the nature and purpose of teaching.[2] Clearly, the movement to change the direction and focus of study in American literature has radical practical and, therefore, theoretical implications for pedagogy, as will be evident to any teacher replacing a traditional anthology of American literature representing fifty or so authors (predominantly male, northern European, Protestant and middle- to upper-class) with the over one hundred thirty voices found in the *Heath Anthology*—voices originating in Zuni, Spanish, Chinese and English, in the experiences of both colonized and colonizer, immigrant and Native American, rich and poor.

This collection, then, is based on the premise that the debate over the nature of the study of American culture must be as much pedagogical as it is theoretical and that, in fact, the radical critique known as multiculturalism must consciously resist the traditional academic split between research and teaching, scholarship and classroom practice, in order to *be* a truly radical critique. I see this collection as part of the beginnings of this theoretical-pedagogical critique and, therefore, as suggestive rather than definitive of this critique. In the preface to *Reconstructing American Literature*, Paul Lauter similarly describes that collection of multicultural syllabi not as an end in itself but as a "tool in a larger effort"—the effort described in the title of that work (xi). Continuing this effort, this collection hopes to initiate the creation of what might be thought of as a new genre, the theoretical-pedagogical essay.

"New" is, of course, a relative term. Certainly the works listed in note 2 prove that pedagogical theory is not new; there are books and journals devoted to the topic, most obviously in the fields of education and, as I mention below, composition studies. From a historical perspective, Paul Lauter points out in his Afterword that the lack of interest in pedagogy over the last two decades really represents a suppression of movements for radical pedagogical revision that accompanied the social and academic activism of the sixties, the same activism responsible for the contemporary multicultural movement.

Still, as a quick survey of the works-cited list shows, most of the important recent work in college-level pedagogy comes from a relatively small group of publishers, most notably the National Council of Teachers of English and the University of Illinois Press. Within the discipline as a whole, pedagogical theory is still positioned as a specialized subcategory ancillary to the "main" activities of theory and scholarship. By "new," then, I mean not so much the creation of a new form as the demarginalization of the study of pedagogy within literary and cultural studies and a restructuring of literary criticism to match the restructuring of American literature, a restructuring that deconstructs the crippling institutional and intellectual oppositions between theory and practice, scholarship and teaching.

II

The history of the old canon helps explain why the attempt to reconstruct American literature is as much about pedagogical theory as it is about literary criticism. When critics talk about "canon revision" in American literature, they are usually referring to a revision of the New Critical canon. Lauter traces the process through which in the nineteen-twenties critical authority for the evaluation and interpretation of literature was consolidated on college campuses in the hands of a small, demographically homogeneous group of professors—mainly male, upper-class, from northern European Protestant backgrounds—who began to develop various strands of formalist and modernist literary theories into a set of critical principles that valorized formal complexity, self-conscious irony and aesthetic distance—the collection of aesthetic perspectives known as the "New Criticism."[3] Lauter goes on to show, as does Jane Tompkins in *Sensational Designs*, how the narrow cultural perspective represented by these scholars along with the narrowly defined set of formalist aesthetic ideals they developed (the emphasis on formal experimentation, irony and ambiguity), worked to narrow the number of texts included in literary anthologies and taught in classrooms.

This account of the development of New Critical theory is only part of the story, however, because, as Lauter also demonstrates in the Afterword, in the case of the New Criticism, the argument about *what* to read and why was connected with an argument about *how* to read. Obviously much of the academic success of the New Criticism lay in the positions of professional status held by the New Critics as well as in their membership in the dominant cultural group, but much of the institutional success of New Critical theory—its enshrinement in literary anthologies, classroom syllabi and teaching strategies—lay in the pedagogical foundation that the New Critics built. Unlike most recent literary criticism, pedagogical theory was a part of New Critical theory right from the beginning. As Tompkins has shown, this eminently teachable pedagogy became part of a self-reinforcing process of literary evaluation (*Sensational Designs* 194). Works like *Understanding Poetry*, *Understanding Fiction* and the textbooks they generated both taught a way of reading poetry and provided a justification for the valorization of those literary texts deemed most amenable to such a method of reading. Open almost any standard textbook designed for introductory literature classes, and you will find the New Criticism: analysis of theme, tone, setting, imagery and irony as entities in and of themselves, with scant attention to social, historical or political context—or rather, with the assumption that social context is secondary to considerations of formal analysis. In the Afterword, Lauter describes this institutionalization of New Critical methodology as the "pedagogical canon."

The revolution in literary scholarship over the past twenty years has countered the narrowness of the New Critical canon by bringing long neglected texts not only to light but now into print as well. Pioneering work by organizations like the Feminist Press have led to projects like the Rutgers University Press "American Women Writers" series, The *Heath Anthology of American Litera-ture* and the recent proliferation of texts and readers featuring a greater selection of works by women and minority writers. Introductory literary texts now contain Alice Walker, Tillie Olsen and Leslie Marmon Silko along with Nathaniel Hawthorne, William Faulkner and John Updike. But if "multiculturalism" has become, in one sense, mainstream and sometimes seems as much a marketing strategy as a sociopolitical movement, it is because while those introductory texts now feature a more diverse index of authors, the (New) critical strategies recommended for the analysis of these texts remain unchanged.

As a result, while the names of some of the authors being read are different, the reading experience itself remains defined by the focus on the "close reading" of texts as part of an analysis and appreciation of the formal complexity of those texts. Literary merit is still defined in New Critical terms, with one of two results for the classroom. Either texts by women, working class, and minority writers are taught to show that these writers can write "just as well" as the traditional canonical writers (since their previous exclusion from the canon suggests that they were somehow deficient), or texts are chosen in order to be "representative"—a strategy that can lead either to reductionism (Kate Chopin provides the "women's" perspective), tokenism or often both. In other words, unless changing *what* we read involves changing *how* we read, we will not be able to articulate the difference made by reconstructing American literature or by studying texts previously absent in the classroom—indeed, we will not be able to account adequately for that absence by any other means but by those critical-pedagogical ideas that "justified" that absence in the first place.

But if the last twenty years has seen a revolution in scholarship devoted to the discovery and publication of texts by writers belonging to other than the dominant cultural group, they have also witnessed revolutions in both literary criticism and pedagogical theory. Crucial to the New Critical enterprise was not simply the assertion of an alternative form of criticism, but the claim to have developed a kind of an objective science of criticism—the confidence expressed in titles like *Understanding Poetry* and *Understanding Fiction*, and in terms like the "affective fallacy" and the "intentional fallacy." While Brooks and Warren didn't claim to understand everything there is about a given poem or story, they still felt their methods represented the proper way to that understanding. If Wimsatt and Beardsley would concede that the affective and intentional fallacies were almost universal readers' reactions, and that these reactions were not without critical interest, they were still *fallacies* as far as literary criticism was concerned. Perhaps the title of Brooks's famous essay against a certain type of critical practice most neatly captures this sense of theoretical certainty, indeed, almost papal infallibility: "The Heresy of Paraphrase."

While important critiques of the New Criticism have existed from the start, particularly in the reader-oriented, multidisciplinary approach of Louise Rosenblatt, such theoretical certainty has come in for a battering over the last generation from the diverse group of theoretical schools, tendencies and strategies commonly referred to as "poststructuralism" (a term as variously defined and elusive as "multiculturalism"). While the diversity of these critical positions is itself one of the defining characteristics of poststructuralism, and while many critics who could be described as poststructuralists violently disagree with one another, poststructuralist criticisms—whether deconstructionist, feminist, New Historicist, reader-response, or poststructuralist Marxist—do share certain perspectives. Ironically—or perhaps "paradoxically" is the better word—the most important perspective they have in common might be the radical questioning of the idea of "in common" itself as part of a focus on the cultural construction and operation of difference. Rather than trying to achieve a consensus of how reading should work when done "correctly," or trying to settle on "standards" of literary merit, these theorists explore why and how readings and evaluations differ as a function of social, ethnic, gender and historical position. Instead of using theory to arrive at a single index of literary value, poststructuralists analyze what Barbara Herrnstein Smith calls "contingencies of value." Her work can be taken as representative of the general poststructuralist view that "all value is radically contingent, being neither a fixed attribute, an inherent quality, or an objective property of things but, rather, an effect of multiple, continuously changing, and continuously interacting variables or, to put this another way, the products of a dynamics of a system" (30).

This move from absolutes to contingencies (a move a member of my undergraduate class in literary criticism ironically/paradoxically described as "common sense") has involved a radical decentering of authority in matters of literary interpretation and evaluation, and helps explain why the process of "canon revision" referred to in the title of this book is really a process of canon elimination, specifically, the elimination of the idea of the canon as representing a centralized source of cultural authority.[4] This same theoretical movement toward the examination of contingency also removes the "text itself," as it used to be called, from its central position as the stable determiner of the reading experience.

However, the traditional classroom is, if nothing else, a centralized place, typically involving a single instructor, a single syllabus, and a single lecture. Thus, the newly "multicultural" versions of the introductory textbooks referred to above represent a collision not only between canon revision and the New Criticism, but also between the decentralized assumptions of poststructuralism and the institutional and pedagogical centralization of the traditional classroom. But just as poststructuralist literary theory of the last twenty years has moved from absolutes to contingencies, from centers to margins, so too has pedagogical theory moved towards decentralized classrooms and the questioning of teacherly authority. Again, as Lauter more specifically documents in the Afterword, the same social activism (the civil rights and women's rights movements, most specifically) that led to the opening of the university both to women and minority students and to the study of the cultural experiences of women and minorities also generated a move towards more democratic pedagogies that acknowledge and build on the diversity of cultural experience in the United States, a diversity represented by the increasingly heterogeneous college student population.

The Brazilian educator Paolo Freire stands as both an example of, and primary influence on, this pedagogical trend towards the decentered classroom. In his classic *Pedagogy of the Oppressed*, he writes of the need to move from a "banking" model of education—where knowledge is a commodity "owned" by the instructor and "deposited" into the empty heads of the students—to a "problem posing" model of education building on a critical analysis of the contradictions and struggles encountered by students in their immediate social situations. Thus, Freire argues for a concentration on process and the student over content and the teacher. My shorthand use of "process" and "content" is itself more strategic and contingent than absolute, however; rather than asserting a clear separation between process and content, Freire's pedagogy focuses on developing a critical awareness of how process leads to content—in short, how knowledge is created. As a result, Freire's pedagogy works toward students becoming active producers, rather than passive consumers, of knowledge and culture.

In the field of textual studies, the greatest work done on the application of the process model of pedagogy to the teaching of reading and writing over the last twenty years has come from composition studies, a field that has come into its own concomitantly with Women's Studies, African American Studies and other activist academic movements. Whereas the lecture model is still the norm in many literature classes in the United States, in composition there has been an increasing emphasis on what is called the student-centered classroom, with classes focused as much if not more on the process of writing than the end product. Peer review of student writing, along with alternative evaluation strategies like deferred and portfolio grading, is now fairly commonplace in the composition classroom.

Feminist theory, with its analysis of the centralized strategies of patriarchal power, has likewise questioned the centralized, top-down model of the traditional lecture class. Just as composition theorists have studied how to overcome traditional pedagogical methods that have silenced writing students and prevented them from developing an authentic sense of voice, feminist pedagogy has also developed strategies to counter silencing in the classroom, in this case, the systematic silencing of women's voices and privileging of men's.

Still, for all these simultaneous developments in literary and pedagogical theory, only recently has literary theory acknowledged pedagogical theory. Just as composition programs are often marginalized adjuncts of English departments, regardless of the scholarly and pedagogical success of these programs, pedagogy has long been the repressed Other of literary studies. That how to teach is something that "goes without saying" has been signified by nobody saying anything about it. Tompkins describes this repression of the pedagogical by saying that for most traditional college professors, "teaching was exactly like sex . . . something you weren't supposed to talk about or focus on in any way but that you were supposed to be able to do properly when the time came" ("Pedagogy" 655). The fact that an essay collection like the present one has few recent predecessors is another indication of this fact; its existence, however, points to how this situation is changing.

The essays included here are representative of the revolutions in scholarship, literary theory and pedagogy defined above. Many are written by newly credentialed academics. This newness manifests itself in a diminished allegiance to the canonical past; in fact, many of the scholars represented here have been attracted to literary study by these revolutions in scholarship and theory, as evidenced by the feminist and African American studies perspectives found in these essays. Similarly, more and more new literary scholars have studied composition and pedagogical theory as part of graduate student teaching training and, as a result, carry with them both an awareness of and a respect for pedagogy and pedagogical theory.

Regardless of when the writers received their Ph.D.'s, however, their essays share the fundamental concerns of the theoretical and pedagogical trends I have outlined here: as much focus on *how* to teach as on *what* to teach as part of a larger trend to deconstruct the traditional binary opposition between "theory" and "practice," a dynamic view of education as a dialogic process of cultural analysis rather than the static transmission of information, a commitment to involve students as participants in culture rather than consumers of it, the use of what Freire calls "problem posing" and what Gregory Jay in his opening essay calls "problematics" as organizing structures of classroom instruction. Above all, these essays are radical in the sense that they call for a fundamental rethinking of the goals of literary instruction and the social purpose of cultural analysis. Embracing both the question of how and the question of what we teach, these essays insist on asking the question of *why* we teach.

III

If, as I have said, these essays are theoretically radical (whether overtly or implicitly), they also range in their scope, from Gregory Jay's call to reinvent the nature of literary studies in general to essays like Anne L. Bower's, rooted in classroom practice and focused on the challenges posed by adapting radical theory to both the institutionally conservative sites of instruction and the institutional situations of the instructors. As a result, I have grouped the essays into three loose categories focused on rethinking the practice of study and instruction in American Literature at the levels of the profession as a whole, the individual course, and the interaction between student and teacher. As with the collection as a whole, these groupings are meant to be suggestive rather than definitive, and towards this end, each section is completed with an essay that serves as a transition to the following section.

The first section, "Literary Studies as Text: Rethinking the Profession," features essays that draw attention to the premises and purposes of literary studies in general as one of their main topics, although, as I have said, this question works as an operating problematic in all of the essays in the collection. Gregory Jay's essay, "The End of 'American' Literature," sets the tone for the section and the collection as a whole with his sweeping call for a restructuring of American literary studies, beginning with his opening sentence, "It is time to stop teaching 'American' literature," and continuing with his call for a "forceful uprooting of the conceptual model defining the field itself" based on his vision of the purpose of both scholarship and pedagogy: "Teachers have the responsibility to empower previously marginalized texts and readers, and to teach in a way that we risk surprising and painful changes in the interpretive habits, expectations, and values of our students—and of ourselves."

The following essays in the section work as both endorsements and important qualifications of Jay's powerful and articulate call for a truly radical multiculturalism embracing both the content of college curricula and pedagogical theory. Cornel Bonca's "In the Big Muddy: Art and Politics in the Classroom" cautions that the necessary focus on the political dimensions of canon revision or revolution should not blind us to questions of aesthetics, particularly as they relate to students' experience of literature. Renny Christopher likewise challenges the foundations of traditional literary study by examining the experiences of students—in this case, working-class students (and academics) who find the middle-class culture of the university frustrating and alienating, particularly as embodied in the traditional canon of literature not only mainly written by members of the middle and upper classes, but also taught from middle- and upper-class perspectives.

Bruce Goebel's essay, "Imagining Difference: *Textual Power and the Transgression of the Self*," discusses the work of Robert Scholes—a powerful voice in the effort to link critical theory with pedagogical practice—in the context of considering how to achieve the goal of teaching students "to imaginatively transgress" their own social positions in order to consider other cultural perspectives; in other words, as a way to realize Jay's call for a pedagogy that risks "surprising and painful changes in . . . interpretive habits, expectations, and values." Susan Danielson links a general discussion of pedagogical goals and theories to examples of classroom practice, specifically, the description of her class on "The woman question" in American culture. While her essay works as a fascinating and detailed example of what a "new" course in American literature/culture might look like (and thus anticipates the further examples of such classes in the next section), her introductory and concluding sections set her class within a personal feminist analysis of academic culture and raise questions about what difference a single class can make within the institutional structure of the traditional English department. Finally, Barbara Roche Rico and Sandra Mano explore the dangers of marginalization or tokenization in constructing a multicultural syllabus. They argue for the necessity of building a sociohistorical context for the discussion of the social construction of ethnicity as a way to "acknowledge the possibility of difference, of uniqueness."

The next section, "The Canon as Text: Rethinking the Survey," takes us directly into the classroom, but just as the essays in the previous section were not simply "theory," these essays are not just "practice," and each essay connects specific classroom activities to questions of the overall purpose of literary study. As Martha J. Cutter writes in her essay describing her (sub)version of the survey class in American literature:

At the base of all our discussions of the canon and of ways of teaching the survey course must be some discussion of why we teach, what the purposes of education are, and in the end, what kind of readers we want our students to be. For if we do not consider such issues, our own teaching practices will replicate the very structures of authority and domination which the canon presents, the very structure we seek to escape.

Although not all of the essays in this section deal with the survey class per se, the survey class does embody most of the traditional theoretical attitudes about literature that form the basis for most college curricula in literature: the breakdown of texts into distinct and separable "periods" and "schools," the emphasis on chronological sequencing, the focus on individual "masterpieces" as determined by formalist-modernist and other dominant cultural values, the treatment of sociohistorical context as mere "background."[5] Thus whether the classes under discussion in the following essays are officially designated as surveys or not, each of the writers in this section must confront and subvert these theoretical assumptions that have become embedded in institutional practice.

The first three essays explore the consequences of introducing noncanonical texts into traditionally canonical classes (two surveys of American literature and a class in American modernism), and all argue for the importance of not just adding the noncanonical texts but in placing them in deliberate opposition or dialogue with canonical texts. Both Cutter and Anne Stavney describe classes in which they deliberately counterpoise canonical and noncanonical texts as part of a process of questioning and undermining the myth of a unitary cultural history implied by traditional and institutionally embedded terms such as realism or modernism.

Jeanne Holland takes this process a step further, in a way similar to Rico and Mano, by examining the attractions and dangers of using Native American culture as a means of critiquing the dominant Euro-American culture. Wishing to avoid the reductive racism of viewing Indians as either uncivilized primitives or noble savages, she provides specific strategies for creating a sense of the autonomy, diversity and complexity of Native American cultures within the confines of the traditional survey class.

Irene Moser addresses the same problems of ethnocentrism and facile cultural comparisons in the teaching of Native American literature by advocating a rhetorical approach. Rather than seeing Native American texts as representations of static, monolithic belief systems, such a pedagogy encourages students to regard these texts as part of an ongoing process of cultural negotiation and persuasion—an approach similar to Jane Tompkins's use of the idea of cultural work to emphasize the dynamic operation of texts in specific cultural situations.

Michele Lise Tarter's essay describes her transformation of a survey class with the most imposing institutional title of all— "Masterpieces of American Literature"—into a feminist exploration of American cultural history based on "the dynamic of experiential learning in the classroom." In "Sharing Responsibility for American Lit: 'A Spectacular and Dangerous World of Choice,'" Anne L. Bower goes one step further than Tarter by proposing the most radical version of the student-centered classroom, involving students in the creation and teaching of the survey class—the "sharing responsibility" of her title. In many ways the pivotal essay in this collection, the issues of professional and pedagogical authority raised by Bower serve as transitions to the final section of the book on the nature of authority in the classroom.

This final section, "The Teacher as Text: Rethinking Authority in the Classroom," on the one hand completes a movement in the collection from the global issues implied in "Literary Studies as Text" to a consideration of the politics of the personal relation between teacher and student in the classroom, but on the other represents the fundamental struggle Jay describes as impelling the reconstruction of American literature: the empowerment of previously marginalized texts and *readers* —not just the students in the class, but those students who might especially be called the "noncanonical" student body (women, members of ethnic minorities, working-class students, older students).[6] The essays in this last section remind us that the locus of political struggle in education—and by extension, scholarship—is the power relationship between teacher and student.

The first two essays in this section deal with the cultural preconceptions and analytical limitations students bring to the class as a result of a lifetime spent in a mass media culture driven by the values of consumerism, cultural conformity and the refusal to confront issues of social injustice. Peter Caccavari begins by analyzing negative student reactions to classes featuring noncanonical texts and a non-lecture-oriented pedagogy. Caccavari uses his initial puzzlement and frustration at students who apparently desire centralized, nondemocratic, patriarchal authority as a means toward a deeper questioning of the complex interplay of insecurity and suspicion that goes on in the classroom and of the meaning of a truly democratic classroom.

Melba Joyce Boyd's essay, condensed from a book in progress, deals not with the complacency of middle-class students but with the frustration, anger and confusion of Afro-American students she describes as suffering from a cultural "loss of memory" that precludes any effective understanding of the social, economic and historical conditions responsible for that frustration, anger and confusion. In response, she gives an outline for a radically innovative, multidisciplinary pedagogical strategy geared to the imagination of students brought up in a culture dominated by the visual image. Building on the multicultural, improvisatory jazz tradition, she constructs a holistic, multimedia pedagogy that, like jazz, "engages the energy of multidimensional layers of experience and projects us beyond our cultural contradictions and various predilections."

Next, William J. Savage, Jr. examines the dynamics of classroom authority from the ambiguous position of professional authority held by the graduate student teaching assistant. Turning the marginality of the graduate student T.A. into an advantage, Savage argues that graduate student teachers are uniquely situated to challenge not only the canon, but the "canonical" structures of pedagogical authority: "Potentially more revolutionary than alterations in the roster of acceptable texts . . . would be a reevaluation of how pedagogical authority is understood, institutionalized, and acted upon."

Jane Tompkins's concluding essay in this section is a part of that reevaluation. In the last few years, Tompkins has been using her authority as a tenured full professor and widely respected leader in the theoretical reconstruction of American literature to raise fundamental questions about the nature of professional and pedagogical authority. Her essay, "The Dream of Authority," originally written for a conference panel on the issue of political responsibility in the classroom, suggests that "the political responsibilities of teachers lie first of all in their *way of being*, and not in any doctrine they espouse or in any texts they do or do not teach." Reflecting on her childhood experiences with authority and terror in the classroom, Tompkins takes the question of classroom authority back to its source, arguing:

> Teaching political responsibility begins at home, psychologically speaking; it begins with a frank assessment of one's own encounters with power at an early age, and the attempt to trace the connections between that past and one's present patterns of action and thought.

Finally, Paul Lauter's Afterword sets the collection in historical perspective by drawing a bridge from the pedagogical reform movements of the sixties to their contemporary revival as exemplified by these essays. Noting how many of the writers in this book insist on the collective nature of the construction of knowledge and culture as a counterweight to the traditional American ideology of individualism, Lauter's historical analysis helps reinforce a similar sense of collective enterprise for the pedagogical revision movement itself.

This sense of a common purpose and effort is as crucial for the critique of the pedagogical canon as it is for challenges to the literary canon. While these essays provide concrete examples of how theory and practice can meet in a multicultural pedagogy, they also make clear that the myriad pedagogical challenges created by the restructuring of American literature will never be "solved" in a definitive way. This need for an ongoing pedagogical critique demonstrates both the intellectual strength and a potential institutional weakness of multicultural studies. The New Criticism was centripetal in function: it focused on a refinement of critical ideals and a concomitant narrowing of the literary canon. While such a centripetal movement was part of the elitism and securing of cultural privilege that formed the political context of the New Criticism, this centralizing tendency allowed for the swift institutionalization of New Critical methodology in terms of course offerings, anthologies and lists of examination texts in graduate schools.

The pedagogies described in this collection, on the contrary, are centrifugal in operation, part of a decentralizing intellectual movement that stresses a diversity of methodologies, a constant critical self-examination of those methodologies and the idea of experimentation as the norm. Bower, for example, uses the metaphors of the studio and the laboratory to describe this new pedagogy, drawing on their implications of creativity, experiential learning and questioning. While this centrifugal movement works to create a more democratic and just educational practice, it also stands in opposition to the centralized institutional structures and pedagogical practices of the university in general and the traditional classroom in particular. Thus, a truly multicultural pedagogy cannot simply fit in with business as usual and with totalizing ideas about the nature of culture and the nature of teaching. In contrast, the essays in this collection tend towards the context-specific, carefully describing the particular demographic and institutional settings of the classes under discussion. This pedagogical insistence on the importance of the particular and the local may seem more arduous and time-consuming than relying on standardized ideas about "understanding poetry" in general and on standardized texts and anthologies featuring the traditional "classics," but this focus on context provides a flexibility and sensitivity that are the pedagogical strengths of the approaches discussed in this collection. While essays like Caccavari's and Goebel's rightly describe the difficulties in preventing even the most conscientiously multicultural literature classes from regressing into set lectures that merely reinforce rather than challenge dominant cultural beliefs and stereotypes, the results reported by Bower, Tarter and others suggest the possibilities not just for increased student "participation" but for making the classroom the site of radical cultural critique involving both students and teacher. If the institutional structures and professional demands of academia seem to work against the implementation of radical multicultural pedagogies, the essays in this collection provide evidence that in the struggle to reconstruct American literature and deconstruct the canon in the classroom, teachers and students can be on the same side.

NOTES

1. For a comprehensive bibliography of multicultural scholarship, see Ruoff and Ward. Some useful overviews of the debate over the canon can be found in Lauter (*Canons and Contexts, Reconstructing American Literature*), Baym, Tompkins (*Sensational Designs*), Fetterley, Elliot, Kolodny, and Gates ("The Master's Pieces"), as well as the anthologies by Gates, Von Hallberg, Gless and Smith, Simonson and Walker, and Greenblatt and Gunn. The landmark literature anthology in this regard is *The Heath Anthology of American Literature*, but the impact of multicultural scholarship can be seen in the titles and contents of many new texts designed for introductory literature and composition courses.

The most famous (or infamous) challenges to multiculturalism can be found in Bennett, Bloom, Hirsch, D'Souza and Schlesinger.

2. The exceptions include Lauter (*Reconstructing*), and Henricksen and Morgan. For further examples of work linking critical theory in general with pedagogy, see Atkins and Johnson, Cahalan and Downing, Moran and Penfield, Morton and Zavarzadeh, Nelson, Peterfreund, and Scholes.

3. See Lauter, "Race and Gender in the Shaping of the American Literature Canon: A Case Study from the Twenties" in *Canons and Contexts*, 22–47.

4. Of course, denying the intellectual validity of a literary canon does not deny the strategic cultural influence such a canon can wield. In "The Master's-Pieces," for example, Henry Louis Gates, Jr. argues that the creation of a black literary canon by African American writers and critics does not simply repeat the essentialist logic of the white canon, but that it functions as a Derridean supplement to that canon, both exposing its contingency while also exploiting its cultural power. In other words, Gates's use of the idea of a canon of African American

literature already assumes that canons are multiple, an assumption antithetical to the New Critical canon.

5. See Lauter, *Canons and Contexts*, 36–41.

6. College administrators prefer the term "nontraditional" students.

REFERENCES

Atkins, Douglas and Michael L. Johnson, eds. *Writing and Reading Differently: Deconstruction and the Teaching of Composition and Literature*. Lawrence: UP of Kansas, 1985.

Baym, Nina. "Melodramas of Beset Manhood: How Theories of American Fiction Exclude Women Authors." *The New Feminist Criticism: Essays on Women, Literature, and Theory*. Ed. Elaine Showalter. NY: Pantheon Books, 1985. 63–80.

Bennett, William. *To Reclaim a Legacy: Report on the Humanities in Higher Education*. Washington D.C.: National Endowment for the Humanities, 1984.

Bloom, Allan. *The Closing of the American Mind*. NY: Simon and Schuster, 1987.

Brooks, Cleanth and Robert Penn Warren. *Understanding Fiction*. NY: F. S. Crofts and Company, 1943.

——. *Understanding Poetry*. NY: Holt, 1950.

Cahalan, James and David B. Downing, eds. *Practicing Theory in Introductory College Literature Courses*. Urbana: NCTE, 1991.

D'Souza, Dinesh. *Illiberal Education: The Politics of Race and Sex on Campus*. NY: Free Press, 1991.

Elliot, Emory. "New Literary History: Past and Present." *American Literature* 57 (1985): 611–25.

Fetterley, Judith. *The Resisting Reader: A Feminist Approach to American Fiction*. Bloomington: Indiana UP, 1978.

Freire, Paolo. *Pedagogy of the Oppressed*. NY: Continuum, 1970.

Gates, Henry Louis, Jr., ed. *"Race," Writing, and Difference*. Chicago: U of Chicago P, 1986.

————. "The Master's Pieces: On Canon Formation and the African American Tradition." *South Atlantic Quarterly* 89 (1990): 89–112.

Gless, Darryl J. and Barbara Herrnstein Smith, eds. *The Politics of Liberal Education.* Durham: Duke UP, 1992.

Greenblatt, Stephen and Giles Gunn, eds. *Redrawing the Boundaries: The Transformation of English and American Literary Studies.* New York: MLA, 1992.

Henricksen, Bruce and Thäis E. Morgan, eds. *Reorientations: Critical Theories and Pedagogy.* Urbana: U of Illinois P, 1990.

Hirsch, E. D., Jr. *Cultural Literacy: What Every American Needs to Know.* Boston: Houghton Mifflin, 1987.

Kolodny, Annette. "The Integrity of Memory: Creating a New Literary History of the United States." *American Literature* 57 (1985): 291–307.

Lauter, Paul. *Canons and Contexts.* NY: Oxford UP, 1991.

————, ed. *The Heath Anthology of American Literature.* 2 vols. Boston: Heath, 1989.

————, ed. *Reconstructing American Literature: Courses, Syllabi, Issues.* Old Westbury, NY: Feminist, 1983.

Moran, Charles and Elizabeth F. Penfield, eds. *Conversations: Contemporary Critical Theory and the Teaching of Literature.* Urbana: NCTE, 1990.

Morton, Donald and Mas'ud Zavarzadeh, eds. *Theory/Pedagogy/Politics.* Urbana: U of Illinois P, 1991.

Nelson, Cary. *Theory in the Classroom.* Urbana: U of Illinois P, 1986.

Peterfreund, Stuart, ed. *Critical Theory and the Teaching of Literature.* Boston: Northeastern UP, 1985.

Rosenblatt, Louise. *Literature as Exploration.* 4th ed. NY: MLA, 1983.

————. *The Reader, the Text, the Poem: The Transactional Theory of the Literary Work.* Carbondale and Edwardsville: Southern Illinois UP, 1978.

Ruoff, A. LaVonne Brown and Jerry W. Ward, Jr., eds. *Redefining American Literary History.* NY: MLA, 1990.

Schlesinger, Arthur M., Jr. *The Disuniting of America.* Knoxville: Whittle Direct Books, 1991.

Scholes, Robert. *Textual Power: Literary Theory and the Teaching of English.* New Haven: Yale 1985.

Simonson, Rick and Scott Walker, eds. *The Graywolf Annual Five: Multicultural Literacy*. St. Paul: Graywolf P, 1988.

Smith, Barbara Herrnstein. *Contingencies of Value: Alternative Perspectives for Critical Theory*. Cambridge: Harvard UP, 1988.

Tompkins, Jane. "Pedagogy of the Distressed." *College English* 52 (1990): 653–60.

———. *Sensational Designs: The Cultural Work of American Fiction*. NY: Oxford UP, 1985.

Von Hallberg, Robert, ed. *Canons*. Chicago: U of Chicago P, 1984.

Wimsatt, W. K. *The Verbal Icon: Studies in the Meaning of Poetry*. Lexington: U of Kentucky P, 1954.

SECTION ONE

Literary Studies as Text: Rethinking the Profession

The End of "American" Literature
Toward a Multicultural Practice

Gregory S. Jay

> The failure of the melting-pot, far from closing the great
> American democratic experiment, means that it has only
> just begun. Whatever American nationalism turns out to
> be, we see already that it will have a color richer and more
> exciting than our ideal has hitherto encompassed. In a
> world which has dreamed of internationalism, we find
> that we have all unawares been building up the first
> international nation.
>
> —*Randolph Bourne*

It is time to stop teaching "American" literature. The combined
lessons of critical theory, classroom practice, and contemporary
history dictate not only a revision of the curriculum and
pedagogy of "American" literature courses, but a forceful
uprooting of the conceptual model defining the field itself
(Bercovitch; Elliot; Kolodny). On the one hand this means
affirming the reforms that have taken hold at numerous
institutions and in a number of new critical studies and
anthologies, such as *Three American Literatures*, edited by
Houston Baker, and the monumental achievement of Paul Lauter
and his colleagues in *The Heath Anthology of American Literature*.
On the other hand it means pointing out that many of these
reforms have only been pluralist in character. (JanMohamed and
Lloyd make the case against pluralism, while Ravitch upholds
it.) They add a few new texts or authors without dismantling the

3

prejudicial framework which has traditionally prescribed the kinds of works studied in "American" literature courses and the kinds of issues raised in "American" literary scholarship. That scholarship thus continues to depend upon, and reproduce, the oppressive nationalist ideology which is the nightmare side of the "American dream." Our goal should be rather to construct a multicultural and dialogical paradigm for the study of writing in the United States.

The recent work of Adrienne Rich exemplifies a literary and cultural criticism that neither colonizes nor excludes the Other, but tries to read, think, and feel the differences that our bodily locations—in history, in geography, in ethnicity, in gender, in sexual orientation—can make. Rich's "politics of location" would begin not with the continent or nation "but with the geography closest in—the body." She would

> Pick up again the long struggle against lofty and
> privileged abstraction. . . . Even to begin with the body I
> have to say that from the outset that body had more than
> one identity [female, white, Jewish, middle-class,
> Southern, North American, lesbian etc.]. . . . Two thoughts:
> there is no liberation that only knows how to say "I"; there
> is no collective movement that speaks for each of us all the
> way through.
>
> And so even ordinary pronouns become a political
> problem. . . . Once again, Who is *we*? (212–13, 215, 224, 231)

This mapping of the located body graphically resists the abstract liberal humanism which, for all its accomplishments, continued to force the Other to assimilate to the values and interests of an idiosyncratic though hegemonic Western self, and it attacks the complacency of that self in regarding its image as unitary, normative, and universal. Rich's argument closely resembles those made by postmodern anthropologists and ethnographers such as James Clifford, who writes that "once cultures are no longer prefigured visually—as objects, theaters, texts—it becomes possible to think of a cultural poetics that is an interplay of voices, of positioned utterances" (12). For Rich and Clifford multiculturalism is a dialogue among (and within) socially constructed bodies and subject positions. Students of writing in the United States will become like Clifford's "indigenous ethnographers," self-conscious both of the positions they write from and the positions they describe.

Thus I want to heed the warning of Guillermo Gómez-Peña not to "confuse true collaboration with political paternalism, cultural vampirism, voyeurism, economic opportunism, and demagogic multiculturalism" (133). I have to be self-conscious about the politics of the "we" in my own essay. In part it refers to a set of dominant groups I participate in—European-American, male, middle-class, heterosexual, US citizen, educated, institutionalized, and so on—and I speak to those groups about our need to deconstruct the basis of our own privileges. Danger (leading to "demagogic multiculturalism") lies in imagining that oppression is always someone else's responsibility. Before we get too busy celebrating our position at the forefront of the liberation of the culture, we must recognize that we are often the problem. It is our racism, our sexual prejudices, our class anxieties, our empowered desires that we must confront and resist. The unconscious character of these biases means that we cannot be complacent or comfortable even with the conscious avowal of our positions (as in this essay), for that can always be a defensive reassertion of our authority. Some who might read this essay do not belong to many of these privileged groups, so that their relation to the pronoun "we" will be different. In that case "I" and "you" and "we" may also operate performatively, in utopian fashion, as they do in the texts of Walt Whitman and of Rich—as invocations to the possibility of community. "What is it then between us?" asks Whitman: "What is the count of the scores or hundreds of years between us? . . . I too had received identity by my body" (130). In reference to our location in the United States, or the US, the problematic US indicates the specific heterogeneity of our cultural history and the difficulty of speaking for, or about, it in a univocal voice. Thus my decision to use the abbreviation for the remainder of the essay in order both to evoke and symbolically subvert the nation's identity. To play ungrammatically on Rich's question, the motto for American criticism should become: "Once again: Who is US?"

The history and literature of the US have been misrepresented so as to effectively underwrite the power and

values of privileged classes and individuals. We should act on
the now clichéd observation that literary judgments have always
already been political; our responsibility for justice in cultural
education requires more self-criticism than we have yet shown.
We have to make explicit, and sometimes alter, the values at
work in our schools and scholarship (see Giroux). We have to
engage in struggles to change how the cultural history and
writing of the US get institutionalized and reproduced. The
movement toward multicultural literacy reflects more than a
dedication to intellectual and historical accuracy; it expresses our
sense that the legacy of nationalism must be reevaluated and that
multicultural experience is our imperative reality. US
multiculturalism is a living actuality we cannot escape and
whose configurations we must begin to fathom, even as
renascent nationalisms (here and elsewhere) pose serious
political and theoretical questions. A commitment to
multicultural education also belongs to our historical moment as
we witness a renewed interest in democracy, and as we ask how
a democratic culture might be fashioned. The contemporary
failure of democracy in the US derives from oppressive social
practices (material and ideological) that act against certain
marked individuals, categorizing them as marginal to the
interests of the nation. A responsible pedagogy requires a
vigilant criticism of racism and discrimination in all their forms,
aesthetic as well as political. It is the duty of educators to oppose
the practices which today tolerate and even encourage cultural
chauvinism and the violence of bigotry.

Aren't there dangers as well as values in multiculturalism?
Diane Ravitch argues that a proper multiculturalism teaches
respect for the diversity of America's "common culture" (and so
is pluralistic), while a dangerous multiculturalism advocates
conflicting ethnocentrisms and implies that "no common culture
is possible or desirable" (and so is particularistic) (340). But the
choice should not be posed as one between a common culture
and chaotic ethnic rivalries. Any recourse to a notion of a
national culture risks reimposing a biased set of principles or
historical narratives, and Ravitch is conspicuously silent on what
the content of that common culture may be. On the other hand,
she is right to warn that replacing Eurocentrism with a series of

ethnocentrisms would only multiply the original problem. With Elizabeth Meese I would urge that we avoid thinking of multicultural literacy as a process designed to foster or prop up *an identity*, whether of a person or a tradition or a nation or a school of criticism (31–32). Rather multicultural study should put people into a dialogue with the Other—with the subjects that have historically formed the boundaries of their cultural experiences. Essentialism does not have to be the result of affirmative action, especially if one understands the latter as affirmation of the Other and not of one's self. Our commonality is not a substance or essence (Americanness) but a process of social existence predicated on the espoused if not always realized principles of cultural democracy, political rights, community responsibility, social justice, equality of opportunity, and individual freedom. When these principles are subordinated to totalizing ideologies seeking to invent or impose a common culture, then the actual multicultural life of Americans suffers an oppression that is in no one's best interests.

A strong connection ties the historical development of a theory and institutional practice of American literary studies to the modern history of nationalism. The anxiety to invent an American nation and the anxiety to invent a uniquely American literature were historically coincident. As long as we use "American" as an adjective, we reinforce the illusion that there is a transcendental core of values and experiences that are essentially "American," and that literary or cultural studies may be properly shaped by selecting objects and authors according to how well they express this essence. This metaphysical approach has shaped American literary theory ever since the first attempts to invent a uniquely American literature in the 1820s, and has persisted throughout every theory that has used arguments for American exceptionalism. Current revisionary critiques show that the "American" of conventional histories of American literature has usually been white, male, middle- or upper-class, heterosexual, and a spokesman for a definable set of political and social interests. Insofar as women, African and Asian and Native Americans, Hispanics, gays and lesbians, and others make an appearance in such histories, it is usually in terms of their also being made into spokesmen for traditional values and schemes.

Their "assimilation" into American literature comes at the cost of their cultural heritage and obscures their real antagonism and historical difference in relation to the privileged classes.

The "melting pot" is a crock, as great and pernicious a myth in literary history as it is in social and political history. Today we are moving away from the myth of assimilation and into the struggle to create a just multicultural society that respects the values and practices of distinct if interdependent groups. Cultural education must aim to represent historically that ours always has been a multicultural society and that the repression of this heterogeneity (usually in the service of one group) ultimately threatens the cultural vitality and even survival of every group within it. In contrast, past histories of American literature have been active functionaries in reproducing the hegemony of culturally privileged groups. From 1882 to 1912 (and beyond), observes Nina Baym, "textbook writers made literary works and authors display the virtues and achievements of an Anglo-Saxon United States founded by New England Puritans" (459). This narrative served the purpose of "Americanizing" and assimilating the growing industrial and immigrant classes: "Paradoxically, the non-Anglo-Saxon could become American only to the extent of their agreement that only those of Anglo-Saxon lineage were really Americans" (463; see Bourne). At the level of class, the ambitions and disappointments of exploited workers could be mediated by an education in transcendentalism: "What more likely to deflect the (usually foreign-born) poor from their desire to have a substantial piece of the country's settled wealth than exposure to an idealism from whose lofty perspective the materialist struggle would seem unworthy?" (462). Literary history fabricated a symbolic consensus that papered over real social contradiction; as a social practice pedagogy manufactured compliant subject positions (see Graff, *Professing* 130–32, 209–25).

I propose that we replace the idealist paradigm with a geographical and historical one. Our focus of study ought to be "Writing in the United States." The objects of study will be acts of writing committed within and during the colonization, establishment, and ongoing production of the US as a physical, sociopolitical, and multicultural event, including those writings that resist and critique its identification with nationalism. Organizing courses on the bases of national entities inevitably reproduces certain biases and fallacies, and we need to protect against these by including specific theoretical questions and methodological devices in the curriculum. Or we could simply rename our discipline "Comparative American Literature," or establish courses and programs in North American Studies that would integrate the cultural history of the US with those of Canada, Mexico, the near Latin American countries, and the Caribbean, though this could end up repeating the history of colonial imperialism at the level of academic study. Still, the borders between these nations are less the origins of our history than the products of it.

Our peoples and writers have been flowing back and forth over the space these boundaries now delineate since before the colonial adventure began. These borders make little sense when one is studying the histories, say, of Native- or Hispanic- or African-American literature. This crossing of boundaries, as José Saldívar and others argue, becomes the paradoxical center of Mexican-American and Chicano literature, for example, which has been violating borders of nationality and of language since the 1500s (see Saldívar; Gómez-Peña; Rosaldo). How does one categorize a work like Rudolfo Anaya's *Bless Me, Ultima*, which crosses so many of these linguistic and cultural divides? What "Americanist" pedagogy could do justice to the traditions, historical representations, and contexts of utterance in *Black Elk Speaks* or James Welch's *Fools Crow*? Can the borders between Native-, Hispanic-, and Anglo-American literature be drawn without recalling the political treacheries that imposed a series of violated borders upon indigenous peoples and settlers from Mexico, borders that were shifted whenever white economic interest dictated, so that Hispanic- and Native-American cultures come to be an "outside" within the "inside" of "America"?

Within the boundaries of the US, the lines between cultural groups do not form impassable walls, though they often take oppressive shape. Historically these zones are an area of constant passage back and forth, as each culture borrows, imitates, exploits, subjugates, subverts, mimics, ignores, or celebrates the others. The myth of assimilation homogenizes this process by representing it as the progressive acquiescence of every other group to a dominant culture. Writers who analyze this myth often depict the experience instead under the metaphor of "passing"—as in to "pass" for white, for gentile, for straight, for American. The "object of oppression," writes Cherríe Moraga, "is not only someone outside of my skin, but the someone inside my skin" (30). Thus there are borders within, as well as between, our subject positions. This "divided consciousness" (to recall the phrasing of W. E. B. DuBois) affects every group and individual with a specificity that must be understood and felt.

Language is a primary vehicle for passing, and literary critics should study the manner in which the formal development of genres and movements participates in its rituals and contradictions. As we highlight the politics of linguistic assimilation—of the consequences for non-English speaking people who must learn to speak and write the master's tongue—we can exploit the pun in the phrase "Writing in the United States." "Writing" here designates not simply a static set of objects, but the process of verbal or textual production in its historical and dynamic sense, and in the sense of what a speaker or writer experiences when she or he attempts to write within the boundaries of the US (see Baker, *Journey* 1–52; Gates, *Figures* 3–58). If we replace the term "literature" with "writing" we can resist the cultural biases built into the former term and institutionalized by departments that have built their curriculum around the privileged genres developed in modern Europe. Writing, or textuality if you prefer, names events of representation, and so includes previously marginalized forms and media as well as canonical forms produced by marginalized people.

Historically, "Writing in the United States" would begin with Native-American expressive traditions and include those narratives produced by the first European explorers and colonizers, Spanish and French as well as English. This would effectively decenter histories of American literature which have always placed their origins in the Anglo-Saxon culture of Puritan New England (see Reising 49–91). That culture was a culture of the Book—of the Bible—which confronted an oral culture among the Native Americans. The cultural and literary politics of this confrontation require consideration, as does the problematic of translation it dictates. The survival of Native-American discourse henceforth began to depend on its translation into written form, often through the mediation of whites, or on the translation of native experience into white expression in the public speeches and documents produced by Native Americans in defense of their lands and rights. The literary history of the US includes the story of how the destruction of Native-American culture was essential to the literary and political invention of "America," as the struggle for culture coincided with the struggle for land. The boundaries of "Writing in the United States" could thus be drawn geographically and historically, not linguistically, through attention to the demographics of cultural populations, as we witness the dialogical interaction of succeeding generations of natives and arrivals from Europe, Africa, Asia, and Latin America. "Writing in the United States" would then be placed within the history of colonialism and imperialism, as well as nationalism, better providing a foundation for comprehending the current political and social dilemmas facing the US as it reconceives itself as a multicultural society in a multicultural world.

The nationalist biases I have referred to are built into the organization of academic literary study. For about a century we have had departments of English, French, German, Spanish, Portuguese, Italian, and so forth. These were originally conceived as the modern heirs to the tradition of Classical philology, and centered on the study of language, with literature read as an illustration of the history of linguistic development. This philology, like the New Criticism that replaced it, was never entirely a formalism, for it inevitably reproduced the cultural values of the canonical texts it studied. Many language faculties advocated more cultural study in the curriculum, until a basic ambiguity haunted these departments: were they designed to teach the history of a language or the history of a nation? (Graff, *Professing* 55–120). The question, as in the case of English, became vexing when languages crossed national borders and historical periods. When the *interpretation* of literary texts, as opposed to their philological description or use for historical documentation, became of significant institutional concern, the very rationale for language-based departments began to crumble, though we have not yet faced this fact or imagined real alternatives.

"English" is a misnomer for departments offering courses in psychoanalysis, Derrida, postcolonialism, film theory, feminism, Native-American autobiography, and Chicano poetry. "Indeed," says Annette Kolodny, "no longer can we hold to the linguistic insularity implied by the Americanist's presence in departments of *English*" (293). I would side with Kolodny against William Spengemann, who concludes that because "American" does not designate a language, we ought to abandon efforts to conceive an American literary history and instead return to the study of texts written in English, specifically those great texts that have markedly changed the language itself. Spengemann tumbles into tautology and circular reasoning when he advocates a canon based on the linguistic practices of modernism: only those past texts that belong to modernism's history get into the canon, and modernism is the origin of the canon because past experiments in literary language lead to it.

In the study of US writing, the exclusion of texts not written in English or of authors drawing heavily on non-European sources limits the canon with pernicious results. One cannot even adequately interpret works in American English without some knowledge of the various cultures surrounding and informing them. Most writing produced here after the eighteenth century, moreover, borrows words, characters, events, forms, ideas, and concepts from the languages of African-, Hispanic-, Jewish-, Native-, and Asian-Americans. At the same time speakers and writers from these different cultures adapt the English language to create hybrid forms and texts. When analyzing writers such as Frederick Douglass, Isaac Singer, or Leslie Silko, a background in Chaucer or Restoration Drama or Imagist Poetry may be less helpful than studying, say, the traditions of religious representation of the author's native people. The problematics of assimilation and translation inform writing in the US with a complexity that has scarce been recognized or theorized. One could argue that the study of US writing cannot be adequately pursued within the boundaries of the English department, for this comparative project ultimately subverts the very premises of that academic organization.

Though I believe in an historical approach to writing, it will suffer the same deconstruction of boundaries as any approach that tries to impose artificial limits on language or geography. US history cannot be represented a priori as a totality, a unity, or a grand story whose plot and hero we already know. A chief model for modern literary nationalism is that historiography which represents the nation as a collective self, a figurative mind or spirit which is realizing its great soul through the unfolding progress of the national community's history. Not surprisingly, this fiction has often been compared to the *bildungsroman*, and we are familiar with the claims it makes on us, from *The Autobiography of Benjamin Franklin* to the testimony of Oliver North. The metaphorical self used to figure such national histories, of course, turns out to wear the idealized face of a very real class or group of individuals—in the West, what we now handily call white patriarchy. The spiritual story of the nation's quest to realize its dream turns out to be a set of writing practices that participates in the manipulation, exploitation, repression, and even genocide of those subjects deemed peripheral to the tale.

Of course undoing the canon doesn't just mean adding on previously excluded figures; it requires a disturbance of the internal security of the classics themselves. In gay studies, for example, cultural revision extends beyond including avowedly same-sex oriented writers in the curriculum. Gay studies extends to questioning the sexual economies of ambiguous and (supposedly) straight texts—to the ways they police their desires. According to Eve Sedgwick one "could neither dismantle" the canon "insofar as it was seen to be quite genuinely unified by the maintenance of a particular tension of homo/heterosexual definitional panic" nor "ever permit it to be treated as the repository of 'traditional' truths that could be made matter for any true consolidation or congratulation." Since "the problematics of homo/heterosexual definition, in an intensely homophobic culture, are seen to be precisely internal to the central nexuses of that culture," teasing out these contradictions in classic texts reveals the subversiveness and repression integral to them, so that "this canon must always be treated as a loaded gun" (148). Because patriarchy reproduces itself through "the stimulation and glamorization of the energies of male-male desire," it must also incessantly deny, defer, or silence their satisfaction, forming the double-bind characteristic of much male writing; thus she remaps the territory of Leslie Fiedler by exposing the ties that bind homophobia and misogyny. The mask of identity worn by the straight man covers over a split subject, from Hawthorne and Melville to James, Eliot, Fitzgerald, Hemingway, Mailer and beyond.

The literary history of the US ought to be represented not by "*the* American" and "*his* dream," but in terms of how various cultural groups and their forms have interacted during the nation's ongoing construction. As Meese explains, once we abandon notions of literature's intrinsic value and look instead at the contingencies of writing's use values, we may stop thinking in terms of canons altogether. The "history of literature," she writes, "if it seems necessary to create such a thing, might then be a description of the uses to which texts have been put" and of the value writings have had for their subjects (33; see Smith). Such a history would have many protagonists, wearing many faces, speaking many languages, recalling divergent histories, desiring different futures. Syllabi and critical studies could be focussed around contestation rather than unity, putting to work in this area the principle Graff has dubbed "teaching the conflicts." Instead of selecting a set of books and authors that express a previously agreed-upon list of characteristics that are "uniquely American," we could assemble texts that openly conflict with each other's assumptions, terms, narratives, and metaphors. These conflicts, moreover, should unsettle national generalities by reference to the specific pedagogical locality—to the state, region, city, area, and social group of the students, the professor, and the institution.

My own involvement in African-American literature, for example, though precipitated by the Civil Rights movement of the 1960s, received its professional impetus from my being hired—fresh from an education in California and New York—to teach the American literature survey course at the University of Alabama in 1980. I felt strongly the responsibility to develop a multicultural curriculum, with specific attention to black writers. The politics of my pedagogical location would offer me a tough but simple lesson: these students knew a lot more about racism—consciously and unconsciously—than I did. Texts and authors that I thought I knew read differently in their eyes, and to me through them. I began to juxtapose Franklin's *Autobiography* with the *Narrative of the Life of Frederick Douglass.* (The semester ended with a paper contrasting William Faulkner and Alice Walker.) Franklin's optimistic assertion that the individual can rise from poverty and obscurity to fame and power appeared both denied and confirmed by Douglass's escape from slavery and rise to international celebrity. It was intriguing that both men saw the achievement of literacy as the key to freedom, and both made their careers through the material production of books and newspapers. Could both be assimilated to "The American Dream"?

The inescapable differences between them, however, could be found when one located their writings and careers in terms of their historical bodies, especially as regards the relation of the legal system and state power to myths of individual freedom and achievement. Franklin's rise came through his genius for manipulating the legal systems of discourse; Douglass's literacy was literally a crime, and his very claim to "manhood" a violation of the dictates of the state. The ideology of individual accomplishment that Franklin has been used to promote shows up as hollow in Douglass's case, betraying even Douglass's own complicity in it. Trained in that ideology, however, as well as in the discourse of racism, the majority of my white students wanted to read both Franklin and Douglass as presenting allegories of how the individual could triumph no matter the laws or powers of the state, since that belief is precisely what allows the law and the power of the state to go unchallenged and allows the individual to continue in the complacent myth of autonomy.

For many of my black students, who were attending a recently integrated bastion of white academic racism, these materials presented an uneasy situation. They did not desire to be drawn into open hostility with their white classmates and were sensitive to the bad effects of being located in one's historical body. Many were tired of being the token black or being asked to speak for their people on every occasion, rather than for themselves. Their pride in Douglass was muted by their puzzlement over just how to express their feelings in an oppressive context, which included me—a white instructor. Ultimately we had to make these and other local tensions the subject of classroom discussion, to teach these conflicts to each other by openly questioning the relation of reading to race and of race to individual achievement. Many students began to open up, telling personal stories of their experience of racial and class difference; at that point I had to undo my position as the liberal champion, always a dangerous delusion, and reinscribe myself as another white American, one who had grown up in Los Angeles but had never heard of Watts until he watched black rioters burn it down from the cool comfort of his backyard swimming pool. Racism to me had always been someone else's problem; now I began to feel my own participation in its history. I could criticize racism, but I would never be black (just as I could criticize sexism or homophobia, yet never know them quite as women or gays and lesbians did).

At that time I also began teaching a unit on Jewish-American literature. I had to spend hours in the library researching the history of American Judaism and the details of its culture, despite the fact that my own father was a Jew and my great-grandfather an Orthodox rabbi. I was myself, I realized, the split subject of assimilation. Jewish-American literature provides a useful vantage point for multicultural study, since the Jew both belongs to the hegemony of European cultural tradition and has been the excluded Other within the body of that culture. While Jewish-American writers, critics, and intellectuals have been very successful in securing recognition in the US, they have also made the pathos and incompleteness of their assimilation a constant subject of address. (Among literary critics the classic career of assimilation is that of Lionel Trilling, whose dissertation and first book enacted an identification with Matthew Arnold.) The complexity of these realities is captured brilliantly in Tillie Olsen's *Tell Me a Riddle*, where the contrast between Jewish-American and Mexican-American assimilation unfolds a multicultural fable of the politics of recollected identities.

The autobiographical basis of my illustration may seem gratuitous, but it isn't. By bringing the writing home in this way teachers and students begin to feel the friction between ideological myths and particular histories. Anyone who has tried to teach feminism, for example, will testify to how the personal becomes the pedagogical. The dialogue can be confusing, passionate, humiliating, and transformative, demanding that everyone learn better what Teresa de Lauretis calls "the semiotics of experience" (158–86). If we are to recapture the rich diversity of life in the US, we will have to stop masquerading behind assumed poses of abstraction and generality, even if we continue—with Whitman and Rich—to use the "we" pronoun for utopian purposes. As a teacher I cannot speak on behalf of a united cultural vision or tradition, and I don't want to borrow authority from an ideology that gives me power at the cost of truth.

Historically I belong to a class and generation raised in the knowledge of one tradition, and brought by theory, history, and experience to seek a knowledge of others. My bookshelves are filling with texts and authors never mentioned to me in school. It will take years to begin to absorb them or to know how to speak or write with confidence. Of course I could go on writing about Hawthorne or James or Eliot, but that, I think, would be irresponsible. It would also be less difficult and less interesting than meeting the ethical challenge to undertake what Kolodny describes as a "heroic rereading" of those uncanonized works "with which we are least familiar, and especially so when they challenge current notions of art and artifice." Armed with the criticism and scholarship of the past twenty years, revisionists should "immerse themselves in the texts that were never taught in graduate school—*to the exclusion of the works with which they had previously been taught to feel comfortable and competent*" (302).

What practical consequences can be drawn from such a reading lesson? We should probably abandon even a reconstructed version of the American literature survey course. No one or two semester course can possibly live up to the implied claim of historical or representative coverage; coherence is usually bought at the cost of reductive scenarios resting on dubious premises. At best one can construct courses that take the question "What is an American?" as their only assumption and then work through close readings of texts chosen for the radically different answers they provide (for curricular alternatives see Lauter, *Reconstructing*). The result is more of a rainbow coalition than a melting pot. Facile pluralism might be avoided through demonstrations of the real conflicts between texts and cultures. I advocate courses in which the materials are chosen for the ways in which they *actively interfere* with each other's experiences, languages, and values and for their power to expand the horizon of the student's cultural literacy to encompass peoples he or she has scarcely acknowledged as real.

The socially constructed ignorance of teachers and students will be a hard obstacle to multicultural literacy, for the knowledges it requires have been largely excluded from the mainstream classroom, dissertation, and published critical study. Teachers have enough trouble trying to supply their students with information on the literary forms, historical contexts, and cultural values shaping *The Scarlet Letter* or *The Red Badge of Courage* or *The Waste Land*. Think of the remedial work for everyone when we assign David Walker's *Appeal*, Catharine Sedgwick's *Hope Leslie*, Harriet Jacobs's *Incidents in the Life of a Slave Girl*, Judith Fetterley's anthology *Provisions: A Reader from 19th Century American Women*, William Wells Brown's *Clotel*, Whitman's *Calamus*, Charlotte Gilman's *Herland*, Jacob Riis's *How the Other Half Lives*, Agnes Smedley's *Daughter of Earth*, the poetry and prose of Langston Hughes, the *corridos* of the Southwest, Scott Momaday's *House Made of Dawn*, Audre Lorde's *Zami*, Maxine Hong Kingston's *The Woman Warrior*, or the stories of Bharati Mukherjee.

In terms of method, this reeducation sharpens our ability to discern the various ways a text can participate in (or even produce) its context; in terms of pedagogy, it makes the literature classroom part of a general project of historical recollection, analysis, and criticism; in terms of politics, it confronts the institution, the teacher, and the student with the imperative to appreciate the achievements of distinct cultural groups, which cannot be whitewashed with humanistic cliches about the universality of art, the eternal truths of the soul, or the human condition. In sum, a multicultural pedagogy initiates a cultural re-vision, so that everyone involved comes not only to understand another person's point of view, but to see her or his own culture from the outsider's perspective. This decentering of cultural chauvinism can only be healthy in the long run, especially if it leads each of us to stop thinking of ourselves as subjects of only one position or culture.

From the standpoint of literary theory, this approach treats written works as active agents in the socio-political process. This need not mean, as numerous critics have shown, abandoning attention to the formal properties of writing. On the contrary, it strengthens that focus by locating the historical and material specificity of those forms and by charting how they take effect, are appropriated or transformed in concrete contexts. This *does* mean that purely formalist generic categories such as "the novel" or "the elegy" or "tragedy" be called back from the hazy pedagogy of a naive aestheticism. Theorists from Virginia Woolf and Kenneth Burke to Jameson and Baker and beyond have shown that forms of writing are socially symbolic actions. Styles are linguistic and material practices that negotiate between the binary illusions of documentation and fabrication, or history and fiction. In other words, a renovated rhetorical criticism can frame the written work as an historical utterance, as addressed both to the cultural traditions it draws upon and to the audiences it assumes or even transforms (see Mailloux). Such forms as the slave narrative (produced for abolitionists) or the Native-American autobiography (as told to an ethnographer) provide rich opportunities for deconstructing our categories and concepts of literary authorship and production.

Clearly a multicultural reconception of "Writing in the United States" will lead us to change drastically or eventually abandon the conventional historical narratives, period designations, and major themes and authors previously dominating "American literature." "Colonial" American writing, as I have already suggested, looks quite different from the standpoint of postcolonial politics and theory today, and that period will be utterly recast when Hispanic and Native-American and non-Puritan texts are allowed their just representation. What would be the effect of designating Columbus's *Journal*, the *Narrative of Alvar Nuñez Cabeza de Vaca*, or the creation myths of Native peoples as the origins of US literature, rather than Bradford's *Of Plymouth Plantation*? To take another example, the already shop-worn idea of "The American Renaissance," probably the most famous and persistent of our period myths, ought to be replaced by one that does not reinforce the idea that all culture—even all Western culture—has its authorized origins in Graeco-Roman civilization. The period of 1812–1865 would better be called that of "America During the Wars," since the final colonial war and the wars to take the property of the Native Americans and Mexican-Americans and to keep enslaved the bodies of African-Americans dominated the socio-political scene and heavily determined its literary output, including that of such canonical figures as Cooper, Hawthorne, Melville, Emerson, and Thoreau. This designation would bring back the historical context and along with it the verbal productions of those marginalized groups or cultures which were busy representing themselves in a rich array of spoken and written discourses. The transformation of this period has already begun through emphasis on Native- and African-American texts and on the writing of women in this period, many of whom were actively engaged in these political struggles. Likewise the era of "Modernism" as the period of Eliot, Pound, Stevens, Williams, Hemingway, and Faulkner has been shattered by questions about the gender and race limitations of this historical construct, prompting renewed attention to Stein, H. D., Moore, and Barnes and a reconsideration of the Harlem Renaissance.

Take finally the currently fashionable tag "postmodern," originally used in literary studies to categorize the self-reflexive fiction of white men (Barth, Coover, Barthelme, Vonnegut, Pynchon) who struggled with the legacy of their modernist fathers. In the popular formulation of Jean-Francois Lyotard, postmodernism names a period without "metanarratives," a sort of extended epistemological and semiotic version of what we used to call the death of God. From his locations in Paris and Irvine, however, Lyotard sees this as the crisis of peculiarly disembodied, abstract, and metaphysical concepts, whereas these metanarratives belong to the ideological apparatus of identifiable institutional and historical groups. As Edward Said points out in his critique of Lyotard, the (supposed) breakdown of the metanarratives of "emancipation" and "enlightenment" cannot be comprehended as solely an internal event of Western civilization. The collapse of Western metaphysical metanarratives, especially those of what is called "The Subject," are (and it's no coincidence) contemporary with the struggle of non-European populations and countries for historical self-determination—for the freedom to be agents rather than subjects.

According to Said, Lyotard '"*separates* Western postmodernism from the non-European world, and from the consequences of European modernism—and modernization—in the colonized world." Moreover, the crisis of legitimacy characterizing Western modernism involved

> the disturbing appearance in Europe of various Others, whose provenance was the imperial domain. In the works of Eliot, Conrad, Mann, Proust, Woolf, Pound, Lawrence, Joyce, Forster, alterity and difference are systematically associated with strangers, who, whether women, natives, or sexual eccentrics, erupt into vision, there to challenge and resist settled metropolitan histories, forms, modes of thought. (222–23)

Once one puts the color back into postmodernism, if you will, then the period's inseparability from postcolonialism appears crucial. And this is not simply a matter of discerning the origins of modernism's traumatized consciousness in the West's confrontation with its Others or even of deconstructing the representations of those Others passed off by dominant discourses. Postcolonialism means recognizing, or at least trying to find a way to read, the texts produced by dominated peoples, and acknowledging their participation in narratives of resistance. The literary and cultural works of the marginalized during the nineteenth and twentieth centuries, then, suddenly appear as part of the ongoing development of a postmodern literature, insofar as they contradict the metanarratives of Western modernism. One could argue that, among "Americans" writing in English, a different canon of postmoderns could be compiled from the explosion of texts by contemporary African-, Asian-, and Native-American writers (see Vizenor).

Themes, like periods, derive from and are determined by a previously canonized set of texts and authors. The classic themes of American literature—the Virgin Land, the Frontier West, the Individual's conflict with Society, the City versus the Country, Innocence versus Experience, Europe versus America, Dream versus Reality, and so on—simply make no sense when applied to marginalized texts and traditions, including those produced by women. Thematic criticism can be especially discriminatory since themes are by definition repeated elements of a totality or metanarrative centered in an historically limited point of view, though thematic criticism regularly universalizes that perspective and so transforms an angle of insight into an oppressive ideological fabrication. The cartoon simplicity of these themes serves as a mask for this ideological pretension: it presents a partial experience in the form of an eternal verity, thus at once obstructing any analysis of the historical construction of that perception or any analysis of viewpoints that don't conform to the theme or which lose their difference and cultural truth when they are made to conform to the theme.

To supplement or replace periods and themes as points for organizing classes and critical studies, I would offer rather a list of problematics whose analysis would put texts from different cultures within the US into dialogue with one another. Unlike a theme, a problematic does not designate a moment in the history of the consciousness of a privileged subject. A problematic rather indicates an event in culture made up simultaneously of material conditions and conceptual forms that direct the possibilities of representation. A problematic acts as one of the determinants of a representation, though it does not operate as an origin. A problematic indicates how and where the struggle for meaning *takes place*. Each of us could construct a list of problematics conditioning US writing, but for illustrative purposes I would argue for the following: (1) origins, (2) power, (3) civilization, (4) tradition, (5) assimilation, (6) translation, (7) bodies, (8) literacy, and (9) borders. While these problematics have indeed been addressed by some writers, and thus may appear to be themes, I want to resist reducing them to intentionalities or structures of consciousness. Having touched on most already, I want to end by saying something more about origins and power.

The deconstruction of metaphysical ideas about origins played a key role in the development of poststructuralist criticism and initially was resisted by advocates of marginalized groups, who rightly insisted on the need to affirm and recollect the difference of their beginnings (Gates, "The Master's Pieces"). I think we have a consensus today that no choice exists between essentialism and nihilism, as they are two sides of the same metaphysical coin. Because of the historic destruction of dominated (sub)cultures by privileged classes, much writing by women and persons of color tries to recover traditions rather than rebel against them. But as Michael Fischer argues, ethnicity is less an essence than a constantly traversed borderland of differences, "something reinvented and reinterpreted in each generation by each individual. . . . Ethnicity is not something that is simply passed on from generation to generation, taught and learned; it is something dynamic, often unsuccessfully repressed or avoided" (195). This process of recollection does not entail a simple nostalgia or the dream of recreating a lost world: more painfully and complexly it involves a risky translation of recovered fragments into imagined futures by way of often hostile presents.

"The constituency of 'the ethnic,'" writes R. Radhakrishnan, "occupies quite literally a 'pre-post'-erous space where it has to actualize, enfranchize, and empower its own 'identity' and coextensively engage in the deconstruction of the very logic of 'identity' and its binary and exclusionary politics" (199). What should be resisted are myths of origin that function in totalitarian fashion; what should be solicited are myths of beginning that delineate the historical and cultural specifics of a group's experiences and interactions (see Said's *Beginnings*). In multicultural studies we examine multiple sites of origin and multiple claims to foundational perspectives. Rather than adjudicate between these claims in a timeless philosophical tribunal, the student of culture ought to analyze the historical development of the conditions for these narratives and the consequences of their interactions. This would mean, for example, contrasting the disparate creation myths of Native and Puritan Americans and speculating upon how the values embodied in these myths shaped the outcome of the conflict between these groups.

Thus a deconstructive thinking about origins can work along with a politically charged criticism that affirms a dialogue with the Other, so that multicultural study need not lead to the metaphysical dead end of "identity politics." This point is made with exemplary tact by Meese in her chapter on Silko's *Ceremony* (29–49). The novel's choice of a "half-breed" protagonist and multiracial cast of characters and the plot turns that entangle them make it impossible, she argues, to interpret it as calling for a return to a fabled purity of Indian identity. Instead a more intricate process of "crossing cultures" gets represented and played out, one that analyzes the changing economy of values between acculturated subjects—and between that economy and the values of the reader.

Michel Foucault stressed the inseparability of knowledge and power, a problematic he revolutionized by using his experience as a gay man to rethink its traditional scenario. Multicultural studies cannot evade the question of power, since power is both a prime subject for analysis and a constitutive element of the situation of the analysis: the student and the professor are empowered in relation to the object of study, and this disciplinary power usually has its affiliations with distributions of power along lines of gender, region, class, age, ethnicity, and so on. While texts may be studied as expressions of struggles for power, and while we may reflect self-consciously on how scholarship participates in the institutions of power, we should not forget the cautions offered by poststructuralism regarding the fallacies of reference and mimesis. We cannot assume the veracity of a text's representations, and the powers of a text are certainly not confined to its correspondence to an objectively verifiable reality. We must discern how texts take power—how they gain power through the modes of their composition as well as through the modes of their (re)production.

The canonical status of a text is often justified by reference to its superior "power" and its endurance ascribed to the timeless claim it makes on readers. In response we need to question the aesthetics of power and the power of aesthetics.

Once one demonstrates that the power of a text to move a reader is a culturally produced effect—that literary "taste" is not natural but taught, and taught in a way that reproduces values that go beyond aesthetics—then the issue of power becomes of vital pedagogical concern. Yet no teacher or text can ensure that the student will receive the letter as it is prescribed. No pedagogy or text, no matter the care of its address, can predetermine exactly the effect it has on everyone, for everyone's subjectivity is plural. Moreover texts are not clear messages or simple unities but occasions when a mediation of conflicts is symbolically enacted. Teachers have the responsibility to empower previously marginalized texts and readers, and to teach in a way that we risk surprising and painful changes in the interpretive habits, expectations, and values of our students—and of ourselves. If we acknowledge that the aesthetic power of a text is a function of the distribution of material and cultural power in society, our pedagogy cannot help but become politically embroiled. In teaching students to value other cultures and other world views we necessarily draw them with us into conflicts with the dominant culture that has produced and sustained our identities and which has the power to enforce its opinions as law. At the same time, we as readers and writers may become agents of change, not just subjects of discourse; we may draw or take power from the canon, from history, from the institution, and turn it in unexpected directions. "We" can fight the power.

Works Cited

Baker, Houston A., Jr. *The Journey Back: Issues in Black Literature and Criticism.* Chicago: U of Chicago P, 1980.

———, ed. *Three American Literatures.* NY: MLA, 1982.

Baym, Nina. "Early Histories of American Literature: A Chapter in the History of New England." *American Literary History* 1 (1989): 459–88.

Bercovitch, Sacvan. "America as Canon and Context: Literary History in a Time of Dissensus." *American Literature* 58 (1986): 99–108.

Bourne, Randolph. "Trans-National America." *Atlantic Monthly*, July 1916: 86–97.

Clifford, James. Introduction. "Partial Truths." Clifford and Marcus 1–26.

Clifford, James, and George E. Marcus, eds. *Writing Culture: The Poetics and Politics of Ethnography*. Berkeley: U of California P, 1986.

de Lauretis, Teresa. *Alice Doesn't: Feminism, Semiotics, Cinema*. Bloomington: Indiana UP, 1984.

Elliot, Emory. "New Literary History: Past and Present." *American Literature* 57 (1985): 611–25.

———. "The Politics of Literary History." *American Literature* 59 (1987): 268–76.

Fischer, Michael M. J. "Ethnicity and the Post-Modern Arts of Memory." Clifford and Marcus 194–233.

Foucault, Michel. Afterword. "The Subject and Power." *Michel Foucault: Beyond Structuralism and Hermeneutics*. Ed. Herbert L. Dreyfuss and Paul Rabinow. 2nd ed. Chicago: U of Chicago P, 1983.

Gates, Henry Louis, Jr. *Figures in Black: Words, Signs, and the "Racial" Self*. NY: Oxford UP, 1987.

———. "The Master's Pieces: On Canon Formation and the African American Tradition." *South Atlantic Quarterly* 89 (1990): 89–112.

Giroux, Henry A. "Liberal Arts Education and the Struggle for Public Life: Dreaming About Democracy." *South Atlantic Quarterly* 89 (1990): 113–38.

Gómez-Peña, Guillermo. "Documented/Undocumented." *The Graywolf Annual Five: Multicultural Literacy*. Ed. Rick Simonson and Scott Walker. Saint Paul: Graywolf, 1988.

Graff, Gerald. *Professing Literature: An Institutional History*. Chicago: U of Chicago P, 1987.

———. "Teach the Conflicts." *South Atlantic Quarterly* 89 (1990): 51–68.

JanMohamed, Abdul R., and David Lloyd. Introduction. Special issue on "The Nature and Context of Minority Discourse." Vol. 1. *Cultural Critique* 6 (1987): 5–12.

Kolodny, Annette. "The Integrity of Memory: Creating a New Literary History of the United States." *American Literature* 57 (1985): 291–307.

Lauter, Paul, ed. *The Heath Anthology of American Literature.* 2 vols. Boston: Heath, 1989.

————, ed. *Reconstructing American Literature: Courses, Syllabi, Issues.* Old Westbury, NY: Feminist P, 1983.

Lyotard, Jean-Francois. *The Postmodern Condition: A Report on Knowledge.* Trans. Geoff Bennington and Brian Massumi. Minneapolis: U of Minnesota P, 1984.

Mailloux, Steven. *Rhetorical Power.* Ithaca: Cornell UP, 1989.

Meese, Elizabeth. *(Ex)Tensions: Refiguring Feminist Criticism.* Urbana: U of Illinois P, 1990.

Moraga, Cherríe. "La Guera." *This Bridge Called My Back: Writings by Radical Women of Color.* Ed. Cherríe Moraga and Gloria Anzaldúa. NY: Kitchen Table P, 1983.

Radhakrishnan, R. "Ethnic Identity and Post-Structuralist Differance." *Cultural Critique* 6 (1987): 199–220 .

Ravitch, Diane. "Multiculturalism: E Pluribus Plures." *American Scholar* (Summer 1990): 337–54.

Reising, Russell. *The Unusable Past: Theory and the Study of American Literature.* NY: Methuen, 1986.

Rich, Adrienne. *Blood, Bread, and Poetry: Selected Prose 1979–1985.* NY: Norton, 1986.

Rosaldo, Renato. "Politics, Patriarchs, and Laughter." *Cultural Critique* 6 (1987): 65–86.

Said, Edward W. *Beginnings: Intention and Method.* NY: Basic, 1975.

————. "Representing the Colonized: Anthropology's Interlocutors." *Critical Inquiry* 15 (1989): 205–25.

Saldívar, José David. "The Limits of Cultural Studies." *American Literary History* 2 (1990): 251–66 .

Sedgwick, Eve Kosofsky. "Pedagogy in the Context of an Antihomophobic Project." *South Atlantic Quarterly* 89 (1990): 139–56.

Smith, Barbara Herrnstein. *Contingencies of Value: Alternative Perspectives for Critical Theory.* Cambridge: Harvard UP, 1988.

Spengemann, William. "American Things/Literary Things: The Problem of American Literary History." *American Literature* 57 (1985): 456–81.

Vizenor, Gerald. "A Postmodern Introduction." *Narrative Chance: Postmodern Discourse on Native American Indian Literatures.* Albuquerque: U of New Mexico P, 1989: 3–16.

Whitman, Walt. *Leaves of Grass and Selected Prose.* Ed. Lawrence Buell. NY: Random, 1981.

In the Big Muddy
Art and Politics in the Classroom

Cornel Bonca

> There is no document of civilization that is not at the same time a document of barbarism.
>
> —*Walter Benjamin,*
> *"Theses on the Philosophy of History"*

> Waist deep in the big muddy . . .
>
> —*Bruce Springsteen,*
> *"Big Muddy"*

If I could propose a single suggestion for teachers interested in exploring the issues brought about by the recent debate on the canon, it would be to adopt Benjamin's sentence as an epigraph to their literature class syllabi. Let it stand there, perched atop what otherwise would seem to students a harmless list of texts. Let them stare at it and wonder. Those who do so long enough, and honestly enough, might just start hearing one hand clap.

That is, of course, if they can first get past their intellectual panic, which often sets in when anyone confronts the uncanny. But then I can think of nothing better for a class of nineteen-year-olds than genuine intellectual panic. If I could offer a second suggestion, it would be that libraries and college entrance portals dig Benjamin's words into their walls—though I won't hold my breath—because colleges and universities could use a good dose of honest intellectual panic, too. Now it's true that for some time, academic journals and the popular press have been filled with reports of the crisis of liberal humanistic education, but rather than engage this very real crisis's trenchant contradictions, which Benjamin has captured with aphoristic economy, mostly what we professors and critics have done is harden our polarized positions—(traditionalists on one side and the left on the other), preach mostly to the converted, and willfully misconstrue, even condescend to the other side.[1] We haven't waded deep enough in the big muddy, as that junior college dropout Bruce Springsteen would say, and our students, hungry for the many ways literature can illuminate and liberate their lives, suffer from our failure.

Look at Benjamin's claim again: "There is no document of civilization that is not at the same time a document of barbarism." In a politically correct era, it's a good idea, as Gide once warned his own interpreters, not to understand Benjamin too quickly. Of course he is saying that documents of civilization—art, literature, history, philosophy, science—are written by the privileged, or at least by those who have benefited from the repressive order that the privileged have imposed, and that for the modern historian "cultural treasures . . . have an origin which he cannot contemplate without horror. They owe their existence not only to the efforts of the great minds and talents who have created them, but also to the anonymous toil of their contemporaries" (256). "Civilization" requires for its creation, in other words, conditions that for the many are barbarous, and often betrays its barbarism in the very art that is supposed to rise above brutality.[2] This isn't exactly news, yet it is our inability to hold the paradox in our minds that makes it so ominous.[3] Many academic traditionalists think it is inflammatory, excessively "political," even irrelevant to yoke cultural treasures with horror, "great minds and talents" with repressive ideology. Why stain the best that has been thought and said ("the documents of civilization") with history's slaughter bench, or with our temporary political obsessions (sure to look strange and skewed fifty years from now), when art provides us our only opportunity to rise above history, to rescue fragments against our ruin? The traditionalists deny the yoking, or at least its importance, in order to protect the formal autonomy of art or the integrity of the Great Works.

For their part, many on the academic left— poststructuralists; New Historicists; proponents of multiculturalism; analysts of race, class, and gender— domesticate Benjamin's haunted statement to serve what seems to me an equally limited vision. They take up, say, T. S. Eliot's totalizing tendencies (his appeal to myth as formal organizing principle, the idea of "Tradition"), and then link them with his Anglo-royalist politics (and sometimes to his racism). The link, fortified by the poststructuralist joining of "totalization" with "totalitarianism," casts such a deep shadow over the poetry that it becomes virtually impossible—even frivolous—to appreciate the poetry's formal innovations and extraordinary emotional reach, both down to the depths of nihilist grief and upwards toward the grace of religious revelation. Eliot's "great mind and talent" are discounted in order to foreground his unacceptable politics.[4]

The traditionalists want to deny that a document of civilization participates in barbarism, while the left wants to deny that a document of barbarism can still be a great civilized work, a "cultural treasure." Both sides miss Benjamin's tortured point: civilization *coexists* with barbarism in the same document, and neither cancels out the other. If a document of civilization can be a document of hideous barbarism, that same barbaric document can remain a remarkable document of civilization. Eliot's poems, for all their troublesome appeals to dubious forms of authority, are still stunning works of art, the envy of thousands of writers who came after him, and are still able to generate deeply resonant responses in his readers. Eliot is a reminder of the consolations *and* costs of art in a world drenched in horror.

In this essay, I'd like to explore how we might make this paradox, this frightening juxtaposition of civilization and barbarism, available to students in such a way that they will see imaginative literature as a powerful muddy river, the site of a running struggle in writers and readers to achieve aesthetic wonder *and* social illumination, purity of aesthetic form *and* urgency of political engagement, *jouissance and* social consciousness, goals that often directly contradict each other. Along the way, students might recognize that the *stakes* of writing and reading literature are vertiginously, heartbreakingly high—as are the stakes of all great passions, all leaps into dangerous rivers—and worth a lifetime of brave, eternally frustrating, and loving attention.

II

Scott Fitzgerald wrote that the "test of a first-class intelligence is the ability to hold two opposing ideas in the mind at the same time, and still retain the ability to function" (69). Fitzgerald's "first-class intelligence" has always seemed to me a very American rewriting of Keats's "man of Achievement," the man of "negative capability" who was able to dwell "in uncertainties, mysteries, doubts, without any irritable reaching after fact and reason" (104). Fitzgerald's formulation came in the famous *Crack Up* essay, which he wrote in the stark dawn of clarity following the worst of his breakdowns, and it ought to give us all pause, since, from the mid-1960s on, the whole enterprise of liberal education has been cracking up and breaking down, much as Fitzgerald's delicate sensibility did. I'm tempted to suggest that if we want our students to experience literature with the kind of impact that will lead to a lifelong engagement with it—which after all, ought to be our main goal in teaching literature—we need simply to acquire a first-class intelligence, achieve some negative capability. I'm not being altogether glib here. These days, profoundly irritated by the juggernauts of structuralism and deconstruction, which together have done a spectacular job of shaking the humanistic foundations upon which liberal education makes its appeal, we do reach too quickly after the consolations of "fact and reason" (or the contemporary equivalent of such, which is *theory)* rather than dwelling in the uncertainties of our trade.[5] Poststructuralism is a tidal wave of Enlightenment revisionism: "reason" is now just a form of rhetoric; "truth" is another word for "power"; "objective knowledge" is a disguise for propaganda; "humanity" is a code for the universalized values of dominant white males; the "self" is an accidental net of discourse, soon to disappear from history altogether; and "freedom," well, freedom is just another word for something we never had to lose to begin with. The critique is devastating for liberal education, since it is founded on the belief that the "self" can use "reason" to acquire "knowledge" that will help it "liberate" itself from the local prejudices of time and place in order to discover, if not truth itself, at least a certain clarity and "humanity." Poststructuralism means, among other things, the twilight of liberal education's idols, and most of the education establishment has been scrambling ever since, to try to find new terms to justify what it does for a living.

The academic left, that loose-knit group of scholars—often quite contentious with one another—who have made self-conscious and overt leftist political thinking (inspired by Foucault, Fanon, and feminism, not by Marx) central to the literary critical scene, have arrived to fill the void of purpose in liberal education, and they have done more than anyone else to shake up our thinking about that shadowy notion called the canon. Though they engage in the kind of internecine haggling common to any robust group of scholars, I think it's fair to say that they generally agree with Foucault that Euro-, phallogo- and logo-centric concepts like "truth," "reality," "knowledge," "culture," "beauty," "sanity," "white," "male," and "the self," disguise ideological power grids of class, gender, and race hidden below the surface of discourse that are designed to empower certain groups and marginalize others. The Western tradition, in fact, for many leftists, is mostly one long document of barbarism, a sweeping record of the manipulation of discourse in the service of the privileged few and at the expense of oppressed billions, and thus the purpose of an education in the "human sciences" (which replaces the "liberal arts") is to uncover the manipulations, to give voice back to the silenced and disenfranchised, to deconstruct the deceptive platitudes about Great Works and artistic excellence that have dominated Western discourse, and to replace them with the concept of "diversity." In other words, education's purpose is to politicize in an overt way a cultural process which has disguised its political nature all along. To these ends, these leftists have called for a revision of the canon to include writers of previously underrepresented groups, and have undertaken the theoretical project of showing that definitions of "art," "excellence," "beauty," and other aesthetic concepts are inextricably bound up with the race, class, and gender biases of the definers, who up till now have been overwhelmingly white, well-off, and male.

The left, all in all, is a zealous force at the moment, possessed of a moral fervor and a mobilizing anger that has re-energized several disciplines, bringing literature departments in particular bracingly out of the formalism of the previous forty years and discovering new ways for students—a radically different and more diverse population than those who attended college before the 1960s—to connect with history and literature. At the same time, there has come to be something droningly predictable about leftist criticism, not to mention sanctimonious (especially when white male critics perform their acts of absolution), humorless (a female stage director I know relished this joke: Q: "How many feminists does it take to screw in a light bulb?" A: "That's not funny"), stiflingly materialistic, and as ham-fisted as thirties communist literary criticism in its attempts to discuss a text's aesthetic power. Too many on the left seem excessively satisfied, in other words, with showing that documents of civilization are documents of barbarism, without acknowledging that the reverse is also true. Because of this, the left seems to do only half of what a literary work demands in a classroom.

The traditionalists, a similarly loose group, as contentious with each other as is the left (perhaps even more so), are composed of the Blooms, the Bennetts, and the Great Books editors at the reactionary end of the spectrum; the straggling remnants of the Age of Eliot in the academy; post-old-left New York intellectuals at *Partisan Review* and *Salmagundi*; and a large body of humanistic scholars throughout the nation who wish all this canon hubbub would go away so they could go about their work in peace. Traditionalists disagree about many things, but they are united by their conviction that art is not just another form of discourse, that it is indeed "privileged"—not by criteria reducible to race, class, and gender, however, but by formal and aesthetic values (harmony; integrity; subtlety; complexity; sensitivity; wit, perhaps; or a work's ability to inspire awe, mystery, wonder, pleasure, vividness) that, if not "universal," are certainly time-honored enough that we can celebrate them as being part of the long and distinguished line called the Western tradition. Great literature deserves our respect and careful attention, for it has survived the vagaries of historical circumstance and goes some way toward redeeming the admittedly horrible history out of which it was born. For the traditionalist, if you want a document of barbarism, watch a Nazi film of Jews being shot into a mass grave. Don't put that in the same category as *The Four Quartets.*

But the traditionalist response is as inadequate to the demands of teaching imaginative literature as is the left's. Suffice it to say that traditionalists have been unable to answer the poststructuralist critique, specifically the charge that aesthetic judgments are ultimately just expressions of subjective taste reinforced by a self-interested cultural hierarchy. But I do want to suggest that traditionalists suffer, ironically enough, from the same problem that the leftists suffer: they refuse to acknowledge fully the *para-doxa*—the side-by-sideness—of civilization and barbarism, the *equal* claims that a work of literature asks us to make of its art and its politics. Traditionalists want art to keep its hands clean of politics, just as leftists insist that art is always already politics, and thus seek to keep their hands clean of the unruly energies of art.

I'm not going to claim I have an answer to the paradox—I don't think there is one—but I do think that holding the two opposing ideas of civilization and barbarism—the simultaneous demands of art and politics—in the mind at the same time, is the best way to run a classroom and create a syllabus. D. H. Lawrence's genius is *more* vital to me, not less, because of his sexist and authoritarian impulses; the soaring lyricism of *The Duino Elegies* is more wondrous to me precisely because it is equally capable of inspiring saintliness and fascism, maybe both at once (a point Pynchon's *Gravity's Rainbow,* by the way, makes with extraordinary power). Furthermore, I like how saying these things affects my students. The note taking stops, and a certain increased density of thought fills the room, a more uncomfortable, ungrounded, a more *panicky* thinking, which is the kind of thinking that is necessary before a student can let go of typical preconceptions such as "the true artist is above politics" or, on the other hand, "good artists are politically correct." All students (undergraduates especially) need to float awhile in the void, need to feel the danger of seeing their moral and intellectual compasses go haywire. They need to feel the walls of their mental categories teeter and fall so that they can sit amidst their ruins and begin reconstructing them piece by piece, more aware this time of how tenuous and fraught with difficulty all intellectual activity is.

I don't think this happens sufficiently when a course emphasizes aesthetic concerns at the expense of history and politics or, on the other hand, when a course emphasizes the left's political agenda at the expense of aesthetic concerns. Let me give examples of what happens in each of these cases. Take the question of style in Hemingway. To read a sentence as simple as "It was a fine morning" from *The Sun Also Rises* is to sense the enormous authority Hemingway was able to steal from the taut straight-shooting tones of Midwest vernacular as well as the painstaking effort it took for him to accommodate this minimalist voice to a form dominated by his genteel precursors. There is an excitement to the *sound* of *The Sun Also Rises* that is similar to what people must have felt when they first heard, say, Elvis's "Sun Sessions."[6] But to read this same sentence in *Across the River and Into the Trees* is to sense how the pressures of a modern style can overburden a work and slacken its energies if that style is not continually rethought and renewed. These are not small issues in a classroom; they are vital to anyone interested not so much in "discourse," but in the struggles of craft, in engagements with the sensual texture of words that, for a writer, are every bit as important as a painter making up his or her palette. They are especially exciting for those—and English major rosters are replete with them—who are interested in writing.

To limit discussion of Hemingway to his craft, of course, deprives the student of the fuller implications of his work. For Hemingway's style—leanly macho (keeping emotion close to the vest) and often disdainfully authoritative—is a perfect fit for his content, which glorifies exclusively male pursuits, especially violence, and is frequently homophobic, women-hating, and anti-Semitic. We can claim, as some have, that Hemingway's shabby politics makes discussion of his artistic talent beside the point: I know people with Ph.D.'s who refuse to read him on principle.[7] But this seems absurd to me. I have a Jewish friend—steeped from birth in the Jewish tradition and as aware as anyone that the Holocaust began within fifteen years after Hemingway made Robert Cohn the object of his ridicule and bile in the novel—who keeps going back to Hemingway's work with the complex feelings one has toward a long-standing lover. He knows that an artist can have despicable ideas and still be an artist. Great artists, he knows, tend not to be very nice people, but are men and women with abiding obsessions that are usually accompanied by a morass of prejudices and bad mental habits that nonetheless allow them—are sometimes even instrumental in allowing them—to focus their tumultuous imaginations. What if my friend discovered somehow that a Pole read *The Sun Also Rises* in 1940, and the experience tipped his decision towards turning in a family of Jews hiding in a Warsaw attic? Would that make *The Sun Also Rises* less great a book? No, he'd say, just more dangerous, as dangerous and muddy as are all places where passionate minds meet. This conclusion seems immensely more powerful—and more likely to propel students into a lifelong passion for literature—than merely denouncing Hemingway's obvious stupidities.

On the other hand, what happens when we examine a novel—say, Toni Morrison's *Beloved*—as a document of barbarism, as a document primarily of political ideology? Many of the episodes—Paul D's horror in the chain gang, the murder of Sixo, Sethe's assault by the white boys while her husband looks on, Halle's subsequent insanity, Sethe's brutal murder of her baby girl so the child would never have to enter a life of slavery—are so wrenching and so obviously have their origins in the institution of slavery itself that as readers we are ready to assent to Stamp Paid's meditation:

> Whitepeople believed that whatever the manners, under every dark skin was a jungle. Swift unnavigable waters, swinging screaming baboons, sleeping snakes, red gums ready for their sweet white blood. . . . But it wasn't the jungle blacks brought with them to this place from the other (livable) place. It was the jungle whitefolks planted

in them. And it grew. It spread. In, through and after life,
it spread, until it invaded the whites who had made it.
Touched them every one. Changed and altered them.
Made them bloody, silly, worse than even they wanted to
be, so scared were they of the jungle they had made. The
screaming baboon lived under their own white skin; the
red gums were their own.

Meantime, the secret spread of this new kind of
whitefolks' jungle was hidden, silent, except once in a
while when you could hear its mumbling in places like
124. (198–9)

The sadism of whites—the jungle inside them—this reading
goes, first created slavery, and the destruction of African tribal
culture and its family traditions, as well as the dehumanization,
horror, insanity, and death that African Americans have endured
ever since, have even inflicted on each other, are all inarguably
connected to white oppression. Whatever love and tenderness
can be salvaged from this historical condition is as miraculous as
a ghost shaking the walls of 124. This is ideologically potent
material, and where I teach, at a state university (in Orange
County, California) serving a predominantly white and middle-
class population, it is tempting to simply hammer this point
home and hope to change some idle minds about American
racism, past and present.

But if that's all one does, then one is doing a profound
disservice to a writer who has expended as much careful effort
finding her voice as Hemingway did. To perform on *Beloved* an
ideological analysis is only one part (necessary as that is) of
engaging it. Unlike, say, Susana Rowson's early nineteenth-
century novel, *Charlotte Temple*, which is being used more and
more in American literature classes as an illustration of the way
ideology functions in a text, *Beloved* is not *used up* by ideological
analysis. *Charlotte Temple* doesn't repay rereading. Once you
grasp the fact that it depicts a fully operative patriarchal
universe that even its author participates in, there's nothing left
to say. The novel simply lacks richness; after we process its
ideological implications, there's no supplementary energy to the
book. As Keats would say, "there is nothing to be intense
upon."[8] *Beloved*, on the other hand, is one of the most awesome
fictional performances American literature has produced in

years. The passage I quoted above is caught up not just in the horror of African American history, but in the *wonder* of it; the prose excites in a reader a feeling for the vastness, the sheer *unbelievability*, of the African American legacy—and not just as an abstract notion but as an idea planted deep in a single man's beleaguered soul (Stamp Paid's) and expressed in his own living and unmistakable voice. The passage has surprise, emotional tensile strength, power, that is, the ability to move even minds that want to resist it. As professors, we need to address ourselves to the alchemic wonder Morrison inspires here, even if we have no legitimate paradigms for what makes it beautiful. In a literature class, ideas of aesthetic quality, emotional power, and wonder should always be kept bouncing, highly and visibly.

Sandra Gilbert has written that "not only is the personal the political; the aesthetic is the political; the literary is the political; the rhetorical is the political" (31). I agree. But unless we want to be thoughtlessly reductive, we have to acknowledge that if this is true, then the political is also the aesthetic, the literary, the rhetorical. When dealing with works of the imagination, neither side of the equation should have priority. Harold Bloom, gadfly that he is, once suggested that, all "writing" being equal, why not, when we perform a Freudian interpretation of Shakespeare, follow it up with a Shakespearean interpretation of Freud? Imagine what we might learn if we applied Shakespeare's intuition about character and emotion, his humor and passion and fearlessness, to Freudian ideology. In the same spirit, why not ask a class which has just trashed *Lady Chatterley's Lover* for its sexism to imagine a full Lawrentian reading of late twentieth-century feminism? Imagine a Kafkaesque reading of Foucault! Or an Eliotic interpretation of Terry Eagleton! We could expect strange and wondrous things: brilliant dances of intuition, flashes of insight that a theorist would take dozens of pages to develop, and startling revelations that emerge from a master craftsman's scrutiny of academic prose. It probably wouldn't be pretty—and it would be no more fair than a contemporary theorist's condemnation of an artist for having outmoded political views—but it would offer a necessary tonic to those for whom politics is the primary yardstick for critical analysis. It would pitch the virtues and vices of art versus the virtues and vices of politics in a very direct way; leave students standing waist deep in the big muddy, swamped (if only for the moment) by imaginative literature's manifold conflicting interests; and give them a compelling direction to sort our their own feelings over a lifetime's worth of reading.

III

I know I'm not alone in finding the final page of *The Great Gatsby* one of the most haunting passages in American literature. I've read the book, and that ending, perhaps fifty times, and it has never failed to move me with the feeling that *this is as good as words get; this is what words are meant to do.* It never fails to remind me why I entered a profession that was about the power of words—rather than, say, computer programming or carpentry. And I think one of the biggest reasons I feel so partial to that ending is because it is one of the greatest documents of civilization and barbarism we have in this country's literature. It is easy to read it as a romanticization of (sexual and economic) imperialism by those Dutch sailors who set their European gaze on "the fresh green breast of the new world" they aimed to despoil like they'd despoiled virgins everywhere else.[9] This is not really a wrong reading, just half of one. Because the passage, like the book, acknowledges the barbaric tragedy of the American past at the same time it rings with the wonder of the American odyssey woven into that tragedy. We do beat on, boats against the current, but it is a deep powerful muddy river we dip our oars into, and Fitzgerald knew that. And the past we seek? It's just as muddy but, all the same, commensurate with *our* capacity for wonder *because* it is both civilized and barbaric, beautiful and damned, and finally able to inspire such thrillingly vivid words to force us to confront it.

In this essay, while I've spoken to the necessity of a "first-class intelligence" mediating the demands of art and politics in the classroom, I have doubtless come off as leaning toward the demands of art rather than politics. Carolyn Heilbrun wrote back in 1979 that "the spirit has largely gone from our studies"; English studies were still mired in the "same old [formalist] stuff," she said, lacking the relevance and vitality that feminist political perspectives could bring it (28). She may have been right in 1979, but by 1992, I think the pendulum has swung the other way, and I sense another flagging in spirit, this time precipitated by the abdication of our responsibilities to treat the same old formalist stuff with the same passion with which we treat the new political perspectives. We have developed a daunting theoretical scaffolding to analyze the political implications of works of art, but we as a profession have begun to abandon talk of beauty and aesthetic power. Novelists and poets certainly haven't stopped talking about these things—that's why there is so little dialogue between artists and critics these days—but we have begun to, and if we don't change, our teaching will stagnate. And our students—whose desire that art and literature give them beauty, excitement, pleasure, and illumination is as powerful as their longing for love (remember what that was like?)—will abandon literature for art that does give them those things—Rap (that language-infatuated phenomenon), postpunk rock, David Lynch movies—and we will end up getting through to fewer students than we already do.

NOTES

1. John Searle, in his essay "The Storm Over the University," points out that "the frustrating feature of the recent debate is that the underlying assumptions seldom come out into the open" (36). For Searle, these assumptions have to do with whether the canon should be construed in primarily "political"—as opposed to literary or aesthetic—terms. The left says yes, the traditionalists say no, and both snap derisively at the other for being obtuse and close-minded. See also the very excitable and entertaining exchange of letters, typical of the current debate, between Gerald Graff, Barbara Herrnstein Smith and Searle that followed Searle's essay in *NYRB*'s February 14, 1991 issue (pp. 48–50) and its May 16, 1991 issue (pp. 62–30).

2. George Steiner makes the point this way: "Numerous representative achievements—literary, artistic, philosophic—are inseparable from the milieu of absolutism, of extreme injustice, even of

gross violence, in which they flourished. To be argued seriously, the question of 'the guilt of civilization,' must include not only colonialism and the rapacities of empire but the true nature of the relations between the production of great art and thought, on the one hand, and of regimes of violent and repressive order, on the other" (64).

3. And the paradox hits closer to home than many of us like to think. For instance, state-funded universities in California, and the unions that represent their workers, battled all through the summer of 1992 to ensure that their budgets would take a lesser "hit" during California's fiscal crisis than those of other state-funded institutions. They succeeded. Both the budgets of the University of California and California State University—when we consider both budget cuts and shifts from state to county and city budgets—were spared the gutting that took place, for instance, in the California welfare system, the Medi-Cal system (which serves the medical needs of the poor), and other "safety net" programs. Curiously, there was little outcry from professors. Budget priority issues are always complicated, of course, but my point is that the state education system benefits *at the expense* of other programs, usually those with less powerful constituencies, i.e. the poor, the uneducated, the historically unrepresented. The civilized documents that academics at the University of California and California State University produce in the form of research thus have their barbaric undertow. This essay, in fact, was written under that system and can't escape implication in the paradox I have been describing.

4. See Andrew Ross (chapters 1–3) and Terry Eagleton (146–151) for examples of such views.

5. It might be objected here that neither Fitzgerald's nor Keats's notions are free of an aestheticism which makes them dubious devices for mediating the paradoxes of civilization and barbarism, art and politics. Fitzgerald links a "first-rate intelligence" with "a literary man" who is "never going to have the power of a man of strong political or religious conviction" but who will be "certainly more independent" (70). As for Keats, he says that negative capability "pursued through volumes would perhaps take us no further than this, that with a great poet the sense of Beauty overwhelms every other consideration, or rather obliterates all consideration" (104). My response to this is that I see no reason why both their ideas still can't be adapted to our present difficulties. Neither idea is inherently quietistic; neither idea paralyzes the mind. What each does is put the individual in a *temporary* state of suspension where wonder rushes in. What poets, readers, and students *do* with this wonder afterwards, in a political context, is left up to them.

6. I use the Elvis Presley comparison for a reason that goes beyond the obvious one—that students can relate to it. Like Elvis, whose style was an amalgam of borrowed styles (country and western, rhythm and blues, pop) which he turned into something that seemed "new," Hemingway was a borrower (from Gertrude Stein, Sherwood Anderson, Turgenev, and others) who forged his debts to others into a style that seemed "new" and became vastly influential.

7. Such attitudes aren't limited to my immediate acquaintance, apparently. John Duvall, in his recent *Faulkner's Marginal Bodies: Invisible Outlaws and Unspeakable Communities,* says: that "writers of the earlier part of [the twentieth] century seem hopelessly backward in their sense of men and women, so much so that calls for moratoriums on reading their texts seem almost correct."

8. Someone like Jane Tompkins would disagree with this assessment. Her *Sensational Designs* is partly an attempt to rescue the "sentimental women's novel" from academic oblivion. More bluntly than most new historicists, Tompkins admits that her project "involves, in its most ambitious form, a redefinition of literature and literary study, for it sees literary texts not as works of art embodying themes in complex forms, but as attempts to redefine the social order, articulating and proposing solutions for the problems that shape a particular historical moment" (xi). But even after one reads Tompkins's impressively mounted argument explaining, for example, why Little Eva's death in *Uncle Tom's Cabin* is a typological reenactment of Christ's Passion that moved millions to Christian love and helped end slavery in America, *Uncle Tom's Cabin still* reads to me like a sticky, emotionally oppressive book. It might have moved millions to good thoughts and deeds, but so do Jerry Lewis's telethons, and he's not going to find himself in the canon any time soon.

9. See Annette Kolodny.

WORKS CITED

Benjamin, Walter. "Theses on the Philosophy of History." *Illuminations.* Ed. Hannah Arendt. Trans. Harry Zohn. NY: Schocken, 1969.

Duvall, John. *Faulkner's Marginal Bodies: Invisible Outlaws and Unspeakable Communities.* Austin: U of Texas P, 1990.

Eagleton, Terry. *Criticism and Ideology*. London: Humanities Press, 1976.

Fitzgerald, F. Scott . *The Crack Up*. Ed. Edmund Wilson. NY: New Directions, 1956.

Gilbert, Sandra M. "What Do Feminist Critics Want? A Postcard from the Volcano," in *The New Feminist Criticism: Essays on Women, Literature, Theory*. Ed. Elaine Showalter. NY: Pantheon, 1985.

Heilbrun, Carolyn. "Bringing the Spirit Back to English Studies," in *The New Feminist Criticism: Essays on Women, Literature, Theory*. Ed. Elaine Showalter. NY: Pantheon, 1985.

Keats, John. *The Selected Letters of John Keats*. Ed. Lionel Trilling. Garden City, NY: Doubleday, 1956.

Kolodny, Annette. *The Lay of the Land: Metaphor as Experience and History in American Life and Letters*. Chapel Hill: U of North Carolina P, 1975.

Morrison, Toni. *Beloved*. NY: Penguin, 1987.

Ross, Andrew. *The Failure of Modernism: Symptoms of American Poetry*. NY: Columbia UP, 1986.

Searle, John. "The Storm Over the University." *New York Review of Books*, 6 Dec. 1990: 34–42.

Springsteen, Bruce. *Lucky Town*, Columbia 53001, 1992.

Steiner, George. *In Bluebeard's Castle: Some Notes on the Redefinition of Culture*. New Haven: Yale UP, 1971.

Tompkins, Jane. *Sensational Designs: The Cultural Work of American Fiction, 1790–1860*. NY: Oxford UP, 1985.

Cultural Borders
Working-Class Literature's Challenge to the Canon

Renny Christopher

Jake Ryan and Charles Sackrey write in *Strangers in Paradise: Academics from the Working Class* that a college degree is certification that one belongs to the middle class; in other words, the institution of college stands as a guard at a metaphorical border. This statement carries deep implications about the nature of the education and socialization process being carried on within the university. If these implications are true, if what's actually happening within the university is that students are being socialized and acculturated into the ways of the middle class, then in what ways does the inclusion of working-class literature in the curriculum challenge not only the traditional canon, but the definitions of literature and of education itself?

If the very forms of literature and criticism are shaped by and for the middle class, how can working-class literature remap those contexts? If the novel is, as Ian Watt identifies it, a bourgeois art form, can there be a working-class novel? How have working-class authors attempted to imprint themselves into American literature? How do they cross borders, attempt to redefine borders, and remain entrapped within borders? And what challenges are posed by incorporating working-class materials into the curriculum? How do those materials sit side by side with other texts? How do diverse students respond to them? What tensions arise between working-class and middle-class students in discussions of these texts?

I would like to begin to address some of these questions by discussing three particular works by working-class writers and the ways in which diverse students responded to these works in a class I taught at the University of California, Santa Cruz, called "White Working-Class Literature in the U.S." UCSC is an elite university; the median student family income is the second highest of any university in the state. UCSC has few working-class students, few reentry students, and the worst retention rate for minority students of any campus of the UC system.

The novels of Carolyn Chute, *The Beans of Egypt, Maine* (1985) and *Letourneau's Used Auto Parts* (1988), stretch the borders of literature. The reception of her work by reviewers reveals in sometimes gross and shocking ways the class bias of the literary establishment, as when one reviewer writes that Chute's characters present a good case for "mandatory sterilization." Chute's work presents non-upwardly-mobile characters and so challenges some fundamental assumptions of American literature, as does the work of Agnes Smedley, whose autobiographical novel *Daughter of Earth* (1929) presents an upwardly mobile character who remains ungrateful for and unappreciative of her upward mobility. A short story by Dorothy Allison, "Steal Away," (from her collection *Trash*, 1988) introduces the metaphor of theft for a working-class character getting a college education; the character steals her professors' books, defaces them, and replaces them on the professors' shelves, in an attempt to imprint herself onto the university the way that the university is attempting to imprint itself upon her.

I will begin with the most difficult of the three works, Chute's *The Beans of Egypt, Maine*. This work violates the conventions of the bourgeois novel in several ways, not the least of which is that it presents the lives of non-upwardly-mobile poor people. Perhaps "non mobile" is the better description, because one of the book's biggest transgressions is that it lacks not only a plot, but that mobility which is the hallmark of the bourgeois. Chute's characters go nowhere. The bourgeois novel is conventionally structured around some sort of movement—a quest, a search, a striving for career, for love, for fulfillment, for a better address. Chute's characters aren't striving for anything. They're struggling to stay alive, but *struggling* isn't the same thing as *striving*. Alice Bloom, in a review of Chute's second novel, *Letorneau's Used Auto Parts*, writes that Chute's material is "lives that have never been put into art before, much less into the novel which is, whatever its subject, style, or structure, a record of movement" (546).

Chute shows that the novel need not be bourgeois, that although it might have arisen as *the* bourgeois art form, as Ian Watt suggests in *The Rise of the Novel*, it can be wrested from its origins and profoundly reconfigured. Chute's (and Smedley's) novels show that the working-class novel is created out of a different set of conflicts than the bourgeois novel, which requires not only movement, but teleological movement. Chute's novel contains almost no movement at all; Smedley's contains movement, but not teleological movement.

The Beans of Egypt, Maine has several sections. I will focus on the one called "Meat," in which Beal Bean, one of the main characters, is killed by the police. Beal has been injured at work; he has a splinter in his eye which has caused the eye to swell shut. He and Earlene, his wife, can't afford medical care, and with Beal out of work, also can't afford food for their baby, whose hunger cries run through the section. Beal takes his rifle and attempts to go hunting (poaching, for which his cousin Reuben is serving time) for food, but being too sick, he fails. It is Beal who is transformed into meat by the police when he takes a few shots at the house of the affluent new neighbors across the street.

Earlene, who narrates the chapter, has taken notice of the neighbors. She and her friend Rosie notice the new house:

> I look over and think what a crazy thing this new house is. Until now, there ain't been neighbors . . . and now we got 'em. I says, "It's a pretty place."
>
> She whistles. "They got moocho, that's for sure." She rubs her fingers together. She says, "Earlene, what's them class folks gonna think of *this*?" She leans back on the legs of the chair and picks at the tarpaper wall.
>
> I shrug. (184)

Beal is driven to destruction by his lack of control, his lack of ability to provide food for his family. He has been unwilling to consider the idea of seeking government relief when Earlene suggests that she might try to get food stamps to feed the baby. Beal objects out of both pride and fear. In his world, people don't seek that kind of help because they believe in self-reliance; in this way the white working poor share the belief in a common American myth subscribed to by those of higher-class status. For all their poverty, none of the Beans are on public assistance; they don't believe in it.

Beal is also motivated by fear, though. He has been working "under the table," and he believes that seeking free medical treatment for his eye or food stamps for the baby would expose his tax-dodging activities:

> And do you know what would happen to us if they find out I've been workin' under the table this long? Guh-uh-uh-government gets out the old fuh-uh-feelers . . . Once you get in the old welfare game, they got a trail on you . . . 'cause, lady . . . when you're poor, you stink! (177, ellipses in original)

Beal's attitude reflects both pride and self-awareness, but also reflects the well-justified fear of those who have no real knowledge of the workings of government, and no recourse against it. A few of the middle-class students in my course thought that Beal was paranoid and unreasonable, and should have gone on welfare. Other students felt that Beal was right in his attitudes, and that the novel thus pointed out a terrible contradiction in the American system—that those willing to work, those who believed in American ideals, were nonetheless unable to support their families.

Beal's ultimate way out is to turn his anger, directed at himself (and Earlene) for a long time, toward the most visible sign of injustice: the neighbor's fancy new house.

> He is sightin' with his good eye on what's left of them broad new windows across the road. Another shot. Glass buckles. But cops work fast to remove the problem. . . . He is beautifully lightweight. The hand and the rifle remain unseparated, not ever letting go. (192)

Beal's choice of a target for his anger is not, of course, random.

This section of the novel is the most problematic for students, for an interesting reason. Many readers will identify more with the people who live in the nice house and who drive by in their Chrysler with the children in car seats wearing "matchin' chocolate-color coats" (189) than with Beal and Earlene. Readers who have never been poor are probably more likely to identify with the neighbors than with the Beans. It is clear from the reviews of the novel that many readers can't identify with the Beans at all (such as the *Newsweek* reviewer, who said that the characters look like "prime candidates for compulsory sterilization").

For any readers who identify with the neighbors, Beal will be shooting at them. This is emblematic of a larger problem: Chute's portrayal of the conditions of the people she calls "the working poor" puts many middle-class readers into the position of feeling liberal guilt. This was certainly the case with some of the students in my class, who were made uncomfortable by the book. They were reluctant to criticize it, because it made them feel disenfranchised; they felt that they had no place from which to criticize the novel.

The novel is therefore an interesting teaching tool, to get the privileged students into this position. Putting them into this position may serve as a "teachable moment," decentering their assumptions about the world and allowing them to gain new perceptions and insights. Further, the privileged students are then put into the position usually occupied by the working-class students. One working-class student in this class, Mardi, told me that for the first time, she felt able to "just talk about the books," because they intersected with her life. In classes where the books came from a middle-class milieu, she felt it necessary to talk about her own experience in order to connect with the material, for which she often "got slammed." This was the most interesting comment from any of the students (she told me this in office hours, not in class), because it revealed in a very clear way one more of the many hidden disadvantages working-class students face in the university.

I think this student's comment is an important one. Her experience with literature classes was similar to mine as a working-class undergraduate from a poor rural high school encountering the American literature canon. A story from my own experience might help to illustrate the point further. In my first year of college I took a course called "Classic American Writers." The classic writers turned out to be Hawthorne, Melville, Emerson, Thoreau, and Whitman. The professor taught the class in what I now recognize as a very New Critical style. At the time, with typical undergraduate faith, I believed that was the only way to teach a literature class, and that those were the only "classic" American writers. I had no context to tell me otherwise.

My problem was that I was completely unable to make a connection with these works. I thought Hester Prynne should have just told the old farts to go to hell; I never got far enough into *Moby Dick* to get to the whaling stuff that I might have liked because my father had been a fisherman, because the book was so alienating and boring; I simply couldn't see what Emerson was about at all; as for Thoreau, I thought somebody who'd go live in the woods when he didn't have to was nuts. And although Whitman kept insisting that he was one with the slaves and the dockworkers, I thought he was just an egomaniac. (Yes, that's exactly what I thought; I have my old journals still. Not a very promising beginning for a future literature professor.)

The problem was twofold. First, I had no class consciousness; at that time I didn't identify with the working class. I came from the non-unionized, rural, white working class, and we simply didn't think about class at all. I thought the whole world was going to be basically similar to where I came from. When it turned out not to be, I had no way of understanding why and how, because no one ever taught me about class issues as an undergraduate. Therefore I had no explanation of why I felt alienated from "classic" American literature (and the problem only worsened later when I took "Modern American Poetry" and read Williams, Frost, Stevens, Pound and Eliot, and nobody else). Second, the teaching style worked to prevent me from making any connection. If I had been taught about the history and the context from which these writers emerged, I might have been able to start to understand them on their own terms, instead of unsuccessfully trying to relate them to my terms, as my student Mardi was trying to do with bourgeois literature. The professor never supplied any critical context; I had no idea, then, that these dead white men were simply F. O. Matthiessen's "American Renaissance" writers. I thought they had been canonized by some absent literature god, and that they were the only choice.

By a circuitous and lengthy path, I somehow ended up in graduate school anyway (although "Classic American Writers" and other classes like it actually caused me to drop out and stay out for several years). In graduate school I took a course called "The Other American Renaissance," based on Jane Tompkins's reexamination of women writers of the pre-Civil War period. In that class I was introduced to *Ruth Hall* by Fanny Fern. That novel describes the trials of a woman trying to support herself through writing. There was something I could connect with, immediately and viscerally. That was a novel I understood, because although the main character was actually a fallen bourgeois, not a working-class woman, nonetheless she was cast into the world of labor, and the novel was written from the inside of that experience.

What reading that novel did was make me intensely regret my earlier brushes with the canon. It showed me clearly how the canon operates to keep out those who have traditionally been kept out. This is one of the ways in which the canon is a self-perpetuating system. Works from outside the canon thus may disrupt the system by allowing into the circle of readers people like me and my student Mardi, people who are supposed to be excluded.

The Beans of Egypt, Maine doesn't really draw clear lines between middle-class and working-class readers, though, because Chute's characters are not really working-class, they are working poor, and there is a great deal of difference between working-class culture and underclass culture. Some working-class students might find it as hard to deal with *The Beans* as some middle-class students might. But Agnes Smedley's *Daughter of Earth* draws much clearer lines in reader response.

Smedley's autobiographical novel traces the life of Marie Rogers, daughter of a man who abandoned his family and a woman who worked as a laundress to support her children. Her flights of imagination were discouraged by her mother, who whipped her for being a liar (7). Marie manages to get an education, and eventually leaves the West of her youth for New York in the 1930s, where she becomes involved with a group of intellectual socialists who have little interest in, or compassion for, a true member of the working class.

> When I was introduced to them they automatically extended a hand, but their eyes were on someone else and they were speaking to others. I might have been one of the chairs they were gripping in passing. . . . Many of them belonged to those interesting and charming intellectuals who idealize the workers, from afar, believing that within the working-class lies buried some magic force and knowledge which, at the critical moment, will manifest itself. . . . Those who really talked with me tried to discourage me from studying in the university, saying life and experience was of more value than books. Some found my naivete interesting and did not wish to see it disturbed. (230–1)

Since many working-class students have encountered similar patronizing attitudes during their own college careers, Smedley's description of Marie's experiences with the socialist intellectuals is familiar and even comforting to them, in that they find themselves not to have been the only people to have experienced such treatment. Smedley's novel shows that such class prejudices have a long history.

Marie Rogers eventually becomes involved with the Indian independence movement, and becomes romantically involved with an Indian man. Her involvement with the movement lands her in trouble—ultimately in jail—with American authorities; sexual double standards equally destroy her relationship with Anand, the Indian intellectual. Marie ends up fleeing the country, declaring "I hate life . . . I hate love!" (390), deeply bitter and resentful over the things she has learned about the educated world she so desperately aspired to when she was young.

Thus Marie is an upwardly mobile character who refuses to appreciate her upward mobility, refuses to see the middle class intellectual world as "better" than the world she comes from, after all. She is especially appalled when one of her circle of intellectual friends suggests that she abandon her siblings, whom she is trying to support and educate.

> My life was my own, she said; I had not brought my brothers or sister into existence, nor was I ever responsible for them. If I really had a social conscience, I would go on and study and prepare myself for better work . . . . I never could quickly reply to such arguments. The ties that bound me to my brothers were very strong. (245)

She lives by a value system in which family and loyalty to others are of primary importance; her middle class friends live by a value system in which individualism and self-promotion are of primary importance.

Exploring these issues in the novel provides a platform for productive discussions about value conflicts and the costs of upward mobility. Such discussions have different importance for different students. For middle-class students, they afford an opportunity to see that middle-class values are not neutral or universal (something which many middle-class students, in my experience, have not yet realized). For working-class students, they afford an opportunity to talk about the merits and costs of upward mobility, and the expectations on both sides: those of the upwardly mobile individual, and those of the society which she is moving into.

Dorothy Allison's story "Steal Away" also divides students along class lines. It introduces the important metaphor of theft of education for working-class students. Since university education is meant for middle-class students, theft seems to me to be an appropriate metaphor. Allison's narrator steals merchandise in order to help make up the gap between means and expenses during her college career, but in the story's central metaphor, she also steals her education itself.

She steals both out of need and out of anger. When she is barred from registration because her scholarship check is late, she steals crystal goblets and ashtrays from the Hilton Hotel, takes them down to the pier and throws them off, at sunset, one at a time. "Sight and sound, it was better than a movie" (82). In my class, almost all the working-class students understood the narrator's motivation, while almost none of the middle-class students did. The middle-class students spoke out about how they were shocked by the narrator's destructiveness.

When her scholarship is cut, she carts "surplus" to St. Vincent DePaul, who pay small prices for it.

> They had hardwood stools in the studios, and stacking fileboxes no one had opened in years. I wore a cloth cap when I took them, and my no-nonsense expression. I was so calm that one of the professors helped me clear paper off the third one. He was distracted, discussing Jackson Pollack with a very pale woman whose hands were marked with artist's tush. "Glad they finally decided to get these out of here," was all he said to me, never once looking up into my face. My anger came up from my stomach with an acid taste. I went back for his clipboard and papers, but his desk was locked and my file broke on the rim. In compensation I took the silk lining out of the pockets of the corduroy coat he'd left thrown over a stool. The silk made a lemongrass sachet I gave my mother for her birthday, and every time I saw him in that jacket I smiled. (82–83)

The narrator's anger at the professor arises out of her invisibility when she's masquerading as a worker. This scene echoes the experience of a friend of mine who, after leaving graduate school, worked at the same university as a janitor. The professors who'd been on his dissertation committee failed to see, recognize, or acknowledge him when they passed him and his mop bucket in the hallway.

But most importantly, the narrator tries to imprint herself on the university. A female professor expresses an interest in her, but "didn't want to hear about my summers working in the mop factory" (83). The narrator begins stealing the professor's books off her shelf, writing in the margins, and replacing them. It is this act of literally writing herself into the consciousness of her professor, into the heart and life of the university, that helps her to preserve her selfhood while she is being educated.

Moreover, her thieving helps her to stay connected to her family. Her last act, driving away from graduation, is to steal the commemorative roses off the college sign, and present them to her mother.

This story is capable of provoking intense discussion over the issues of both metaphorical and literal theft. (Two quarters after I taught this class, an article appeared in the university newspaper about students who shoplift to make their way through school.)

Teaching these and other works by working-class writers challenges students in productive and dangerous ways. Productive, because the introduction of such discordant material into the curriculum brings in contentious viewpoints that open up students' discussions and papers and allow them to examine both their own attitudes and the educational process itself. Dangerous, because in-depth examination of these works leads to a reevaluation of the basis of university education, just as works by feminists and writers of color have for the past several years. So far, the inclusion of works from the "expanded canon" has brought about reform without bringing about revolution. Works by working-class authors who have not wholly embraced upward mobility suggest that a revolution—at least in thinking—is called for.

WORKS CITED

Allison, Dorothy. *Trash*. NY: Firebrand Books, 1988.

Bloom, Alice. "Adults Only." *The Hudson Review*. 41 (1988): 539–47.

Chute, Carolyn. *The Beans of Egypt, Maine*. NY: Ticknor & Fields, 1985.

Fern, Fanny. *Ruth Hall*. New Brunswick: Rutgers UP, 1986.

Prescott, Peter. Review of *The Beans of Egypt, Maine*. *Newsweek*. 25 February 1985: 86.

Ryan, Jake, and Charles Sackrey. *Strangers in Paradise: Academics from the Working Class*. Boston: South End P, 1984.

Smedley, Agnes. *Daughter of Earth*. NY: The Feminist P, 1973.

Tompkins, Jane. *Sensational Designs*. NY: Oxford UP, 1985.

Watt, Ian. *The Rise of the Novel*. Berkeley: U of California P, 1957.

Imagining Difference
Textual Power *and the Transgression of the Self*

Bruce A. Goebel

> The purpose of humanistic study is to learn what it has
> meant to be human in other times and places, what it
> means now, and how to speculate about what it ought to
> mean and what it might mean in the human future. The
> best texts for this should be determined locally, by local
> conditions, limited and facilitated by local wisdom.
> > —*Robert Scholes,*
> > "Aiming a Canon at the Curriculum"

> The study of literature can force no one to be humane, but
> apparently the study of literature can make it possible to
> be more humane than would otherwise be the case.
> > —*Gordon Mills,*
> > *Hamlet's Castle*

Robert Scholes's *Textual Power* offers one of the more thoughtful
attempts to bridge the distance between the practice of teaching
and the current debates in literary theory. The primary aim of
Scholes's argument is to question the persistent influence of New
Criticism on the teaching of literature. Denying that literature
courses should be reserved for the study of great works, he
advocates an approach to teaching literature that is more
conducive to students' social and political responsibilities in a
democracy. This suggestion presents a significant improvement

in pedagogical thinking; however, Scholes's emphasis on criticism as an art of resistance renders his approach problematic for teachers of multiethnic literature who find that inherent student opposition to cultural differences inhibits the ethical reading of some texts.

Scholes begins by suggesting that the needs of students and the mandate of liberal education far exceed the narrow scope of traditional approaches to literature and claims that the teacher must give students

> the kind of knowledge and skill that will enable them to make sense of their own worlds, to determine their own interests, both individual and collective, to see through the manipulations of all sorts of texts in all sorts of media, and to express their own views in some appropriate manner. (15–16)

Implicitly, he proposes teaching students to exercise their autonomy, to recognize the right to different perspectives, and to challenge totalized visions of the world. In effect, Scholes calls for a complete reversal of the New Critical perspective. Reverence for masterpieces is replaced by suspicion. In so doing, he emphasizes the importance of cultural knowledge as a necessary complement to students' critical skills, recalling that, under the aegis of New Criticism,

> we have sometimes behaved as if certain skills, such as composition and even close reading of poems, could be developed apart from knowledge, especially apart from historical knowledge. We are paying the price for that error now. (16)

Ignorance of cultural and historical knowledge leaves one incapable of comparative critical judgment.

Such knowledge is necessarily multicultural if it is to allow students the breadth of vision necessary for informed choice. When the texts taught in a literature course only reflect a narrow sampling of the possible social positions that can be occupied by the author, narrator, and characters, students cannot achieve much perspective. If the life experiences they read about only mirror their own, they may be encouraged to believe that their life-style is the only legitimate one. If, on the other hand, the literary experiences with which they come in contact never reflect their own, as has been the case for many women and people of color, then they may be led to believe either that their own lives are somehow invalidated or that the experience of literature has little to offer them. The lack of cultural diversity within the traditional literary canon denies students, regardless of ethnic background, opportunity to see alternative values and life-styles and, thus, inhibits their ability to make critical judgments and decisions. In other words, they lack "textual power."

Insisting that "we must stop 'teaching literature' and start 'studying texts'" (16), Scholes advocates a literature course that will empower students politically, in the broadest sense of that term, making them aware of and skillful with the ways language is used as a means to power. Implicitly, he sees students at the mercy of far more skillful players in a competitive language game.[1] As a result, he claims that the "great aim or end of liberal education" is to teach students "to resist the very texts from which they derive textual pleasure: to analyze, to dissect, to oppose" (62). Rather than passively consume canonical masterpieces, students should uncover their hidden values and challenge them. For Scholes the introductory literature class should be an extended lesson in resistance to a dominant discourse, a course based on the teaching of critical judgment. Theoretically, if students can learn the rules and skills of the deadly serious language games to which they are subjected, they can become players capable of positively affecting their own lives and the lives of those around them. As he suggests, "textual power is ultimately power to change the world" (165).

From Scholes's point of view, teaching literature as the aesthetic appreciation of canonized texts equates with teaching submission to the textual power of others. New Critical approaches are, in this sense, dehumanizing. For this reason, the object of study in an introductory literature course should be "textuality: textual knowledge and textual skills" (20). Essentially, such an emphasis changes the focus from teaching the acceptable interpretations of a small number of approved texts to teaching how meaning is generated through any text by the interaction between the author, the readers, and the communities that surround them. An appreciation of aesthetic values gives way to an inquiry into language and values and a skeptical regard for the intent behind every text.

The development of textual power requires attention to three fundamental aspects of textual study: reading, interpretation, and criticism. Reading is primarily an unconscious act facilitated by the reader's knowledge of the cultural context and the narrative codes used by the author of a given text. From this knowledge, readers can quickly recognize (usually unconsciously) character types or anticipate the plot development of familiar genres. While readers might have difficulty defining narrative codes—indeed, may never have thought of stories as being somehow codified—their lifelong experience with the popular stories and images of their culture make them quite adept at reading these codes. For example, when I ask my students to outline the generic plot structure of a television detective show, they quickly produce characters and events that include an opening crime scene; the introduction of a tough, masculine detective and an attractive, female client; the gathering of clues; a close call with the perpetrator (usually about a half hour into the show); a developing romantic connection between detective and client; more clues; a successful chase scene; and a closing romantic embrace. Of course they have greater difficulty uncovering the implicit values hidden in such a narrative code. Nevertheless, their familiarity aids their act of reading.

This is not to say that the relative ease of reading somehow implies that reading is unimportant. Scholes insists:

> Without a serious act of "reading"—of a book, a face, or a tone of voice—we will never be able to agree or disagree with another person, since we will have turned all others into mirrors of ourselves. Reading—as a submission to the intentions of another—is the first step in all thought and communication. It is essential; but it is incomplete. It requires both interpretation and criticism for completion. (40)

Careful reading is essential. And, as long as the texts that students read do not radically violate the cultural knowledge or narrative codes they have previously experienced, they will probably submit themselves to those texts. In this sense, reading is the dominant act when the repertoire of symbols in the text coincide with those of one's own communities.

However, when the cultural knowledge and codes of the text to which the reader is asked to submit significantly differ from those of the reader, then the act of reading not only feels incomplete but is much less likely to be performed "seriously." When readers encounter such a violation of their textual expectations, they are forced into the role of interpreters. Scholes defines the act of interpretation as a response to the failure of reading to adequately make sense of a text, a failure that may occur due to either an "excess in meaning in a text" or a "deficiency of knowledge in the reader" (22). On one level, interpretation requires that the reader fill most of the major gaps between his own cultural knowledge and that of the author. Interpretation at this level can be as simple as looking up unknown words or as time-consuming as reading histories of the social context surrounding the production of the text. On another level, however, interpretation requires that the reader answer the question, "What does this story mean?"—a question unasked in the realm of reading. The resulting inquiry necessarily leads to authorial intent, however problematic the location of such intent may be. Students must discover, through identification of themes and narrative codes, what they believe are the aesthetic and political designs of the author and recognize how language has been manipulated to facilitate those designs, as well as the ways it may escape such intent.

The end result of the act of interpretation is the tentative identification of a text's most probable meanings and an understanding of the vision of the world it offers and the values implicit within that vision. Such a definition implies that the act of interpreting a Native American novel, such as Leslie Marmon Silko's *Ceremony*, can not be completed without an exploration of Silko's life and her tribal affiliation, values, and historical and literary heritage. Ethically, readers must make the attempt to understand the text from the perspective of the social context from which it was written. Unlike New Criticism, the interpretive act that Scholes describes necessarily places the literary text in the social, political, and aesthetic context from which it arises. Even a "purely" aesthetic judgment of such a novel would require a knowledge of the evolution of Native American oral tradition and the brief history of its conflation with the novel form.

Only after a serious act of interpretation can students make the leap to valid criticism. Learning to critique themes or the narrative codes that contain themes is the ultimate goal for students of textual studies and requires that they measure the values and the alternative social positions of the text against their own. For Scholes, criticism is the site for opposition or resistance to the hegemonic messages of texts and represents a radical declaration of autonomy. If students can identify the themes and values of texts through careful attention to style, form, and content and can judge the corresponding political implications, then they can resist them.

The ability to critique other visions of the world, other value systems, is the foundation of textual power. Thus, the three fundamental aspects of textual power form a hierarchy: "We move from a submission to textual authority in reading, through a sharing of textual power in interpretation, toward an assertion of power through opposition in criticism" (39). The two major responsibilities of teachers of literary studies are "to devise ways for our students to perform these productive activities" through their own creation of oral and written texts and to "assist students in perceiving the aura of codification that surrounds every verbal text" (24).

While insisting that criticism is more politically important, Scholes presents a pedagogical strategy which emphasizes the difficulty students have with interpretation. Their lack of cultural knowledge inhibits their ability to fill in the gaps left between the author's vision and their own, making it difficult to adequately recognize and understand the themes. This problem is intensified in an introductory literature course by the tendency to read a wide variety of authors, each one presenting new contexts and new repertoires of symbols. Under such conditions, students are often overwhelmed, rarely attaining a minimum understanding of one text or author before rushing on to the next. As a result, they feel frustrated rather than empowered. For this reason, Scholes suggests that teachers should structure their introductory course around a "triangle" of three writers who each receive extended attention. By doing so, they allow students to become acquainted with the social context of that author and the chosen texts and can begin to see the complex "aura of codification" that surrounds that author's work. As students read subsequent selections by that author, they need less and less assistance, finding that their acquired cultural knowledge enables them to complete the interpretive process among themselves.

Structuring introductory courses around such a triangle of three writers makes sense; however, such a pedagogical decision places a tremendous significance upon the choice of authors and texts. Scholes chooses to begin with Ernest Hemingway. While agreeing with Scholes's general project, I find the *initiation* of a course with Hemingway inappropriate not only for my purposes but for some of his own stated goals as well. He believes Hemingway "is justified by fame, by accessibility, and by the uses to which his work can be put" (25) and chooses *In Our Time* as the best text with which to begin. He explains how he would carefully guide students through class discussions, taking them sequentially through a series of short interchapters and pushing them to uncover Hemingway's narrative codes which will reveal, in turn, the way the world of his literary vision operates. Scholes supplements discussions with group work, research, the reading of a variety of interpretations, and only a few brief lectures. Through his approach, the student's inquiry should lead, inevitably, to "cultural history itself," and subsequently, they will gradually begin to see Hemingway's social and aesthetic position in a much broader context, as one vision of the world among many.

Achieving this perspective is crucial because that is what allows the student to take the step into criticism. As he puts it:

> The move from interpretation to criticism is not simply a destructive negation. . . not a mere rejection of ideas and values proposed by a text. It is a differentiation of the subjectivity of the critic from that of the author, an assertion of textual power against that of the primary text. Even agreement is significant only if the critic's subjectivity is differentiated from the author's. (40)

Criticism, as a declaration of autonomy, requires both a recognition of difference between one's own social position as a subject and agent in the world and the social and aesthetic position of the author and characters in the text. Consequently, it also requires an evaluative judgment.

In theory, students should recognize, in their contact with *In Our Time*, the often destructive nature of Hemingway's vision of masculinity with its aestheticization of violence and death and its misogynist tendencies. In fact, Scholes justifies the inclusion of Hemingway in his syllabus because it allows for a discussion of issues of sexism. He insists that "we need to position Hemingway as an Other, a distinct subjectivity, in order to criticize him and define ourselves against him" (50), adding that the

> critical project we are embarked upon here consists of finding a stance sufficiently antagonistic to Hemingway's to bring his "untold" perspectives to light. The act of freeing ourselves from the power of his text depends upon our finding a position outside the assumptions upon which the text is based. (70)

I believe he is exactly right. But this is precisely where his oppositional approach to literature and his choice of Hemingway become problematic. Having stated the need for this act of freeing, he quickly implies that it can be done by discussing the implicit values of modernist aesthetics, suggesting that if we can recognize Hemingway's "love affair with violence and death, [that] should allow us to position ourselves critically: with him or against him—or both—by choice" (73). But that is not necessarily the case.

As Scholes admits, "establishing a critical perspective is especially hard for students, whose own thoughts and values are likely to be constantly wavering and far from clear" (55). And those values that they are sure of may not be conducive to an oppositional stance to Hemingway. After all, many of Hemingway's values are still deeply embedded in mainstream American culture. Is it illogical to believe that students share many of Hemingway's more violent, patriarchal values when even such a long-standing liberal as Daniel Patrick Moynihan justifies the United States' military response to Iraq's invasion of

Kuwait by proudly stating, "You must understand that Americans are a warrior nation"? The experience of reading Hemingway probably does not enable—let alone require students (particularly, white male students) to step outside their own social positions.

Scholes chose Hemingway for his course because students would find themselves "culturally at home" in his work. As a result, for them to position Hemingway as Other, they must position *themselves* as Other—since the distinction between Hemingway's vision of the world and their own is not clear. Viewing one's self as Other, or, more appropriately, to see one's self through another's eyes—is not easy. Such an act takes practice and necessarily requires a knowledge of alternative positions. Many of the students in Scholes's hypothetical class would not be able to make such a leap outside themselves, though they would probably be observant enough to perceive what he wanted them to say. Despite any exploration of modernist aesthetics, most of them are left with no real choice. Subjects of a culture that often glorifies misogyny, violence, and death, they are offered Hemingway's vision of glorified misogyny, violence, and death. Without a well-defined alternative on which to stand, they must accept Hemingway's vision, even while acknowledging it as potentially suspect. Indeed, considering the conservative, preservationist nature of the self, many of them will privately resist any attempt to create an Other of Hemingway. While outwardly surrendering to Scholes's authority and debunking the suspect values, they would learn to be hypocritical, not critical.

The concept of textual power, evolving out of Scholes's earlier, more structuralist concerns, is a valuable improvement in pedagogical strategy. His careful attention to the processes of reading, interpretation, and criticism, the polysemic nature of language, the intertextuality of knowledge, and the power that resides in our awareness of and abilities with these facets of literature form a valuable theoretical foundation for teaching. However, applying his strategy is more difficult than he lets on and requires more attention to the background of students and their limitations in making the imaginative leaps he implies. Since his definition for wielding textual power necessarily includes the act of choice predicated upon a knowledge of alternatives, his initial textual choice undermines the efficacy of his pedagogical project.

The task of teaching textual power should be combined with teaching students to imaginatively transgress their own social positions. They must know their own collective value systems in the context of other value systems, if they are to make comparative judgments. However, in order to acquire such knowledge, they must be able to distance themselves from themselves by imagining what it would be like to be different from what they are. To a degree, literature is inherently capable of facilitating this goal. It can, to apply Jane Tompkins's useful phrase, perform "cultural work" by adding to the reader's repertoire of symbols and alternative social positions. In its capacity to transmit large amounts of information about the values and life-styles of differing cultures, literature can provide the diverse knowledge necessary for adequate contextualization of alternative social positions and lay the foundation for the kind of informed choice that autonomy requires. In its explicit modeling of the imaginative act itself, literature can reveal a variety of methods of perceiving the self and the world, methods that can deny the definitive validity of any sole perspective. And, in the power of its poetic qualities and its ability to assist readers in recreating sensations, experiences, and entire worlds, literature can—if only temporarily—grant them the distance required for self-reflective judgment.

However, some texts are more conducive to this self-liberating goal. Of course, any discussion of appropriateness borders on the impolitic. Such textual choices, for me, do not constitute a judgment of aesthetic quality with selected texts somehow representing better literature than those not selected. Rather, the textual selections that I make merely reflect a knowledge from personal experience that, given the nature of introductory courses and the goals that I hope to achieve, certain texts simply work better in the classroom than others.

When choosing the triangle of three writers for my course, I begin with texts that offer cultural perspectives that often radically differ, politically oppose, and aesthetically violate the perspectives of the majority of my students and myself. In

Textual Power, Scholes acknowledges that students need to "confront difference," but he implicitly, and inadvertently, devalues the act of knowing difference in a number of ways. His choice of Hemingway as representative of difference is problematic, and while he does suggest teaching Ursula LeGuin's *Left Hand of Darkness* to foreground alternative views of gender, his inclusion of her text seems a marginal addition to the more important issue of opposing the textual power of canonical texts. Indeed, the continual emphasis on opposition undermines the initial submission to difference that he claims is so necessary. That initial submission is not easy.

Contrary to the hierarchy of difficulty in reading, interpretation, and criticism, many students are quite willing to skip the first two processes and immediately make the leap (albeit poorly) into critical judgment of texts that offer visions of the world radically different from their own. Often, as soon as they suspect the threat of difference in a text, in the first few pages or even prior to reading, they quickly reject it. Their reading and interpretation from that point on is oppositional indeed, and it is appealing, since the act of rejection absolves them of the need for careful attention. Try teaching Adrienne Rich's poem "From an Old House in America" after telling students of her feminist history and sexual preference. The subsequent discussion will likely reveal a lack of careful reading and consist of preformed, sexist statements about homosexuals and feminists.

Textual power, like any other means to power, can be misused and abused. Taught without ethical context, textual power is as easily a hegemonic weapon as it is an emancipatory tool. To teach textual power primarily as a tool of opposition denies its equally important role in cooperation, negotiation, and reconciliation. This should be true of a student's reading of canonical and noncanonical texts. After all, Hemingway has much to teach us. Henry Giroux suggests that in "a revitalized discourse of democracy" textual power

> should not be based exclusively on a language of critique, one that, for example, limits its focus . . . to the elimination of relations of subordination and inequality. This is an important political concern but in both theoretical and

political terms it is woefully incomplete. As part of a
radical project, the discourse of democracy also needs a
language of possibility, one that combines a strategy of
opposition with a strategy for structuring a new social
order. (172)

When teaching an introductory course, I try to select texts with
the potential to perform such work. I construct a syllabus that
offers alternative positions for students to imaginatively assume.
Because of the time constraints of such a course, the idea of
centering the course on a triangle of writers, or perhaps a
triangle of three distinct social positions occupied by writers
with similar concerns, is a sound one. I have had the most
success when the first two legs of this triangle rest upon radical
difference.

Most recently, I have selected Leslie Silko's *Ceremony* and
Marilynne Robinson's *Housekeeping* to complement
Hemingway's *In Our Time*. Silko's critique of racism,
industrialized violence, and environmental degradation and
Robinson's challenge to patriarchal, materialist values offer
students perspectives with which they are not familiar. Only
after exploring such alternative positions do I return to
Hemingway and expect my students to critique his work with
any depth of perspective. In the past, I have also juxtaposed Zora
Neale Hurston's *Their Eyes Were Watching God*, Maxine Hong
Kingston's *Woman Warrior*, and John Irving's *The World According
to Garp*. In this fashion the texts selected for a course can speak to
and argue with one another and confront students with the
necessity for making critical judgments.

An ethical critique requires the ability to imaginatively
transgress the boundaries of the self and its corresponding value
system. Gordon Mills suggests that

> if people leave a literary classroom without having
> enhanced their readiness for experiencing a semblance [an
> aesthetic transgression of the self] in a mature way, the
> classroom has failed. If people do not also carry with them
> from the literary classroom a capacity for using semblance
> as an instrument in examining many of the problems of
> their real world, then—in my opinion—the classroom has
> failed again. (37)

I agree and further advocate offering students texts whose aesthetic experience directly implicates them in "the problems of their real world." Such an idea may offend traditionalists who continue to see introductory literature courses as an initiation into the major courses with their more thoroughly entrenched canonized masterpieces, but an introductory literature course is not an "introductory" course in that sense. It can be more accurately thought of as a "conclusion to literature" course, since few of the students who take it will ever take another literature course again. When perceived in this light, priorities change drastically. Knowing that this may be my last chance to influence their attitudes about literature, culture, and their awareness of the power of language, the way I design the course becomes crucial. As Jonathan Smith suggests:

> subject matter, thought of in some lineal progression, cannot be our organizing principle. . . The notion of the survey, of "coverage," becomes ludicrous. As long as we do not allow ourselves to be misled by the notion that every introductory course is an introduction to the major program, and the major is a preparation for graduate study in the same field—a notion that has neither factual nor educational warrant—then, *there is nothing that must be taught*, there is nothing that cannot be left out. (728, emphases his)

In fact, the notion of coverage is one of the most pernicious pedagogical traditions in that it places quantity over quality, speed over careful teaching, brief exposure over personally engaged knowing. The brief duration of a semester severely limits what I can do for my students. In the face of this temporal limitation, I resist the temptation to speed up and, instead, slow down, become more focused, and be absolutely sure of my objectives.

I share Robert Scholes's conviction that students should leave the classroom wielding textual power. However, the oppositional emphasis that he places on such power makes it problematic when dealing with cultural contexts that differ from that of the reader. When teaching multi-ethnic literature, much of the focus must rest on helping students develop the self-transgressive imagination necessary for a competent interpretation. This interpretation should take into account the social and historical influences that informed the production of the text and that currently inform the reader's construction of meaning. Only then can students ethically make comparative, critical judgments about an author's vision of reality and the value system implied within that vision. Such a process will not only aid students in their contact with multi-ethnic literature, but may very well empower them to successfully negotiate the cultural differences that they encounter in their own lives and the political decisions they make regarding people different from themselves.

NOTES

1. In many ways, Scholes's prescription for textual power and the implicit conceptions of society and culture that underlie it parallel Jean-Francois Lyotard's claim, in *The Postmodern Condition*, that only equal ability with and access to all sources of knowledge will bring "justice" to the mercenary and aggressive language games of postmodern culture.

WORKS CITED

hooks, bell. *Talking Back: Thinking Feminist: Thinking Black.* Boston: South End P, 1989.

Giroux, Henry A. *Teachers as Intellectuals: Toward a Critical Pedagogy of Learning.* NY: Bergin and Garvey, 1988.

Lyotard, Jean-Francois. *The Postmodern Condition: A Report on Knowledge.* Trans. Geoff Bennington and Brian Massumi. Minneapolis: U of Minnesota P, 1984.

Mills, Gordon. *Hamlet's Castle: The Study of Literature as Social Experience.* Austin: U of Texas P, 1976.

Rorty, Richard. "The Opening of American Minds." *Harpers Magazine,* July 1989: 18–22.

Scholes, Robert. *Textual Power: Literary Theory and the Teaching of English.* New Haven: Yale UP, 1985.

Smith, Jonathan. "'Narratives into Problems': The College Introductory Course and the Study of Religion." *Journal of the American Academy of Religion* 56 (Winter 1988): 727–39.

Domestic Strains
*The Woman Question, Free Love,
and Nineteenth-Century American Fiction*

Susan Danielson

The summer before I taught my first American Survey class I asked the head of my department, also an "Americanist," for advice on books to order, pedagogical approaches, goals to aim for in my teaching. In retrospect, I believe he was thoroughly disarmed by my query: "Don't worry," he quipped, "You know what to do. Go ahead and do it." I might attribute his dismissal to an underlying sexism and arrogance that some feminists see pervading male academia; however, I had met with a similar situation just four years before on the eve of teaching my first women's literature course by one of my feminist colleagues. At least for these two associates there seemed no particular way in which I was to conceive of these courses, no larger curricular framework into which they were to fit; I, an autonomous individual, might do as I pleased—anything less, I gathered, would be an infringement on my academic freedom or a signal of my gross incompetence. Or perhaps from their perspective, it did not matter what I did in the classroom, since all classrooms are created equal, that is, equally impotent to affect student lives or the creation of knowledge. Or perhaps they trusted I would know what to do because there was, from their perspectives, only one thing to be done and I, being a good girl, would "do the right thing."

I had often found myself facing a similar indifference in my domestic life. Would my spouse mind if I applied for a grant in another state for next summer? How could I be supportive of his work toward tenure while pursuing my own career goals? Would he be home in time to watch the kids so I could get to my meeting? Each question, whether of major or minor significance, met with silence. Though we came from opposite sides of the country, from rural and urban backgrounds, and from different religious faiths, there was no need to discuss how to raise our children or organize our lives. Since we were married, I would, of course, know to "do the right thing," or perhaps, our love, if it were really "true," was to transcend such "superficial" differences. Like my colleagues, my spouse never seemed to recognize any need for discussion on what I considered to be crucial, although domestic, matters.

Governing both my public and domestic life is some universal secret code to which I am supposed to have access, in lieu of which I am left to do precisely as I like. Despite the fact I have faced this silence for many years, I have been consistently uncomfortable with it. None of the explanations I have come up with to account for this situation squares with my own, dare I say it ?—passionate interest in what I do and the arenas in which I get to do it. As a university teacher I am engaged in a public, community-based enterprise, not a private, entrepreneurial practice; I believe it involves more than a self-aggrandizing inquiry into my field. In my roles as wife and mother I am also not an autonomous being, but employed in (albeit unacknowledged) public work without which society would not be able to function. The strains that arise within each of these separate spheres and from their interpenetration (that is, of the individual and the communities in which she/he finds her or himself) is the material out of which literature is constructed; to suppress the complexity and importance of that interaction is to deny the need for any discourse beyond the most rudimentary— "pass the salt," "fill in the blanks," "turn over."

When faculty claim disinterest in curricular matters, either through an appeal to aesthetic transcendence, or to protect the free play of ideas in the university marketplace, or because they distrust the engagement of "enthusiasm," the literature curriculum becomes enshrined in romantic idealizations appropriate to a fifteenth-century monastery: removed from the world, alone with their (texts) God, scholars are left to commune and reflect on what are known to be (notice the passive voice) the central metaphysical issues of the day. And when this silence (about the shape, content, or viability of, in this case, the canon in American literary studies) is questioned, an alarm of crisis proportions is sounded by the dons of the educational superstructure. Calls for national unity based on a consensual model of educational goals and values (summarized recently by Arthur Schlesinger, Jr. in *Time*) are issued in the name of protecting us from the impending economic Armageddon that will surely befall us if we sink below some universally understood but unarticulated standard of literacy and competence. As J. Wade Gilley warned in his recent work *Thinking about Higher Education: The 1990s and Beyond* : "If schools do not improve fast enough, what will colleges do? How will they provide the number and quality of graduates required for America to compete in a tough international economy?" (9).

Rather than capitulate to these ardent cries, scholars like Gerald Graff have refused to be silent and instead challenge their conceptualizations of curriculum that are articulated at such an abstract level that they appear to be essentially static, ahistorical, and universal: "Implicit in the idea of a democratic culture . . . is that *thought is an inherently political and contested activity*" (24, emphases Graff's). Graff's double thrust, "political and contested," both destabilizes and domesticates a rigid concept of curriculum by drawing it into a debate, into the realm of "American" "democratic" values. He shifts the focus away from the "content" of the canon (or "curriculum," if you will) onto the values, beliefs, and purposes that inform its shape and their effect on the students who are its audience. Recognizing the inevitability of a "politicized" university, Graff urges us not to take sides, but to teach the ideological conflicts at work in the texts we chose to read. Rather than becoming less intellectually rigorous, such a curriculum will make "education more rigorous, by asking students to take an active part in an intellectual conversation" (34). For better or for worse, the shape of the educational consensus longed for by Schlesinger appears to be in the process of renegotiation.

Unfortunately, what appears to be a challenge to the traditional curriculum can evaporate into a reenforcement of the status quo when approached through Charles Altieri's recent plea for preserving both authorial intention and the canon. Drawing on the same vocabulary as Graff, Altieri appeals to those concerned with the values, beliefs, and purposes of literary study:

> A vital canon provides the richest imperatives to make ourselves new: in the works it preserves we find alternatives to what the dominant culture imposes on us; and in the modes of questioning and comparing that we develop for adapting the canon, we find ways of organizing psychic energies capable of engaging and even extending our own age's most radical thinking about the psyche. (10)

Underlying such assertive, ministerial prose are at least two assumptions about the value of literary study: 1) the world of "literature" and the dominant culture are distinct *and* oppositional entities—"literature" exists outside and against the culture in which it was written; good literature reinforces this separation and valorizes literature over society; and 2) working on the canon ("modes of questioning and comparing") provides an arena in which to put contemporary theory into practice. Both propositions are at first seductive: often our students say they go to literature to find out how to live. Like the eighteenth-century conduct books out of which some of our earliest novels developed, the works in the canon would show us in Thoreauvian fashion "how I lived and what I lived for." But the worlds set forth in these works, whether the creation of Susan Warner or Nathaniel Hawthorne, never existed outside the cultural and psychological climates that gave them birth, climates that no longer exist. While our first response to their fiction may be to "identify" with their characters or the moral dilemmas that the narrators address, for us to go deeper (whether stylistically, thematically, or philosophically), we would be well advised to unpack the cultural worlds in which these authors wrote. Such a process may expose the essential complexity underlying their seemingly transparent prose.

Similarly, the influence of empirical thinking on literary criticism in the form of New Criticism is limited; contemporary theoretical approaches—feminist, poststructuralist, deconstructive, reader-response—ask that we engage a text beyond itself, though they may differ as to the context within which they would place that text. Altieri's belief that through literary study "we make ourselves new" (10) speaks to an abiding faith in the power of the word, but the power of the lash, the power of money, the power of faith, and the power of the law are equally compelling in this process of refashioning, and all are subject to sociohistorical and psychological forces.

In the course discussed below, "Domestic Strains: The Woman Question, Free Love, and Antebellum Fiction," I attempted to rehistoricize nineteenth-century American literature in full recognition of the inherent limitations of my project. Although I agree with Altieri that we need to "postulate some active principle, independent of the reader, that guides selection of meanings from a range of semantic and cultural possibilities," I have never presumed to claim to interpret "anything more than the potential for constructing certain meanings" (13). By incorporating extraliterary and noncanonical readings in my syllabus, I hoped to make available to my students just that "potential." The construction of meaning through my choice of texts is always inherently unstable. Who knows how the students will read these works? What previously undiscovered meanings will they uncover in their intertextual readings? Who knows what I may learn from them about literature and about life? Rather than silencing the differences between literature written in the past and life as we live it today, "Domestic Strains" offered students the opportunity to examine the formal features of literary style in their relationship with the cultural, social, and philosophical issues of the writer's day as far as I could present them and as far as the students could grasp them in a ten-week quarter.

In *High-Brow, Low-Brow*, Lawrence Levine argues that such an approach may help us "to shed [our] own cultural skin sufficiently to be able to perceive [our literary authors] as nineteenth-century Americans perceived [them], through the prism of nineteenth-century culture " (5). When we recognize the interconnectedness of literature and other cultural constructs (history, science, art), fiction emerges as one of a number of competing strategies through which a society discusses issues of human, national, and even global importance. Replacing writers within their culture, rather than just asserting knowingly their difference from it, demythologizes those few whom we know as our literary greats, while reclaiming historically neglected fiction allows us to acknowledge and follow the various constructions of literary "value." Rather than initiating students into an already predetermined literary club, broadening our field of inquiry offers students the notion of a "shared culture" and the opportunity to participate in its making. Scholars like Graff and Paul Lauter share Altieri and Schlesinger's understanding about the function of education:

> For it is not merely literary concepts and historical configurations that are undergoing reconstruction; it is our consciousness, that set of internal assumptions and outlooks that forms what we see, or even what we look at. (Lauter 116)

Given the importance of that endeavor, I am unwilling to relinquish the curriculum in the name of educational consensus or transcendent literary value.

Structuring "Domestic Strains"

> A new thought has dawned upon the world—that of fidelity to one's self. . . .The freedom of woman is now to be asserted and achieved . . . ; that she go not shuddering and loathing to the bed of the drunkard, or any diseased monster, or any honest and good man whom she does not love, because the law and public opinion require this sacrifice. (*Marriage* 198)

Written in 1851 by health reformer and novelist Mary Gove Nichols, this call to women's self-dependence was one strand of a consistent antebellum challenge to the "cult of true womanhood," whose emphasis on passionlessness, purity, and piety led increasingly to the isolation, demoralization, and oppression of white women. "Domestic Strains," an upper-division American literature course, took for its central inquiry the debate surrounding the "woman question" as presented in several nineteenth-century texts. This thematic approach allowed us to work on several levels at once. It introduced students to historically neglected fiction without relinquishing what many regard as the central texts of our discipline; it familiarized students with the social discourses out of which canonical and historically neglected literary works emerged; and it encouraged students to revise previously held beliefs in light of new information and to reconsider the construction of literary value.

Three interconnected pedagogical strategies supported these goals. First, through a series of student reports on primary source materials, I focused our attention on the "private," female sphere in which marriage, divorce, and sexuality are privileged over the "public," male sphere of business, politics, and philosophy. Second, I subordinated canonical works (in this case, *The Blithedale Romance* and *The Bostonians*) to the reading of historically neglected fiction: *Mary Lyndon: or, Revelations of a Life*, by Mary Gove Nichols (published in 1854), *Incidents in the Life of a Slave Girl* by Harriet Jacobs (finally published in 1860 though also written in 1854), and *Iola LeRoy*, by the most widely read black woman writer of the last century, Frances Harper (published in 1894). Finally, I invited continuous discussions of literary "valuation," asking students to use a reading journal to reflect on the assumptions underlying the ways in which they had traditionally categorized "good" and "bad" literature.

Providing a Context: Free Love, Spiritualism, and the 1850s Divorce Controversy

> [W]hat are the theoretical conceptions, the critical practices, the historical designs, the ideas about function and audience, that must be reconstructed *so that* [historically neglected] works can, indeed, be read? (Lauter, "Canon Theory and Emergent Practice" 136)

In "Domestic Strains," a series of extraliterary readings and student reports on eighteenth- and nineteenth-century advice literature (see appendix I) allowed the social context and debates concerning woman's place to emerge. Social reform movements advocating individualism and communism, women's rights, women's vocations, divorce, free love, and spiritualism had adherents and dissenters in almost every antebellum community; they informed the everyday patois, providing a host of literary allusions and metaphors. The educated elite, the skilled and unskilled laborers, the slaves—all found these movements attractive and compelling: newspapers like "Herald of Health" had a readership of over 100,000 in the early 1850s; Harvard faculty hosted the father of mesmerism, Spurzheim, on his tour of the United States; even such conservatives as Harriet and Catherine Beecher's father, Lyman Beecher, earned his living for a time performing phrenological "readings" of skulls with the soon-to-be publisher Lorenzo Fowler.

The class's early readings of late eighteenth-century epistolary novels (*The Power of Sympathy* and *The Coquette*) and excerpts from Charles Brockden Brown's lengthy conversation concerning marriage in *Alcuin* presented the issues surrounding the "woman question" at the founding of the republic. To declare one sovereign illegitimate and construct a new sovereign raised issues of legitimacy and power on the domestic as well as on the political front; the creation of a "new" democratic man needed a partner, a "republican" woman who could educate children ready to participate in democratic life even as a burgeoning middle class found itself tempted to participate in the privilege of aristocratic culture. Strains already present in the construction of domestic life became more pronounced with the emergence of the antebellum women's rights movement. Throughout the 1840s, marriage reformers publicly challenged the prevailing concept of marital unity which "mandated the wife's subservience to her husband" and "held the distinction of obliterating her legal identity" (Basch 24). They fought for women's right to property and legal redress, finally codifying those demands in the "Declaration of Sentiments," signed in 1848.

By the early 1850s, divorce surfaced as another strategy to contest gender inequities and a Free Love movement emerged that questioned the authority of the state to regulate a marriage contract Free Love adherents believed should be a matter of spiritual affinity between two adults. The ideology of these Free Love radicals, as understood in the mid-1850s, was presented through a series of student reports on Swedenborgianism, Fourierism, Josiah Warren's *Individual Sovereignty*, and Thomas and Mary Gove Nichols' tome *Marriage*. Engrossing class discussions explored the alternative meanings of Free Love under debate in the early 1850s; we puzzled over why our current definition is so at odds with the one offered by the Free Love advocates writing during the previous century. Students were surprised to learn that so many of the reforms sought by the antebellum free lovers are considered common sense today: no-fault divorce and community property, women's right to child custody and property, a woman's right to choose when and with whom she will bear a child.

Through these reports and discussions it became clear to the students that none of these reforms were granted women by a benevolent state or compassionate men; they were no more self-evident than those of the "Declaration of Rights" that we take as common sense today; their originators were often ridiculed and persecuted and their ideas suppressed. In each of these struggles, the genre of the novel provided one forum in which to debate the various calls for changes in private life, offering alternative scenarios to the dominant domestic ideology.

Reading Historically Neglected Fiction

All the nineteenth-century novels chosen for this course participated in the conversation surrounding marriage reform and women's place. All of them either rejected or satirized the dominant literary tradition that featured either antisocial heroic males who escape into the wilderness or domestic heroines who establish themselves through romantic marriage or die alone and abandoned. None applauded the civil marriage of their day, whether the antebellum model based on community approbation or the post bellum model based on individualism and romance. For example, *Mary Lyndon* and *Iola LeRoy* present lengthy arguments in favor of companionate marriages that allow for female vocation and usefulness. *Incidents in the Life of a Slave Girl* goes even further; by its end the protagonist, Linda Brent, repudiates marriage entirely, choosing instead freedom and a home. Though Priscilla and Hollingsworth are joined at the end of *Blithedale Romance*, he has become an emotional cripple and they have no children. And while Verena elopes with Basil, the final sentence of *The Bostonians* warns us that this union will not be blissful:

> But though she was glad, he presently discovered that, beneath her hood, she was in tears. It is to be feared that with the union, so far from brilliant, into which she was about to enter, these were not the last she was destined to shed. (*Bostonians* 433)

Instead of what has often been considered the traditional "American" male hero, most of these works present female heroes, who do not find their voices in the rugged wilderness, the desert island, or the utopian community, but in the heart of nontraditional, socially engaged communities: Mary (of *Mary Lyndon*) among the "enthusiasts" of New York, Linda (of *Incidents*) among the abolitionists of upstate New York, Iola (of *Iola LeRoy*) among the freed slaves of the South, and Olive (of *The Bostonians*) on the suffragist platform. In their insistence on "a woman's fidelity to oneself" and their advocacy of female vocation, the three novels argue for and demonstrate the emotional, spiritual, and physical self-dependence of women.

Reading *Mary Lyndon* and *Incidents* provided students with an alternative understanding to the commonly assumed conceptions of antebellum attitudes towards motherhood and female community, two arenas contemporary feminist scholars often present as stable markers of the "separate sphere" ideology of that period. In *Mary Lyndon*, for example, Mary blames her physical sickliness on her mother's lack of maternal affection and knowledge, and her emotional isolation on the narrow-mindedness and ignorance of the female community. Linda, whose own mother dies early in the novel, rejects the mothering she receives from a grandmother whom she portrays as strong in maternal affection and religious fervor but weak in commitment to freedom. Linda's critique of and plea to the white mistresses of the South and the racist women of the North repeats *Mary Lyndon*'s portrayal of community women as vicious gossips and perpetrators of male violence against women. In both novels few supportive women emerge. Linda and Mary offer themselves as models of a new mother, one who places freedom for herself as a precondition of freedom for her children, and of a new woman who achieves economic self-dependence rather than submit to the sexual advances of men repugnant to them.

While we do not know if Frances Harper ever read *Incidents in the Life of a Slave Girl* or *Mary Lyndon*, her only novel, *Iola LeRoy*, echoes their concerns with women's place, self-dependence, and companionate marriage. Iola rejects the proposal by Dr. Graham not only because he is white and is cautious once he learns of her mixed heritage, but because in marrying him she would escape her duty to her race. When she chooses to marry Dr. Latimer, their relationship is portrayed as one of spiritual affinity and social usefulness, the very themes many antebellum Free Lovers and women's rights advocates felt basic for the true marriage bond.

During class discussions we complicated our understanding of the sociopolitical debates surrounding marriage and women's place by exploring the sociocultural context in which these women wrote, particularly the Divorce Controversy of the early 1850s. Novels like Gove Nichols' *Mary Lyndon*, that clearly support Free Love, woman's vocation, and spiritualism provide a thesis to Hawthorne's antithesis in *The Blithedale Romance*. In American literary criticism Hawthorne is generally portrayed as politically disengaged; however, as Jean Yellin has demonstrated in "Hawthorne and the American National Sin," Hawthorne was deeply conscious of the debates surrounding slavery, abolition, women's rights, and spiritualism in the 1840s and 1850s (75). In his biography of Franklin Pierce, written in hopes of winning a federal appointment in Pierce's administration, Hawthorne rejected abolitionist activities against chattel slavery, echoing "both in meter and in matter the rejection of activism against sexual oppression that he would voice at the end of *The Scarlet Letter*" (Yellin 85).

Our readings and reports, including excerpts from Hawthorne's good friend Charles Webber's *Yeiger's Cabinet* and a letter warning his wife Sophia to avoid mesmerists, suggested that Hawthorne's incorporation into *Blithedale* of references to the spiritualist sciences and attacks on social reformers was more than a mere literary device or metaphor through which to discuss the dark side of the human soul. We came to understand that preoccupation with the pseudosciences of mesmerism, phrenology and water-cure was common among his contemporaries (including Emerson, Thoreau, Whitman, and Melville) and they portended disturbing changes in the emotional, physical, and spiritual relations among men and women. Though Hawthorne, like Emerson and Gove Nichols, distrusted reformers (these "one-idea men" mistook involvement with one cause for what these writers considered to be the more necessary work of spiritual transformation), they each differed in the way such a transformation was to be achieved. Providing a glimpse of the positions within Hawthorne's intellectual community towards these innovations offered students a new lens through which to read his fiction.

Reports on Ann Braude's recent *Radical Spirits* and Gove Nichols' 1852 essay, *Experience in Water-Cure* indicated some of the ways in which spiritualist science offered women options to the inadequate horrors of allopathic medicine and provided them with alternative vocations to unpaid domestic service as wives, mothers, and caregivers. Water-cure procedures, for example, did not require special knowledge of drugs, leeches, or lances; therefore, women's exclusion from medical schools did not disqualify them from becoming practitioners. Mediumship, the central role in mesmerism, allowed women the opportunity to extend the "female" traits of intuition, sensitivity, and passivity from the private into the public realm (Braude 23–4, 91–3). Female mediums often took on forbidden roles without challenging the order of society dictated by separate spheres. Mrs. Sarah J. Hale, editor of Boston's *Ladies Magazine*, summarized what came to be known as "educated motherhood" in her support for the necessity of female participation in "phrenological science":

> Excepting christianity, phrenology will do more to elevate
> woman than any other system has ever done. It gives her a
> participation in the labors of mind. She must understand
> its principles and practice them in the nursery. And her
> influence it is which must mold the minds of her children
> and improve the world. (Hale 6)

Although Hawthorne's letters warning Sophia away from
mesmeric healers are common knowledge, his connections to the
spiritualist and Free Love communities in New England and
New York were interesting revelations for my class.
Hawthorne's brother-in-law, Horace Mann, had a long
familiarity with Mary Gove Nichols—first in Lynn,
Massachusetts, where he bought property adjacent to her
mentor, William Alcott, and later, in the mid-1850s, when he
attempted to have Mary and her husband Thomas driven from
Yellow Springs, Ohio, where they had gone to set up their water-
cure community, Memnonia. Hawthorne's friend and fellow
writer, Charles Webber, was a boarder at Mary Gove's water-
cure spa in New York where he had gone to recover from
alcoholism and dementia. Webber's roman à clef, *Yeiger's
Cabinet: Spiritual Vampirism* attacked feminism, mesmerism, and
Mary Gove Nichols, who may have spurned his advances to her
and certainly interfered with his relationship with her daughter,
Elma. In *Yeiger's Cabinet*, Webber appropriates the narrative that
Mary Gove often told in her health-related articles about her
conversion to water-cure, but from a much different perspective.
Rather than appearing as an "apostle of health" (as Mary Gove
Nichols characterizes her own protagonist), his protagonist gains
her strength from her cabal of power-hungry women and sucks
out the souls of her victims.

In *Blithedale*, written at the same time as *Yeiger's Cabinet*
and *Mary Lyndon*, all four central characters have the
characteristics of a spiritual vampire and a "one-idea man":
Zenobia through her passion for women's rights, Hollingsworth
through his obsession with penal reform, Coverdale through his
physical infirmity and narrative control, and Priscilla through
her embodiment of the passive Cult of True Womanhood.
Priscilla ultimately triumphs, sending Zenobia to her watery
grave (and her death by drowning is suggestive given the

contemporary water-cure craze), emasculating Hollingsworth, and ensnaring our narrator. To reimmerse *Blithedale* in this context is to allow its biting satire and wit to emerge *and* to raise to consciousness its assault on the women's rights, Free Love, and the spiritualist movements of the day.

Similarly, it is not by chance that Verena Tarrant in James' *The Bostonians* is a spiritualist. Like the young Mary Lyndon she is a prototypical medium as outlined by Lawrence Moore, a woman who had experienced a lonely and sickly childhood and as an adolescent felt the beginning stirring of clairvoyance: "mediumship . . . offered the possibility of transforming a miserable life into one that brought happiness for oneself and not infrequently to others" (221).

Alfred Habegger has recently suggested that James wrote *The Bostonians* to avenge the way his father had been maligned during the Divorce Controversy of the 1850s, primarily known through an exchange of letters between Horace Greeley, Henry James, Sr., and Stephen Pearl Andrews published in the *New York Tribune*. By this time in the quarter, students began to anticipate that there may be numerous connections between the elder James and the Free Lovers of the 1850s. In 1848 the elder James translated and wrote a laudatory preface to a pamphlet by Victor Hennequin, "Love in the Phalanstery," a Fourierist tract asserting that in marriage some might lawfully enjoy various partners. Four years later, in a review of Marx Edgeworth Lazarus' *Love vs. Marriage*, James repudiated his earlier position and defended civil marriage and a woman's right to divorce. Finally, in an 1853 essay "Woman and the Woman's Movement," James "ridiculed feminism, opposed the entry of women into the learned professions, and insisted with remarkable emphasis that women were intellectually inferior to men" (Habegger 330).

James's retreat from his more radical position exposed him to ridicule by both Andrews and Lazarus. When Greeley refused to continue the divorce debate in the columns of the *Herald*, Andrews republished the entire tract with an extensive preface. Offering Mary Gove Nichols as the chief proponent of the Free Love radicals ("a lady who couples the most wonderful intuitions—the spiritual 'sphere of woman'—with a truly masculine strength and comprehension of general principles,

such as characterizes the highest order of scientific mind" [98]),
Andrews summarized her position in his own words, conflating
the language of the Declaration of Independence and the call for
woman's self-dependence:

> We say Man has the right to Life, Liberty, and the pursuit
> of Happiness; yet he abuses Life, falls into bondage, and
> seeks and does not find Happiness. . . . If [Woman] is fixed
> in indissoluble marriage with a man she must abhor—a
> selfish, sensual tyrant—who makes her his victim, and
> perpetuates in her children his lust of the flesh and of gain,
> and all the deep damnation of his nature, must woman lie
> prone under all this, suffering and transmitting the disease
> and crime which are its ordained product, because it is
> according to law? (99)

Uncovering these broader connections (or the "radical
similarities") between Hawthorne, James, and Gove Nichols and
between chattel slavery and women's rights, students could
situate literature within its social context and postulate another
set of meanings suppressed by more transcendental or close
readings. Far from denigrating the aesthetic worth of these
novels, such readings emphasize the complexity involved in
textual exegesis, and link literary studies to history, psychology,
social science, medicine, etc. Hypothesizing James Sr.'s
involvement with these antebellum radical positions heightens
the biting irony underlying James Jr.'s later depiction of Verena
as the daughter of a debased and mercenary spiritualist and
reformer, and of her marriage to a southern conservative like
Basil, but also suggests that Olive's ascent to the podium is a
triumph rather than an embarrassment.

Verena's very ability to become a medium makes her
susceptible to both "higher powers" and to Olive and Basil, a
character not very different from her flamboyant charlatan of a
father; and it is Olive's and Basil's single-mindedness (they, like
Hawthorne's Hollingsworth and several of the reformers in *Mary
Lyndon*, are "one-idea" people) that insures that neither will be
able to enter into companionate, spiritual, nurturing
relationships with others. Verena's marriage will clearly stifle
her voice, but it will provide the opportunity for Olive to
discover her own. Women will no longer need to speak as

mediums for otherworldly voices, but, as Elaine Showalter
suggests, in their own right, with their own voice:

> Olive, having loved, lost, and suffered, has also overcome
> silence. When Verena leaves with Basil, Olive must take
> her place on the platform. Her moment of speech is
> offered up as martyrdom presenting herself to the
> disappointed audience to be "hissed and hooted and
> insulted," "trampled to death and torn to pieces." But in
> fact, when she mounts the platform, like "some feminine
> firebrand of Paris revolutions," "the hush was respectful."
> Olive can now speak for the movement; she can realize her
> long-stifled personal longing for eloquence. In losing
> Verena, Olive gains her own voice and fulfills her destiny.
> (30)

But Were They Any Good?

The writing styles of historically neglected novels
provided the occasion for us to discuss the social construction of
literary value raised by feminist critics like Jane Tompkins and
Nina Baym. Students were often dismayed by these decidedly
"old fashioned" works that are frequently digressive and overtly
didactic. *Mary Lyndon*, for example, uses stylistic techniques
inspired by romantic beliefs in spontaneity and the traditional
forms of the Quaker spiritual autobiography, epistolary fiction,
and the roman à clef; *Iola LeRoy* includes lengthy sermons and
outlandish moments of coincidence to emphasize its major
themes of racial uplift, women's vocation, and family unity.
Works like *Mary Lyndon* and *Iola LeRoy* are not easily accessible
from contemporary standards of literary value. Only
engagement with their historical, philosophical, and cultural
milieu such as I attempted to provide in "Domestic Strains"
allows their "stylistic intricacy, psychological subtlety, [and]
epistemological complexity" (Tompkins 126) to emerge.

Reading these works also allowed us to ask how and why
the novel as a genre incorporates and transforms earlier genres.
Mary Lyndon, for example, deliberately subverts the purpose of
the Quaker spiritual autobiographical form; by insisting on

tracing the growth of an individual female consciousness in the here and now, and offering as its hero a woman banned by the Quaker community, it undermines Quaker concern with the otherworld and exposes hypocrisy among the Society of Friends. *Mary Lyndon* appropriates the conversion experience of the spiritual autobiography. For its hero, conversion to the Quakers is not the beginning of sight or the receiving of the "Inner Light"; instead, it is an extension of the sickness and darkness that pervades her childhood. The further Mary moves from the traditional structures of marriage, religion, and public opinion, the clearer her sight becomes.

Written the same year as *Mary Lyndon*, *Incidents in the Life of a Slave Girl* similarly transforms traditional genres like the spiritual autobiography and the emerging slave narrative by presenting a female voice: "Slavery" Jacobs writes, "is terrible for men; but it is far more terrible for women." Rather than following the male slave in his escape narrative to the unambiguously free soil of the North, Linda hides in her grandmother's attic for seven years so she can watch the growth and development of her children before escaping to a North permeated by racial prejudice.

The "new" knowledge of American culture helped my class reconstruct its understanding of nineteenth-century fiction. As we uncovered the various connections I have outlined above, students traced a variety of patterns and themes usually obscured in courses that focus only on canonical figures or employ primarily new critical approaches. For students who were more comfortable with the traditional canonical approach, my insistence on intertextuality and historical context was often frustrating and annoying; they resisted taking an active part in the intellectual conversations of the times and preferred to dismiss alternative possibilities concerning textual meaning and literary value. For others, however, literature took on meaning that had eluded them before; it "made sense" because it spoke to human concerns in embodied voices and offered complex, often contradictory, even illogical responses to moral and ethical questions. Finally, questioning the usual notions of literary value and offering students access to primary sources enriched both the canonical and noncanonical material; it humanized our forebearers and the literary profession. Through continuous in-class discussion and in the writing of their papers, students gained an opportunity to offer original insights into themes and structures rarely addressed in traditional literary criticism, and to explore the ways in which difference in historical time impels the formation of literary taste and social value.

The design of the course discussed above took place during the reign of silence within my department. None of my colleagues ever saw the syllabus or asked what I taught or if I taught anything at all. The course has come and gone seemingly without a ripple—yet it has helped me clarify what it is I do in the classroom and how it is that I wish to do it, and just last week a graduate student shared with me that she had found herself questioning another professor's reading of *The Blithedale Romance* because of the contextualized reading of it she had done in my course.

My questions to my department head and my husband were neither naive, ignorant, or irrelevant, they are the necessary *theoretical* questions "about the presuppositions and principles that underlie our practices" (Graff 21) that we would do well to ask when we enter our classrooms or our homes. How can we expect our students or our children to engage in critical and analytical thinking if we refuse such engagement ourselves?

WORKS CITED

Aiken, Susan Hardy, et al. *Changing Our Minds: Feminist Transformations of Knowledge*. Albany: State U of NY P, 1988.

Altieri, Charles. *Canons and Consequences: Reflections on the Ethical Force of Imaginative Ideals*. Evanston: Northwestern UP, 1990.

Basch, Norma. *In the Eye of the Law: Women, Marriage and Property in Nineteenth-Century New York*. Ithaca: Cornell UP, 1988.

Baym, Nina. "Melodramas of Beset Manhood: How Theories of American Fiction Exclude Women Authors." *The New Feminist*

Criticism: Essays on Women, Literature and Theory. Ed. Elaine Showalter. NY: Pantheon, 1985. 63–80.

Braude, Ann. *Radical Spirits: Spiritualism and Women's Rights in Nineteenth-Century America*. Boston: Beacon P, 1989.

Carby, Hazel. *Reconstructing Womanhood: The Emergence of the Afro-American Woman Novelist*. NY: Oxford UP, 1987.

Danielson, Susan. "Alternative Therapies: Spiritualism and Women's Rights in *Mary Lyndon; or, Revelations of a Life*." Diss. U of Oregon, 1990.

Davidson, Cathy. *Revolution and the Word: The Rise of the Novel in America*. NY: Oxford UP, 1986.

Davis, Lennard, and M. Bella Mirabella, eds. *Left Politics and the Literary Profession*. NY: Columbia UP, 1990.

DuBois, Ellen, et al. *Feminist Scholarship: Kindling in the Groves of Academe*. Urbana: U of Illinois P, 1985.

Fowlkes, Diane, and Charlotte McClure, eds. *Feminist Visions: Towards a Transformation of the Liberal Arts Curriculum*. Tuscaloosa: U of Alabama P, 1984.

Gilley, J. Wade. *Thinking About American Higher Education: The 1990s and Beyond*. NY: Macmillan, 1991.

Graff, Gerald. "Why Theory?" *Left Politics and the Literary Profession*. Eds. Lennard Davis and M. Bella Mirabella. NY: Columbia UP, 1990. 19–35.

Habegger, Alfred. "*The Bostonians* and Henry James Sr.'s Crusade Against Feminism and Free Love." *Women's Studies* 15 (1988): 323–342.

Hale, Sarah Josepha. *Godey's Ladies Magazine* 6.

Harper, Frances E. W. *Iola LeRoy or Shadows Uplifted*. Boston: Beacon P, 1987.

Hawthorne, Nathaniel. *The Blithedale Romance*. NY: Penguin, 1983.

Hennequin, Victor Antoine. *Love in the phalanstery*. NY: Dewitt and Davenport, 1849 [1848].

James, Henry, Jr. *The Bostonians*. NY: Penguin, 1985.

James, Henry, Sr. "The Marriage Question." *New York Daily Tribune,* 18 Sept. 1852.

Lauter, Paul. *Canons and Contexts*. NY: Oxford UP, 1991.

————. "Canon Theory and Emergent Practice." *Left Politics and the Literary Profession*. Eds. Lennard Davis and M. Bella Mirabella. NY: Columbia UP, 1990. 127–146.

Lazarus, Mary Edgeworth. *Love vs. Marriage*. New York: Fowlers and Wells, 1852.

Levine, Lawrence W. *High-Brow, Low-Brow: The Emergence of Cultural Hierarchy in America*. Cambridge: Harvard UP, 1988.

Moore, Lawrence. "The Spiritualist Medium: A Study of Female Professionalism in Victorian America." *American Quarterly* 27 (1975): 200–221

Morton, Donald, and Mas'ud Zavarzadeh, ed. *Theory/Pedagogy/Politics: Texts for Change*. Urbana: U of Illinois P, 1991.

Nichols, Mary Gove. *Mary Lyndon; or, Revelations of a Life*. NY: Stringer, 1854.

Nichols, Thomas, and Mary Gove Nichols. *Marriage: its history, character and results; its sanctities, and its profanities, its science and its facts, demonstrating its influence as a civilized institution on the happiness of the individual and the progress of the race*. Cincinnati: Nicholson and Co., 1854.

Schlesinger, Arthur, Jr. "The Cult of Ethnicity, Good and Bad." *Time*, 8 July 1991: 21.

Showalter, Elaine. *Sex and Anarchy: Gender and Culture at the Fin de Siecle*. NY: Penguin Books, 1990.

Skilbeck, Malcolm. *Curriculum Reform: An Overview of Trends*. Organization for Economic Cooperation and Development, 1990.

Stoehr, Taylor, ed. *Free Love in America: A Documentary History*. New York: AMS Press, 1979.

Swedenborg, Emanuel. *The Delights of Wisdom Pertaining to Conjugal Love to Which Is Added the Pleasures of Insanity Pertaining to Scortatory Love*. NY: American Swedenborg Printing and Publishing Society, 1912.

Tompkins, Jane. *Sensational Designs*. NY: Oxford, 1985.

Webber, Charles. *Yeiger's Cabinet: Spiritual Vampirism; The History of Etherial Softdown and Her Friends of the "New Light."* Philadelphia: Lippencot, 1853.

Yellin, Jean. "Hawthorne and the American National Sin." *The Green American Tradition: Essays and Poems for Sherman Paul*. Baton Rouge: Louisiana State UP, 1989. 75–97.

Appendix I

ENG 461/561: American Literature to 1865/Sue Danielson/Domestic Strains: *The Woman Question in Antebellum Fiction*

> I feel this whole question of women's rights turns on the
> point of the marriage relation, and sooner or later it will be
> the question for discussion.
> —*Elizabeth Cady Stanton to Susan B. Anthony, 1853*

English 461/561 will examine the interconnections of literature and social history by focusing on three significant moments in American literary culture. The complexities surrounding the Woman Question, slavery, marriage, and sexuality provide the frame for our inquiry. There is a LARGE packet at Clean Copy and much material on reserve. Assignments will come from both places, and the unassigned material is just there for your perusal. Class time will be spent with brief lecture and much, I hope, discussion.

Undergraduates will be expected to facilitate class discussion of the assigned reading (I will assign two students each week for this task), and to keep a response journal on class readings and discussions. This journal will form the basis for an end-of-term paper, 5 to 7 pages long (topics to be discussed by mid-quarter).

Graduate students will be expected to present a discussion on one of the books or topics listed below. They will also be expected to write a 10- to 15-page research paper on a topic to be discussed with me.

Please hand in two copies of your paper; I will put one on reserve. You will be expected to read and respond to at least three papers on a form I will prepare for that purpose. The night of finals we can discuss issues raised by the papers.

Jan. 8   Introduction—Video—Historical Context

On reserve—Scott-Smith

Jan. 15   Theoretical Problems

Brown, *The Power or Sympathy*, and Foster, *The Coquette*
Packet—Baym, "Melodramas of Beset Manhood"

Wollstonecraft, excerpt *Vindication*

Tompkins, "Masterpiece Theatre"

Brockden Brown, *Alcuin*

Jan. 22   Foster, continued

Women and Reform Culture

Report—*The Empire of the Mother*

Report—Women in Utopias

Report—Conjugal Relations—Swedenborg and Fourier

Packet—Fuller; excerpt *Declaration of Sentiments*

Baym—*Woman's Fiction*—11–50, 276–315

Jan. 29   Companionate Marriage and the Divorce Controversy

Report—Radical Spirits

Report—"Free Love as a Doctrine of Spiritualism"

On reserve—Nichols, *Marriage: its history, character, and results, its sanctities, and its profanities, its science and its facts*, pp. 90–96, 125–121, 177–188

Abstracts of papers due

Feb. 5   *Blithedale Romance*

Report—Critical Responses to *Blithedale*

Feb. 12   *Mary Lyndon* —complete work in packet

On reserve—Danielson, "Healing Arts"

On reserve—Meyerson

Feb. 19   *Bostonians*

Report—Alfred Habegger and *The Bostonians*

Feb. 26 *Incidents in the Life of a Slave Girl*
          Report—Yellin

Mar. 5 *Iola LeRoy*
          On reserve—Christian, "The Uses of History"
          On reserve—Hazel Carby
          On reserve—Paul Lauter
          Drafts of papers due

READING LIST 461/561

Brown, Hubert Ross. *The Sentimental Novel in America, 1789–1860.* Durham, NC: Duke UP, 1940.

Carby, Hazel V. *Reconstructing Womanhood: The Emergence of the Afro-American Woman Novelist.* NY: Oxford UP, 1987.

Clinton, Catherine. *The Other Civil War: American Women in the Nineteenth-Century.* NY: Hill and Wang, 1984.

Cott, Nancy F. "Passionlessness: An Interpretation of Victorian Sexual Ideology, 1790–1850." *Signs* 4 (1978): 219–236.

Douglas, Ann. *The Feminization of American Culture.* NY: Doubleday, 1988.

Eakin, Paul John. *The New England Girl: Cultural Ideals in Hawthorne, Stowe, Howells, and James.* Athens: U of Georgia P, 1976.

Hogelund, Ronald W. "The Female Appendage: Feminine Life-Style in America, 1820–60." *Our American Sister.* Eds. Jean E. Friedman and William G. Shade.

James, Janet Wilson. *Changing Ideas About Women in the United States, 1776–1825.* NY: Garland, 1981.

Leach, William. *Free Love and Perfect Union: The Feminist Reform of Sex and Society.* NY: Basic Books, 1980.

Moore, R. Lawrence. "The Spiritualist Medium: A Study of Female Professionalism in Victorian America." *American Quarterly* 27 (1975): 200–221.

Nichols, Thomas, and Mary Gove Nichols. *Marriage: its history, character, and results, its sanctities, and its profanities, its science and its facts, demonstrating its influence as a civilized institution on the happiness of the individual and the progress of the race.* Cincinnati: Valentine Nicholson and Co., 1854.

Rose, Anne C. *Transcendentalism as a Social Movement, 1830–50.* New Haven: Yale UP, 1981.

Rosenberg, Rosalind. *Beyond Separate Spheres: Intellectual Roots of Modern Feminism.* New Haven: Yale UP, 1982.

Smith-Rosenberg, Carroll. *Disorderly Conduct: Visions of Gender in Victorian America.* NY: Oxford UP, 1985.

Stoehr, Taylor. *Hawthorne's Mad Scientists: Pseudoscience and Social Science in Nineteenth-Century Life and Letters.* CN: Archon Books, 1978.

———, ed. *Free Love in America: A Documentary History.* NY: AMS Press, 1979.

Taylor, William R., and Christopher Lasch. "Two 'Kindred Spirits': Sorority and Family in New England, 1839–1846." *New England Quarterly* 36 (1963): 23–41.

Walters, Ronald G. *American Reformers: 1815–1860.* NY: Hill and Wang, 1978.

Welter, Barbara. *Dimity Convictions: The American Woman in the Nineteenth Century.* Athens, OH: Ohio UP, 1976.

APPENDIX II

Sample Abstracts of Papers Submitted for "Domestic Strains"

1. "The Power of Letters," by Patrice Gruver Dodd, examines the pivotal role of letters in Hannah Foster's *The Coquette; or, The History of Eliza Wharton: A Novel Founded on Fact* (1797), Harriet A. Jacobs' *Incidents in the Life of a Slave Girl: Written by Herself* (1861), and Mary Gove Nichols' *Mary Lyndon; or, Revelations of a Life: An Autobiography* (1860). Dodd argues that the authors use letters to illustrate and enact the heroines' relative successes and failures in creating themselves as free, autonomous, and powerful women against the backgrounds of patriarchy, chattel slavery, and marriage slavery. In addition, because the use of letters highlights the existence of various perspectives within the works, she demonstrates that the authors' choices of whose letters to show and in what proportions shape both the correspondents' perceptions and the relationships between them.

2. "The Spiritual Vampire as Character Type in *The Blithedale Romance* and Other Works by Nathaniel Hawthorne," by Ken Petri, rereads the *Blithedale Romance* in light of his friend Charles Wilkins Webber's roman à clef, *Spiritual Vampirism: The History of Etherial Softdown and Her Friends of the "New Light,"* published in 1853 to attack health reformer and novelist Mary Gove Nichols and the burgeoning women's rights movement. "After showing the affinities between Hawthorne's Priscilla and Webber's Etherial, I suggest that Hawthorne may have been playing out in his fiction some sort of fear of women; the spiritual vampire type of woman is dangerous, as the man who contacts her runs the risk of losing the essence of vitality which allows him to function in male society."

3. "Marriage and Motherhood: Physical and Spiritual Slavery," by Yvonne Sletmoe, compares Harriet Jacobs' *Incidents in the Life of a Slave Girl* with Mary Gove Nichols' *Mary Lyndon: or, Revelations of a Life*. Set in the mid-1800s, in a nation divided over the grim realities of slavery, two women, in their autobiographies, address two of the major issues facing women of the day: the institutions of marriage and motherhood. Harriet Jacobs' work *Incidents* portrays the dilemmas of motherhood set against the physical reality of slavery. Mary Gove Nichols' work, *Mary Lyndon*, on the other hand, portrays the institution of marriage as it can exist in a state of spiritual slavery.

These autobiographies were written for specific causes; both writers are trying to encourage their readers to see, as in Lyndon's words, "There is a difference between the slave who tamely submits and the one who struggles." Mary and Linda (the hero in *Incidents*) found that the path of resistance lead them, albeit through many hard places, to the ultimate realization of their goal: freedom.

New "Theme(s) for English B"
Reimagining Contexts for Learning in Multiethnic Writing Classes

Barbara Roche Rico
Sandra Mano

Introduction

In his poem "Theme for English B," Langston Hughes writes:

> It's not easy to know what is true for you or me
> at twenty two, my age. But I guess I'm what
> I feel and see and hear, Harlem, I hear you:
> hear you, hear me—we too—you, me, talk on this page.

Hughes' poem addresses the Harlem of the 1920s; yet in many ways, in the Los Angeles and other urban centers of the 1990s, in classrooms across the country, Hughes' questions are still our questions: How do we manage the conversation of the classroom? Who enters the conversation when our students and we "talk on this page"? As writing professionals we have spent much of the last decade debating questions related to pluralism and the canons of our curricula. Those of us who teach courses with a multiethnic focus have devised our own response to the challenges voiced by E. D. Hirsch and Allan Bloom. Few of us would be teaching this material if we truly found that pluralism led us or our students down the slippery slope to cultural illiteracy, or if we believed that to open the canon meant to close one's mind. Many of us would agree with Gadamer that the meaning of a given text resides in the historical place of the interpreter; or with M. M. Bakhtin, who suggests that to endow any object or artifact with aesthetic value is a social act, inseparable from prevailing ideologies. We see in the early anthologies of American literature a tendency to celebrate the nativism of Longfellow over the less accessible poems of Dickinson and Whitman. The pattern can be seen as well with schools of criticism: the New Critics, who valued such features as wit and paradox, helped to strengthen the critical reputation of Donne; the formalists, who stressed the importance of defamiliarization, turned to Sterne's *Tristram Shandy*; the structuralists found inspiration in British romantic poetry and Baudelaire. As the work of Barbara Herrnstein Smith and John Guillory has shown, literary values that are at one moment called "universal" are in essence contingent upon social values, socially constructed systems of belief.

There is no need to reenact the debates of the last decade. It is not so much that these debates have been settled, but scholars have more or less chosen sides and moved on. Questions are being redefined from whether to how. Those of us who have chosen to listen more to the voices of our own students than the caveats of those critics opposed to curricular change have found in multiethnic approaches some new opportunities for intellectual growth, both as teachers and as learners. But after ten years of developing multicultural textbooks and multiethnic courses, we are left to ask, How much has really changed? How much have we been changed by the "broadening of the literary canon"? By making our classes more "multicultural" by including new authors, have we really begun to create an environment in which our students will feel more comfortable to speak their truths in the classroom, and to "talk" to us on the page? Or have we just allowed ourselves to become a little more comfortable?

We might assert that the greatest threat to the development of multiethnic courses, or multiethnic approaches to writing, is not the criticisms of the conservatives, but the complacency of the converted. To see this, we would like to examine a few of the ways in which traditional literature and writing courses have been modified in the last decade to reflect a multicultural perspective.

Thematic Approaches

In the 1980s critics such as Walter Ong, Raymund Paredes, and others proposed the use of multiethnic works in what Ong referred to as "interactive organization." Canonical systems could be put into dialogic relationship to help illuminate thematic correspondences. We have adopted such interactive approaches in our own classrooms, and we have found that they can introduce a new perspective to themes common to the freshman English class: ambitions and responsibilities, the struggle for identity, the search for selfhood, and the attraction and delusion of the American dream. The critique of the American dream, which finds its expression in so much American fiction and drama of the 1940s and 1950s, takes on a new sense of urgency in the literature of historically marginalized groups. Useful discussions have resulted from pairings of Tennessee Williams' *Glass Menagerie* with Sandra Cisneros' short novel *The House on Mango Street*, which treats the life of a young woman growing up in Chicago. In both works there is a strong sense of the individual's alienation from and isolation in the urban landscape, the young person's striving for a better life beyond that of the crowded apartment.

Moreover, the sense of struggle for one's goal despite the opinions of the larger society, which emerges clearly in Eudora Welty's "A Worn Path," is expressed in an interesting way in Tomas Rivera's story "La Noche buena." Rivera's story follows the journey of a woman—the wife of a migrant worker—as she seeks to buy presents for her children on Christmas Eve. Here, too, we can sense the derision that she faces as she tries to negotiate her way through the town, the suspicion of the townspeople, and her resolution not to come home empty-handed.

The issues of familial and cultural tensions, the child's sense of responsibility and his desire for self-respect emerge quite pointedly in a discussion that includes Faulkner's "Barn

Burning" and Richard Wright's "The Man Who Was Almost a Man." The dialogic organization of texts has much to recommend it. It prompts students to explore values from a comparative perspective. As Elizabeth Fox-Genovese has suggested, canonical works help to articulate the values of the society that has produced them. As Ong has pointed out, the interaction of works from dominant and marginalized sectors of society can encourage students to explore works and cultural values from new perspectives:

> A minority literature often mixes what is unfamiliar with the majority with what is familiar. It thus provides not only an organization of experience different from that of the majority culture (and of other minorities), but also an interactive organization. A minority literature often negotiates for its own identity with the majority culture and constantly redefines itself, ultimately bringing the majority culture to redefine itself more adequately, too. (3)

This organization can enable students to see "creative tensions" among works. Speaking about Chicano literature's relation to the dominant culture, Ramon Saldívar has asserted:

> As a part of American literature, narratives by Chicano men and women offer significant representations of the historical drama of nineteenth and twentieth century American life, especially as that life intersects, consciously or not, with what has sometimes been referred to as the Third World. (24)

Explorations of marginalized literature can encourage students to develop new ways of evaluating the literary production of both the marginalized and the dominant cultures. Works from each culture can be seen to problematize the value system of the other.

For an interactive organization to be effective, however, there must be a diligent attention to issues of emphasis, perspective, and balance. Imagine, for example, a class discussion exploring three texts with female protagonists: the traditional Griselda story (recounted in Chaucer's "Clark's Tale"), Maxine Hong Kingston's *Woman Warrior*, and Alice Walker's *Color Purple*. The interactive organization would seem to provide an interesting groundwork for exploring, for example, issues related to gender and class in all three works. We might ask our students to consider how these issues can affect a character's sense of self-determination, or how familial control and more public power structures are related to each other in each text. Such an examination might be fruitful, so long as appropriate attention were paid to the unique voice of each literary work.

This is where issues of perspective and emphasis come in. Without a concerted effort to treat each work on its own terms, an interactive organization might tend to privilege the more established, more canonical work—making the Griselda story the central subtext, while representing Walker's or Hong Kingston's narratives as other versions of that story. In such an organization, the less canonical works can be co-opted to highlight newer elements of the dominant-culture work. What emerges is less a conversation among works than a chiarascuro (to use an admittedly Eurocentric term) in which the values of the other works are determined by their power to set off the more canonical one. In such a formulation, those elements present in Hong Kingston or Walker but absent from the traditional story will be overlooked.

Many anthologies that present themselves as being multicultural illustrate another problem with the thematic approach. Too often the thematic structure is not really interactive at all. Many introductory literature and composition readers, for example, offer dialogic pairings less often than a thematically arranged list of titles—often the same handful of authors, the same "critical war-horses" replicated in each anthology. A few examples will help to make the point: Maya Angelou's "Graduation," Ellison's "Battle Royal," Wakatsuki's "Arrival at Manzanar," Rodriguez's "New American Scholarship Boy," the first chapter from Hong Kingston's *Woman Warrior*, and Martin Luther King's "I Have a Dream" speech. Our intention is less to comment on the works themselves, but to explore some of the ways in which their inclusion—indeed, their ubiquity—in introductory literature and writing collections can prompt students to have a simplistic, perhaps even monologic sense about the issues involved.

In terms of this rather limited "rhetoric of inclusion," we note the presence of the early Richard Rodriguez and, more recently, the emergence of Dinesh D'Souza. The formal elegance of Rodriguez's prose has been noted by many; one wonders whether the reprinting of "New American Scholarship Boy" might be related to the ways in which Rodriguez's rhetoric can be seen to reflect positions valorized by the neoconservative movement. Similarly D'Souza becomes the "ethnic" representative that decries the multicultural trends as "illiberal education." As important as what is included is what is left out: we see much less often the writings of John Okada, Gloria Anzaldúa, or until recently, Malcolm X.

Often what tends to be emphasized by thematic organization and the selection of choices is unity rather than diversity, harmony rather than tension. Such approaches tend to encourage ahistorical readings that overlook or deny the importance of cultural difference. This can prompt students to feel that having read the work of one writer from a representative group will allow them to make general statements about others. Having read Rodriguez, they can generalize about affirmative action or the dangers of bilingualism; having read Hong Kingston, they know how Chinese American women feel about keeping silent. One might be tempted to use Hirsch's phrase in describing this approach as "piecemeal undigested knowledge"—incomplete and devoid of context.

When anthologies do include material focusing on prejudice or inequality, these works are often approached from a safe, and thus nonthreatening, position of historical distance. By reprinting Maya Angelou's "Graduation" or Ellison's "Battle Royal," are we allowing our students to conclude that they are encountering rarefied artifacts from another time, and to assume that the problems encountered by the narrator are not their problems, or the problems of students today? Do we teach these works as on the other side of the *Brown v. Board* decision or the civil rights movement? Do we let them assert that the problems depicted in those stories don't exist anymore? The events of April 1992 in Los Angeles and other urban cities have clearly eliminated this "comfort zone," if it ever indeed existed.

Contextual Approaches

Hughes' poem invites us to acknowledge the importance of context: to listen to the individual, the history, the collective memory, that "talks on this page." To recognize the importance of context is to be aware of the culture that speaks through the writer, that enables him or her to speak; it is also to recognize those elements that keep the student from talking. In our enthusiasm for multiculturalism, we cannot allow our explorations of multiethnic cultures to become self-generating, self-congratulatory retreats. We cannot isolate our examinations of cultural expression from the polarized, balkanized contexts in which we find ourselves living. What "talks on the page" is not only life story, but the controversies of immigration, bilingualism, affirmative action, and racism.

An approach to multiethnic texts that introduces and recognizes the importance of context can draw the interpreter away from a work as an isolated artifact and towards the work as a part of a more complex cultural moment. This includes a consideration of the circumstances of its production and its reception. It raises questions about the audience for that text and the authority that it assumes for itself in relationship with other literary texts and cultural markers. Context means acknowledging difference, uniqueness; as Hughes writes "Will my page be colored that I write? Being me, it will not be white."

To choose a contextual approach rather than a strictly thematic one is to acknowledge the possibility of difference, of uniqueness. Rather than present a multicultural menu on the general theme of insider or outsider, one might enter into the literature of an ethnic group, isolate particularly generative periods in the history of the group. What prompted literary texts to be produced? What sort of texts were produced? In what sense did they relate to each other? What images dominate? How are they transformed? What is the relationship between the author and other authors? In what ways does the culture "talk" on the page? What is the history of the work's reception? How is it received today? One example of how this might work would be an examination of the Internment as history, memory, and image in Japanese-American literature. The issuing of the

Evacuation Order caused individuals both within and outside the Japanese -American community to reconsider the meaning of American constitutional guarantees. As Monica Sone and others have described, both citizen and noncitizen residents had to question whether nationality, national origin, or ethnicity would take precedence over constitutional guarantees.

Much of Japanese-American literature written both during and after the Internment reflects, reflects on, and represents the situation of being "in camp"—what it was like to be deprived of one's land and forced to live under regimented conditions, imprisoned without trial. Marginalized, forced to retire from the commerce and community they had known, detainees were left with little but time—time to consider their circumstances, time to write. There emerged a microcosm that contained not only schools but also newspapers, journals, and literary societies, whose authors and audience were "in camp." A generation used the language of confinement to call attention to its own circumstances and to consider the consequences of that confinement on issues related to identity, affiliation, and belonging.

The Internment provides both an important historical moment and a governing image in much Japanese-American literature, even that written years after the camps had been closed. To explore Japanese-American texts from the perspective of the camps is to establish a context in which a set of texts is allowed to speak, not as the isolated representation of a single ethnic group, but as a part of a particularly generative period of literary production. Themes such as identity and loyalty that are represented in Japanese-American texts become more problematic when viewed in terms of the historical context that helped to shape them: Toshio Mori's short stories which had been accepted for publication just before the War, only to be rejected right after Pearl Harbor, or John Okada's *No-No Boy*, a novel about an internee who refused to serve in the military, written by a man who was himself an internee and a decorated veteran of World War II. These themes, historically grounded in the Japanese-American experience, reemerge in the works of other writers, among them Hisaye Yamamoto. Much of Yamamoto's short fiction (published in popular magazines during the 1950s and 60s, but not collected in book form until the late 1980s) explores the ways in which life in the camp helps to define and dictate the sort of life one would have in the future. "Las Vegas Charley," for example, explores consequences of the internment, the ways in which one character's life continues to be shaped by the political choices made years before. "The Legend of Miss Sasagawara" presents a young woman's coming of age as a person and a writer within the confines of the camp experience.

As the poetry of Lawson Fusao Inada and Janice Mirikitani illustrates, the camp image can sometimes be fused with other historical references to create a more general statement about subjugation and silencing. In Inada's poem "Concentration Constellation," the western landscape is presented as a constellation, each point of which marks the site of an internment camp:

> Begin between the Golden State's
> highest and lowest elevations
> and name that location
>
> Manzanar. Rattlesnake a line
> southward to the zone
> of Arizona, to the home
> of Natives on the reservation
> and call those Gila, Poston . . .
>
> Now regard what sort of shape
> this constellation takes
> It sits there like a jagged scar,
> massive, on the massive landscape.
> It lies there like the rusted wire
> of a twisted and remembered fence.

In the poem the camp image overtakes the geography of the continent, so that the entire southwest is seen in relation to the "constellation" of camps. In the image of Poston, one kind of detention fuses with another as the poet makes note of the reservations built to contain Native American Indians. In Mirikitani's more often quoted "We the Dangerous," the allusions to the Internment coexist alongside allusions to other moments of conquest, subjugation, and annihilation:

We the dangerous
Dwelling in the ocean.
Akin to the jungle.
Close to the earth.

Hiroshima.
Vietnam.
Tule Lake.

And yet we are not devoured.
And yet we are not humbled.
And yet we are not broken.

If Mirikitani's poem asserts a kind of cultural strength—a refusal to be "broken"—many of the other works produced in response to the Internment articulate a refusal to be silenced. In fiction and nonfiction, essays and historical accounts, writers such as David Mura, Garrett Hongo, and Ronald Takaki are asserting the importance of "overcoming the silence" that has marked the community's response to the Internment. Garrett Hongo's essay "Kubota," for example, examines the reciprocal nature of the debts each generation owes the other: to tell the stories. In his chapters treating the Internment in *Strangers from a Different Shore*, Ronald Takaki shows the importance of telling the history from the perspective of an insider.

This approach allows issues to emerge that are important to a particular group. Thus, rather than having a conventional list of "universal themes" imposed from the outside, the class discussion is grounded in themes that have emerged from the historical and cultural experience of the groups. From this perspective, the class can then examine issues such as property, entitlement, loyalty, and responsibilities in a more informed manner. It also provides a new context for more fully examining the issues of competition, resentment, and stereotyping based on race, which seem to have reemerged in some sectors of business and academia. Historical and cultural context helps to inform and ground these discussions.

Just as the Internment has had an effect on the Japanese-American community that has continued long after the closing of the camps, the border has become a significant, recurring image in the writings of Chicanos. While some of our students may feel secure in their assumptions that the border is established and needs only to be protected with greater resolve, much of the history and literature of Chicanos problematizes the issue of the border and, with it, issues related to ownership, entitlement, loyalty, and identity. Indeed, from the signing of the Treaty of Guadalupe Hidalgo in 1848, in which Mexico ceded much of its land to the United States, the issue of border crossing has been a pervasive theme in Chicano literature.

An exploration of Chicano literature from a contextual perspective might involve an examination of the border as a legal, historical, and metaphorical construct in Chicano narratives from the signing of the treaty to the present, or it might focus on the writings that helped to shape the "Chicano movement," from the mid 1960s, when the concerns of the farm workers movement helped to bring to the forefront again issues related to the legal and economic status of those who had crossed the border to find employment.

Gloria Anzaldúa's mixed-mode essay *Borderlands/La Frontera* calls the border "una hedira abierta where the Third World grates against the first and bleeds" (193). In presenting another history of immigration (which notes the illegal immigration to Mexican territory in the 1800s), another view of the Alamo ("the symbol that legitimized the white imperialist takeover"), Anzaldúa offers another way of contextualizing the border culture:

> We have a tradition of migration, a tradition of long walks. Today we are witnessing *la migración de los pueblos mexicanos*, the return odyssey to the historical/ mythological Aztlán. This time the traffic is from south to north.
>
> *El retorno* to the promised land first began with the Indians from the interior of Mexico and the *mestizos* that came with the *conquistadores* in the 1500s. Immigration continued in the next three centuries, and in this century, it continued with the *braceros* who helped to build our railroads and who picked our fruit. Today thousands of Mexicans are crossing the border legally and illegally; ten million people without documents have returned to the Southwest. (11, emphases hers)

In Anzaldúa's formulation, the crossing of borders in which the migrants are engaged is less a violation of law than a return to the homeland. The border is not absolute but shifting; like other metaphors, its mobility can serve a multitude of perceptual or rhetorical objectives.

As Anzaldúa suggests elsewhere, the border as a formulation is relevant, not only for the newer immigrant but for anyone who is, as Pat Mora suggests, "bilingual and bicultural." Much of the work of more recent Chicano writers has focused on the intersection of border issues with other issues of affiliation and entitlement. An early chapter of Arturo Islas's *Migrant Souls*, for example, employs irony when describing the family's crossing the border back to Mexico in order to obtain a turkey for their "American style" Thanksgiving celebration. The drive down to the border prompts a discussion of names and their implications:

> On the way to the bridge, Josie made the mistake of asking her father if they were aliens. Sancho put his foot on the brake so hard that Eduviges almost rear-ended the truck. He looked at Josie very hard and said, "I do not ever want to hear you use that word in my presence again. About anybody. We are American citizens of Mexican heritage. We are proud of both countries and have never and will never be that word you just said to me."

When the father is reminded that the newspapers and one of the European-American school children use that word, he responds:

> "The next time she tells you that, you tell her that Mexican and Indian people were in this part of the country long before any gringos, Europeans (he said Yurrop-beans) or anyone else decided it was theirs . . ." She watched him look straight ahead, then in the rearview mirror, then at Josie.
>
> "Don't you see, Josie? When people calls Mexicans those words it makes it easier for them to deport or kill them. Aliens come from outer space . . . Sort of like your mother's family, the blessed Angels, who think they come from heaven. Don't tell her I said that."

Before he made that last comment, Josie was impressed by her father's tone. Sancho seldom became that passionate in their presence about any issue. He laughed at the serious and the pompous, especially religious fanatics. Here the ironic mode—the distance between the narrative voice and that of the father—prevents the father's words from becoming a diatribe. The issues of identity, loyalty, and respect are brought up by a father to his children who wished they had not raised the subject in the first place; the use of "Yurropbeans" adds to both the realism and the irony of the scene, without fully negating what is being asserted. The narrative, which monitors the father's actions (looking forward toward the border and back toward his wife following in the car behind) reinforces the connections between geographical and legal borders and the social borders created by language. Other works extend their examinations of the borders to consider issues of language, class, and gender. Pat Mora's poem "Legal Alien," for example, ponders the ways in which the choice or use of language can be read as affiliation:

> Bi-lingual, Bi-cultural,
> able to slip from "How's life?"
> to "Me'stan volviendo loca,"
> able to sit in a paneled office
> drafting memos in smooth English,
> able to order in fluent Spanish
> at a Mexican restaurant,
> American but hyphenated,
> viewed by Anglos as perhaps exotic,
> perhaps inferior, definitely different,
> viewed by Mexicans as alien.

Like many other Chicana and Chicano poets from Miguel Mendez on, Mora breaks a boundary of convention by having the Spanish and the English coexist in the same poem. In this poem, however, the linguistic coexistence only underlines the dualism about which the poem speaks. While the surface of the poem repeatedly asserts "I am able," the Spanish sentence becomes an acknowledgement of the burden attached to the bicultural, hyphenated existence.

The examples mentioned above show alternatives to the more conventional, thematic approaches of the past. Critical authority is constituted by one's responsiveness not simply to a set of generalized issues, externally imposed onto the text, regardless of its culture. Instead, the thematic considerations are reformulated in response to the historical ones. In this way, the lived experience and earlier forms of cultural production provide a context for what follows. The works of a given author not only assert their difference in terms of their dominant culture; they can also "talk" to each other on the page.

Authority, Marginality, and the Mosaic

The richness of a work can be fairly appraised or fully appreciated only when one has made himself or herself familiar with the context itself in historical, political, or social terms. For those of us from the dominant culture, learning to teach multiethnic literature in a thoughtful way, one must become a student of multiethnic literature. One must exchange a position of relative security for one of risk; one must give up some of one's authority in order to become credible. Barbara Johnson describes this process in her essay on Zora Neale Hurston:

> One of the presuppositions with which I began was that Hurston was situated "outside" the mainstream literary canon and that I, by implication, was an institutional "insider." I soon came to see, however, not only that the insider becomes an outsider the minute she steps out of the inside, but also Hurston's work itself was constantly dramatizing and undercutting just such inside/outside oppositions, transforming the plane geometry of physical space into the complex transactions of discursive exchange. In other words, Hurston could be read not just as an example of the "noncanonical" writer, but as a commentator on the dynamics of any encounter between an inside and an outside, any attempt to make a statement about difference. (172–73)

It is important for those of us teaching the literature of the marginalized to experience in some sense the discomfort that accompanies marginality. Acknowledging this position of vulnerability is essential if one seeks to establish credibility and authority in the classroom. And as Freire and others have suggested, the authority that emerges should be of a new kind, less dependent on hierarchies, more reliant on shared expertise.

One cannot acknowledge one's marginality vis-à-vis a tradition in one moment and then return to the position of critical or generic gatekeeper the next. Many of us would be unwilling to label Cisneros' *Woman Hollering Creek* uneven, for example, lest we seem to be assigning primarily New Critical standards, to be privileging evenness, balance, organic unity as universal values. Yet many who would be reluctant to employ such criteria routinely insist on limiting their choice in introductory writing classes to those works—multiethnic or not—that illustrate and employ the conventions of the analytical essay, the deductive argument; for the perception remains that it is these texts, and not the "more literary ones," that will teach our students how to think critically and how to write. It is our view that to assert this position does justice to neither the works themselves nor the talents of our students. The introduction of multiethnic works into the composition classroom has been challenged by Werner Sollors and others as being incomplete without acknowledging its own incompleteness. In his 1986 essay, "A Critique of Pure Pluralism," for example, Sollors asserts:

> The dominant assumption among serious scholars who study ethnic literary history seems to be that history can best be written by separating the groups that produced such literature in the United States. The published results of this "mosaic" procedure are the readers and compendiums made up of diverse essays on groups of writers who may have little in common except so-called ethnic roots while, at the same time, obvious and important literary and cultural connections are obfuscated. (255)

While deprecating "so-called ethnic roots," Sollors is describing a construct that privileges intracultural factors while devaluing cross-cultural ones. One must acknowledge that any process of categorization is incomplete and to some degree subjective. It remains to be asked, however, whether what Sollors is describing is less a mosaic than an interpretive tunnel. For at the heart of the mosaic is an evershifting relationship between part and whole: the parts comprise the whole, but the meaning of each part is informed by its relationship to the whole. One's perception of the mosaic depends upon one's perspective—the position of the reader, audience, interpreter. Meaning is thus not so much discovered as socially constructed. The responsibility for interpretation is not appropriated by an authority figure, but is retained by the students themselves. As interpreters of cultural artifacts, students of the mosaic are not kept at a distance, but are invited in. In contrast to the silent reverential approach of the chiarascuro, the mosaic approach allows students to establish their own boundaries and assert their own interpretive voices.

WORKS CITED

Anzaldúa, Gloria. *Borderlands/La Frontera: The New Mextiza*. San Francisco: Spinsters—Aunt Lute, 1987.

———. "The Homeland, Aztlán/ El Otro Mexico." *Aztlán: Essays on the Chicano Homeland*. Eds. Rudolfo Anaya and Francisco Lomelí. Albuquerque: U of New Mexico P, 1989. 191–204.

Bercovitch, Sacvan, ed. *Reconstructing American Literary History*. Cambridge: Harvard UP, 1981.

Bloom, Allan. *The Closing of the American Mind*. NY: Simon and Schuster, 1987.

Calderon, Hector, and José David Saldívar, eds. *Criticism in the Borderlands: Studies in Chicano Literature, Culture, and Ideology*. Durham: Duke UP, 1990.

Chin, Frank. "Come All Ye Asian American Writers of the Real and the Fake." *The Big AIIIEEEEE! An Anthology of Chinese American and Japanese American Literature*. Eds. Frank Chin et al. NY: Meridian, 1991. 1–93.

Crawford, John F. "Notes toward a Multicultural Criticism: Three Works by Women of Color." *Gift of Tongues: Challenges in Contemporary American Poetry*. Eds. Marle Harris and Kathleen Aguero. Athens: U of Georgia P. 155–95.

Dickstein, Morris. "Popular Fiction and Critical Values: The Novel as a Challenge to Literary History." *Reconstructing American Literary History*. Ed. Sacvan Bercovitch. Cambridge: Harvard UP, 1981. 29–66.

Fox-Genovese, Elizabeth. "The Claims of Common Culture: Race, Class, and the Canon." *Salmagundi* 72 (1986): 131–43.

Gates, Henry Louis, Jr. *Black Literature and Literary Theory*. NY: Methuen, 1984.

———. "Pluralism and its Discontents." *Profession* 92 (1992): 35–38.

———. *Loose Canons*. NY: Oxford UP, 1992.

Graff, Gerald. *Professing Literature: An Institutional History*. Chicago: U of Chicago P, 1987.

Guillory, John. "Canonical and Non-canonical: A Critique of the Current Debate." *ELH* 54 (1987): 483–527.

Hirsch, E. D., Jr. *Cultural Literacy*. Boston: Houghton Mifflin, 1987.

Inada, Lawson Fusao. *Before the War: Poems as They Happened*. NY: Morrow, 1971.

———. "Of Place and Displacement : The Range of Japanese American Literature." *Three American Literatures: Essays on Chicano, Native American, and Asian Literature for Teachers of American Literature*. Ed. Houston Baker, Jr. NY: MLA, 1982. 54–65.

Islas, Arturo. *Migrant Souls*. NY: Morrow, 1990.

Jameson, Fredric. *The Political Unconscious*. Ithaca: Cornell UP, 1981.

Johnson, Barbara. *A World of Difference*. Baltimore: Johns Hopkins UP, 1989.

Kafka, Phillipa. "Multicultural Introduction to Literature." *Practicing Theory in Introductory College Literature Courses*. Eds. James M. Cahalan and David B. Downing. Urbana: NCTE, 1991. 179–88.

Kim, Elaine. *Asian American Literature*. Philadelphia: Temple UP, 1980.

Krupat, Arnold. *The Voice in the Margin: Native American Literature and the Canon*. Berkeley: U of California P, 1989.

Lauter, Paul. *Canons and Contexts*. NY: Oxford UP, 1990.

Lim, Shirley Geok-lin. "Twelve Asian American Writers in Search of Self-Definition." *Redefining American Literary History*. Eds. A. LaVonne Brown Ruoff and Jerry W. Ward, Jr. NY: MLA, 1990. 237–50.

Mirikitani, Janice. *Awake in the River*. San Francisco: Isthmus, 1978.

Mora, Pat. *Chants*. Houston: Arte Publico, 1984.

Ong, Walter J. "Introduction: On Saying We and Us to Literature." *Three American Literatures: Essays on Chicano, Native American, and Asian Literature for Teachers of American Literature*. Ed. Houston Baker, Jr. NY: MLA, 1982. 3–7.

Paredes, Raymund. "The Evolution of Chicano Literature." *Three American Literatures: Essays on Chicano, Native American, and Asian Literature for Teachers of American Literature*. Ed. Houston Baker, Jr. NY: MLA, 1982. 33–79.

Perkins, David. *Theoretical Issues in Literary History*. Cambridge: Harvard UP, 1990.

Said, Edward. *The World, the Text, and the Critic*. Cambridge: Harvard UP, 1983.

Sollors, Werner. "A Critique of Pure Pluralism." *Reconstructing American Literary History*. Ed. Sacuan Bereovitch. Cambridge: Harvard UP, 1986. 250–279.

SECTION TWO

The Canon as Text:
Rethinking the Survey

If It's Monday This Must Be Melville
A *"Canon, Anticanon" Approach*
to Redefining the American Literature Survey

Martha J. Cutter

I. Overview: Theoretical and Practical Principles; Or, Canon Fodder from the Cultural Wars

Recent debates about the canon have often taken diametrically opposed viewpoints, arguing either for "great works" or for pluralism and diversity. Writers like Allan Bloom and William Bennett call for a return to the "classics"—a return which would shore up an increasingly illiterate and apathetic strata of American students. On the other hand, writers such as Richard Ohmann, Paul Lauter, and Barbara Herrnstein Smith argue that canons are relative, based on contingencies of value and on how well they perform "desired/desirable" functions; this group of critics implicitly or explicitly calls for a pluralistic vision of the canon, one which looks beyond formalist standards to the ideological, social, and cultural functions a text serves.[1] Yet it seems that in this morass of conflicting claims about what the canon was, is, could be, will be, or might be, we have lost our way. We have no working definition of what the canon actually represents, no way of theorizing the relationship between "marginal" and "classic" texts, no conceptual model which could integrate these conflicting visions of the canon. In terms of pedagogy, we have no guideposts, and little criticism which links a theory of the canon with specific teaching practices.

Thus the unwieldy postmodern survey course develops. Caught in the cultural wars or their own notions about what constitutes literary importance, instructors of survey courses feel compelled to "cover" some of the "great" writers. At the same time, most instructors feel they have a duty to integrate the works of women and "minorities" into their courses—a strategy which is both practically and politically correct, for students want to read these works and in fact often enjoy them more than the standard fare which has been dished out in high school. So like our anthologies, which have grown at an astounding rate, our courses have become stuffed—overstuffed, in fact. Teaching a survey course in a postsurvey world is a very difficult task; as texts produced by more and more races and ethnicities become included in discussions of American Literature, the survey becomes an unwieldy "twenty-eight authors in fourteen weeks," "If It's Monday This Must Be Melville" vehicle. Students cannot absorb the plethora of authors, and often feel they are getting only a superficial overview of the literature of the time period (which they are, by the nature of the course). Yet since it seems that both administrators and students will continue to value survey courses, we must find ways of teaching them—ways which respond to the cultural wars we find ourselves caught in, without allowing ourselves to become "canon" fodder. This essay provides a new theoretical model of the canon, as well as an explanation of the pedagogical apparatus which I have used to implement this model.

Critics such as Herrnstein Smith and Frank Kermode have been decoding the canon as text for many years, and I, too, believe that the canon can be read as a text. But I propose that we view the canon as a specific kind of text—a palimpsest, a text which has been written over and upon throughout the course of history, with fragments of earlier, imperfectly erased writing still visible. "Dominant" and "marginal" texts (or "classic" and "minority" works) can thus be envisioned as existing in a dialectical relationship—a relationship in which texts are read through and with each other. In discussing H. D., Shari Benstock argues that her use of the palimpsest does present a dialectical relationship between "text" and "subtext":

> The palimpsest simultaneously documents and destroys its own history, preserving earlier forms in the remnants of imperfectly erased portions of its continuous text while "writing over"—rewriting—the earlier record. . . . Indeed, a palimpsest possesses no single, identifiable source but rather raises various—often conflicting—images that present themselves as origins of the meanings the text provides. These earlier forms are read "through" the contemporary text, coexistent with it in the present moment, but are also (perhaps) discernible as relics, images of an earlier writing. The figure of the palimpsest, of course, constitutes culture as we know it and is present in all writing, since writing repeats and erases, confirms and reverses, its own historical situation. (350–1)

Viewing the canon as a palimpsest which "repeats and erases, confirms and reverses, its own historical situation" allows us to get away from the paradigm of teaching *either* "classic" or "marginal" texts, toward an understanding that "classic" texts and "marginal" works are dependent on each other for meaning. "Marginal" texts can be read through more enfranchised perspectives, and vice versa.[2]

The purpose of the survey course thus becomes not "covering" a specific body of texts (whether classic or not), but *uncovering* dialectical relationships between texts and subtexts. Dominant discourses are dependent on, and in fact cannot be separated from, less enfranchised perspectives. About H. D.'s use of the palimpsest, Benstock also argues that "masculine and feminine myths, male and female 'texts,' are not separate from each other, but entwined and encoded *in* each other by the very fact that they are culturally produced. . . . The second text cannot be 'lifted' from the parent text complete and whole to refute the premises of the primary text" (350). I would argue that this is also the case for marginal and dominant texts, or for what I have come to call in my course "canon" and "anticanon."

The organizing principle of my survey of post-1865 American literature (taught as an upper-level course at Brown University, Swarthmore College, and the University of

Connecticut) is that readings of canonical texts can be informed by, and indeed are dependent on, noncanonical texts; and that noncanonical texts are also dependent on canonical works because they critique the dominant ideologies that enfranchised voices (often) inscribe. Which brings me to a second important aspect of my course: rather than focusing on "literature," I focus on ideology, on seeing texts as repositories of ideas rather than as closed icons.[3] This does not exclude formal analysis of texts, but it shifts the focus to culture, which, as Benstock says, "repeats and erases, confirms and reverses, its own historical situation." The rationale for studying "marginal" texts, then, is not only that it is practically or even politically correct to do so, but that it is culturally and historically correct to do so. If we are interested in understanding how the canon constitutes a play of voices, of text and subtext, then we must utilize an approach which allows this play of voices to be heard.[4]

We can hear the play of dominant and marginal voices more clearly when a "canon, anticanon" approach is used. Because I feel that it is impossible to understand the concerns of "marginal" writers without some exposure to canonical texts, I begin most units with an author whose text supports the dominant ideology of the time period. I then contrast these canonical writers with what I have called, for lack of a better term, the "anticanon": works which in various ways (formally, aesthetically, ideologically) critique hegemonic discourses of the time period and work to create alternative paradigms. "Traditional" literary perspectives can thus play off of and against less centered voices; texts can be read through and against each other as if culture is a palimpsest on which they are inscribed. For students, this is an eye-opening process; having read Black Elk, Zitkala-Sä, and other Native American writers who depict the process of colonization, students never again read Frost's poem "The Gift Outright" (which begins "The land was ours before we were the land's") as a gentle paean to the spirit of America. As Lauter states, a "transformation of perceptions . . . occurs when a traditional literary category is shattered by adding a range of different works to prior accounts of it" (*Canons and Contexts* 110). The process can indeed shatter students' assumptions about literature; in a discussion of

Puddn'head Wilson's treatment of slavery, for example, a first-year student was startled enough to exclaim, "But Twain can't be a racist—he's one of our greatest writers!" Throughout the course, though, my object is not to present traditional writers as racist or sexist, but to see how canonical literary texts usually (but not always) enforce a view of the United States which less enfranchised voices usually (but not always) critique. My object is to uncover the hidden ideologies of the canon and bring less enfranchised perspectives into a more meaningful dialogue with "classic" texts.

However, the "canon, anticanon" approach is not meant to be merely a back-and-forth movement between canonical and noncanonical texts. The course design is also meant to be a rethinking of standard survey courses. Although we might wish to continue opening up the canon, in practice we are limited by the number of weeks in a semester, or by the number of texts a class can afford; as Reed Dasenbrock argues, "our additive rhetoric of 'opening up the canon' meets hard, subtractive logic. We can't teach the new literature in addition to the old canon: something has to give, substitutions have to be made" (65). How do we make these substitutions? I would suggest that substitutions are easier to make if some attention is paid to course design which, as Dasenbrock suggests, must also be rethought. Instead of organizing my course in terms of a linear, chronological progression, I organize it in terms of five units (Slavery and Freedom, The Woman Question, The Frontier, Race, and War); within each unit we see how both centered and "marginal" writers depict their concerns. Each unit is roughly chronological, but the course as a whole is not.

Organizing the course in this way avoids the superficiality of survey courses which attempt to cover all aspects of the texts; I can ask students to focus on the elements of the text which relate to the ideological issues we are discussing, rather than trying to "cover" everything. Furthermore, I can select texts which treat the issues at hand, rather than attempting to choose from an entirely "open" canon. Focusing on specific historical issues also allows me to maintain a strong interdisciplinary focus. As Lauter argues, "any arrangement which systematically separates the texts from the historical contexts in which they are embedded arrests our capacity to read them" (*Canons and Contexts* 120–1). An interdisciplinary focus allows the palimpsest that is the canon—the play of submerged and dominant voices in and with culture—to become clearer.

Using a "canon, anticanon" approach also allows me to emphasize the constructed nature of the canon itself. I do not present the canonical texts as repositories of value or meaning which have endured throughout time, but rather as something which someone has chosen to call canonical, at a particular historical moment. Similarly, the "anticanon" is not meant to be a pejorative term for texts which somehow did not "make it" to the big time, the holy canon status. Rather, the "anticanon" represents texts which for various reasons were not considered "classic." I also do not insist on rigid distinctions between these two groups of texts, although I generally describe texts which support dominant ideologies as the "canon," and texts which undermine these ideologies as the "anticanon."[5] However, a work such as Booker T. Washington's *Up From Slavery* can be an exemplary text for showing students that the canon changes over time. Hailed as the leader of the African American race during his own time, Washington is faulted today for promoting racist ideologies and his autobiography is rarely taught as literature. Ironically enough, then, one of the most contemporaneously canonical writers we study in my course is now, in our own time, the least "canonical" author. Students learn from this discussion that, as Elizabeth Fox-Genovese explains, "The canon, in fact, has never been the true canon, never been the immutable body of sacred texts, that both its defenders and its detractors like to claim. Subject to 'vision and revision,' it has been modified by successive generations" (132).

Yet in a recent class discussion of *Up From Slavery*, I found that even current readings of Washington's text as an endorsement of hegemony could be deconstructed. While examining Washington's comment that "no white American ever thinks that any other race is wholly civilized until he wears the white man's clothes, eats the white man's food, speaks the white man's language, and professes the white man's religion" (67), my class began to realize that his positioning was not that far from our "anticanon" writer, W. E. B. Du Bois. Like slave songs which to white masters meant "happy darky" but to other slaves meant "I'm planning to escape," Washington's text may have a coded ironic subtext which can be read through, and with, the straightforward, dominant text. If Washington's statement is read as an ironic aside meant for a black audience (rather than his conscious emulation of white standards), then a certain double-voicedness creeps into the text. This double-voicedness is similar to what Du Bois describes:

> The Negro is a sort of seventh son, born with a veil, and gifted with second-sight in this American world,—a world which yields him no true self-consciousness, but only lets him see himself through the revelation of the other world. It is a peculiar sensation, this double-consciousness, this sense of always looking at one's self through the eyes of others, of measuring one's soul by the tape of a world that looks on in amused contempt and pity. (45)

I do not mean to conflate the concerns of two very dissimilar writers, but only to suggest that both may be aware of, and seeking to come to terms with, their conflicted and conflictual roles: representing African Americans to white audiences, they must also be self-representational—true to their own concerns and the concerns of their race. Both emphasize a double-voicedness, a speaking between the lines, if you will, which simultaneously articulates *and* critiques dominant ideologies.

The distinction between "canon" and "anticanon" broke down in this instance, as it does so often in this course, as it should. Heeding Gerald Graff's idea that we should teach the conflicts and even build them into our curriculum, I make the canon itself a text, something which can be read and interpreted, both in terms of past and present constructions of authors. The point is not to put literary texts into neat, labelled boxes, but rather to set up meaningful resonances between texts. Ultimately, as I tell students in the course description, the class "is not meant to be a traditional course in American literature from 1865 to 1945 but rather an experimental project in reading both canonical and noncanonical fiction from this time period." To the extent that I can set up meaningful resonances between texts—such as the resonance between Du Bois and Washington—I feel that my experiment has succeeded.

II. From the Texts in the Class to the Class as Text: Theoretical Underpinnings of the "Canon, Anticanon" Course

Beyond choosing texts that question dominant ideologies, I also try to create an educational environment which is radical and questioning. I want my theoretical and pedagogical practices to match the questioning and counter-hegemonic qualities of the texts we read. In other words, I want my classroom to become a text and, hopefully, an "anticanonical" one. Susan Horton has argued that we must recognize that "the *classroom* is also a text, produced by teacher and student in collaboration" (53–54). It is important to consider *what kind of text* we want our classrooms to represent, so that we do not assume an attitude which reinforces canonical authority by using the structures of the past: the "teacher as one who is distanced, objective, holding no relation to students but that of disseminator, determiner of what shall and shall not be poured into them" (54). I will say more about the specifics of my course in the next section, and appendix I contains the course syllabus. Here I wish to explain the theoretical underpinnings of my teaching philosophy and analyze what purpose the study of literature serves; in other words, I wish to "read" my classroom as a text.

In general, I discourage an authoritative view of the canon, the classroom, and my own role in the classroom. I must admit that I am uncomfortable claiming I have "mastered" any text, and I am uncomfortable spouting knowledge to my students as if I am the fount of all information, the source of all meaning. I would agree with Robert Scholes' view that "the ultimate hell at the end of all our good New Critical intentions is textualized in the image of a brilliant instructor explicating a poem before a class of stupefied students. And when I see this very icon being restored to the same position within the same ivied halls, by certain disciples of Derrida—I could weep with frustration" (*Textual Power* 24). Is this what education is all about?

At the base of all our discussions of the canon and of ways of teaching the survey course must be some discussion of why we teach, what the purposes of education are, and in the end, what kind of readers we want our students to be. For if we do not consider such issues, our own teaching practices will replicate the very structures of authority and domination which the canon presents, the very structures we seek to escape; as Barbara Ewell explains, "the current model of university instruction, not unlike the canon, echoes and enforces our cultural attachment to objectivity and a single Truth" (51). I am not inveighing against lecturing per se, or against courses which emphasize the transmission of a certain body of knowledge. However, there are ways of teaching these courses which emphasize both the knowledge and the thinking about this knowledge, both an understanding of "the important facts" and a questioning of why they are important, whether indeed they are facts at all, why these particular facts have been selected, and so on.

I do not want my students to be passive sponges, soaking up the knowledge I transmit, soaking up the "great ideas" texts themselves present. Instead I want my students to be active, resistant readers—readers who can and will engage voraciously with a text, both on its own terms and on theirs; readers who will question my views and defend their own opinions. Certainly, a tall order. But if, as Lauter and others have argued, education is an arena for struggle where what is decided "significantly affects the political economy and important social arrangements" (*Canons and Contexts* viii), then we must begin the struggle in the here and now, by thinking about how we can make our teaching practices reflect our own personal and pedagogical philosophies. We must also struggle to make our teaching practices reflect our philosophies of the canon. If we want to create resistant readers, we can use the idea of the canon to help us. Reading, as Scholes argues, is not only a textual activity; it is a skill which helps students make sense of their environments and resist the continuing assaults of the manipulative structures of their worlds. So if we teach our students to be resistant readers of the canon itself, they may become resistant readers in other contexts.

How does the "canon, anticanon" course foster resistant responses on the part of students? The design of the course encourages resistance to dominant ideologies by presenting both hegemonic and counter-hegemonic texts. In other words, we start with the assumption that dominant discourses can be subjected to examination and critique. Noncanonical texts should be taught precisely because they question ideology, power, and authority; as Christine Froula argues, "the entry of marginal text into the modern literary curriculum not only 'opens up' the canon but opens to question the idea of the canon" (154). More specifically, noncanonical texts often encode radical critiques of both the themes and philosophical *approaches* of canonical documents. Noncanonical texts can thus help liberate us from the grip of canonical authority, as Froula explains:

> Few of us can free ourselves completely from the power ideologies inscribed in the idea of the canon and in many of its texts merely by not reading "canonical" texts, because we have been reading the patriarchal "archetext" all our lives. But we can, through strategies of rereading that expose the deeper structures of authority and through interplay with texts of a different stamp, pursue a kind of collective psychoanalysis, transforming "bogeys" that hide invisible power into investments both visible and alterable. (171)

It is the job of a survey course to engage in precisely just such a "collective psychoanalysis" as Froula advocates. In such a scenario we use "Great Books" as a powerful instrument for change, for when we read them against less enfranchised texts their invisible but often oppressive ideologies become visible. And, to use Bruce Henricksen's phrase, we can also teach them "against the grain" in order to engender more liberating ideologies of power, knowledge, and authority.

The "canon, anticanon" approach fosters such resistant and subversive reading practices. My unit on "The Woman Question," for example, begins with Henry James' *The Bostonians*. Like the canonical gospels or Milton's treatment of Eve (cited by Froula), *The Bostonians* presents a repressive vision of women's search for liberation, and indeed, of feminine nature itself. Yet beyond the text's attitude towards the theme of women, I also ask students to pay attention to its approach towards self-liberation and the achievement of personal authority, both for men and women. My students often conclude that the text holds out little hope of personal liberation. This is particularly true for female characters in *The Bostonians*, but even male characters such as Basil Ransom seem caught in the meshes of James's plot. James's text does not foster an attitude of questioning authority; in fact, it enforces authority—particularly the authority of the text and the author. Moreover, his characters cannot engage in any meaningful questioning of the system they find themselves caught in, of the ideological/cultural nexus of which they are a part.

The second part of this unit involves reading women writers who treat their female characters in a very different way, but who also present a very different approach to the politics of authority and textuality, as well as to the possibility of overcoming a specific cultural entrapment. I am speaking of writers such as Sarah Orne Jewett, Kate Chopin, Mary Wilkins Freeman, and Charlotte Perkins Gilman, all of whom are roughly contemporaneous with James, and all of whom treat "the woman question." Of course, we spend time discussing differences in the imaging of women, and I provide my students with historical information about the medical and cultural views of women during this time period. However, I also encourage my students to think about how these women writers may present a different approach to authority and self-determination, an approach which, like the Gnostic gospels, encourages personal revelation and opposition to the concept of transcendent authority.

Voice becomes an important site of this investigation, for we move from James' specularized women to women like Lucille Wright in Gilman's story "Spoken To," women who turn male specularization upside down through an assertion of female voice. But more than just a reversal of patriarchal paradigms, these women writers emphasize a qualitative difference in the politics of voice and authority. In Freeman's story "A Village Singer," for example, Candace Whitcomb undergoes a radical change of heart and begins questioning the (male) authority figures around her, lambasting, in particular, the minister:

> Candace had had an inborn reverence for clergymen. She had always treated Mr. Pollard with the utmost deference. Indeed, her manner toward all men had been marked by a certain delicate stiffness and dignity. Now she was talking

> to the old minister with the homely freedom with which
> she might have addressed a female gossip over the back
> fence. He could not say much in return. (368)

Candace asserts her own spiritual authority, her own right to
voice and self-determination. Unfortunately, Candace's
liberation is achieved at great personal cost: she becomes ill
shortly after this declaration and dies. Yet her attempt at self-
liberation teaches a lesson which remains. Freeman's text
radically critiques patriarchal treatment of women, but it also
questions the power structure of the world her characters
inhabit, suggesting that this structure is not absolute. In short,
Freeman and other women writers present a paradigm in which
liberation is foregrounded, authority is questioned, and escape
from a specific ideological or cultural entrapment is at least
posited, if not entirely achieved.

R. Radhakrishnan suggests that canonicity is itself a
problem because the canon "establishes and valorizes a
transcendent and universal 'identity' of texts, culture, and
civilization: an identity that persists inviolably despite historical
breaks and ruptures" (121). Thus "the post-pedagogical teacher
should be interested not just in the repudiation of any one canon,
but in the general overthrow of the canonical episteme" (132). I
use the works of writers like Freeman and Gilman to
"overthrow" specific texts but, more importantly, specific
notions about textual and cultural authority. But why teach
Henry James at all, then, or any canonical writer, if our agenda
includes overthrowing the canonical episteme? First, as I
mentioned earlier, I believe students cannot understand the
concerns of "marginal" writers like Freeman and Gilman
without some exposure to more mainstream writers and
ideologies. The anger and madness of many nineteenth-century
female characters becomes more understandable when read
against and with the authorial and cultural structures which
produced that anger and madness. Or as Graff puts it, "neither
difference nor identity can become functional for students and
other outsiders unless the two are experienced *as* difference or
identity" (106). These days I do not think we can assume that
students have read "canonical" texts in high school. Our job
becomes, then, exposing students to *both* hegemonic and

counter-hegemonic texts, and showing how these texts exist in a dialectical, dependent relationship with each other—a relationship which includes *both* affirmation and critique of dominant discourses and paradigms.

Throwing out the canon entirely, then, does not overthrow the canonical episteme; it merely ignores it.[6] What is important is not ceasing to teach a canonical text like *The Bostonians*, but rather reinterpreting it in ways which liberate readers from its confining ideologies. This is a two-step process in which we first must see these ideologies (as presented in the "canon" segment) and then understand that there are alternatives to these ideologies (the "anticanon" segment). To engage in only one of these steps only partially overthrows the oppression of the canon.

III. The Pedagogical Is Political: A Practical Pedagogy of Difference

The theoretical underpinnings of the course are therefore meant to encourage debate and the questioning of authoritative structures. Yet I have also attempted to find a pedagogy which is counter-hegemonic, a pedagogy which encourages debate and dialogue between students and texts, students and other students, and students and instructor. In *Ideology Culture & The Process of Schooling*, Henry Giroux argues that schools are more than mere reflections of hegemonic society; in fact, schools are characterized "by an ongoing struggle between hegemonic and counter-hegemonic forces" (15). My own teaching practices reflect this ongoing struggle, for beyond the content of my course (which portrays the struggle between hegemonic and counter-hegemonic texts), my classroom pedagogy attempts to create the possibility of counter-hegemonic discourses. For as Giroux explains, we must link our theoretical goals with our pedagogical ones: "the content of classroom instruction must be paralleled by a pedagogical style which is consistent with a radical political vision"; power in the classroom "must be both democratized and humanized"(*Ideology* 83). In my own teaching practices, I have made some attempts to "democratize and humanize" the power of the classroom, but I recognize these attempts as starting points, as tentative steps towards a more open pedagogical style. However, since there has been little explicit discussion of counter-hegemonic pedagogical practices, I will be as specific as possible in describing these steps.[7] Both in terms of the course's structure and its assignments, I attempt to create dialogue, flexibility, communal effort, and authorization of student voices.

The structure of the course varies from day to day, but does not generally include lecturing. When necessary, I provide summary sheets containing important historical background, but I also encourage students to bring in information they may have learned from other courses, such as knowledge of Native American ritual, African American trickster myths, or nineteenth-century perspectives on the frontier or on women's rights. As much as possible, I try to shift the focus of attention from my ideas to the ideas of the students. For example, I have students give oral reports, receive class feedback, and then turn these oral reports into papers. Oral reports are staggered throughout the semester (rather than just during the second or last half of the course) in order to increase the input from students throughout the course. The grading of these oral reports/papers has a collaborative component, since students are evaluated both on the content of their paper and on whether they have benefitted from other students' comments. I also frequently have students work in groups discusing topics which I or a group member has devised. Each week I use a variety of techniques to shift the focus of discussion onto students and to make a certain percentage of the class "experts" on particular topics or texts.

These structural strategies have worked to varying degrees. The first class to which I taught the course was small—twelve students, all of whom were highly motivated and independent readers of texts. They ranged in years, but all seemed committed to the "canon, anticanon" project, and had in fact selected the course for the "radical" stance it took to the notion of the canon. These students took on responsibility for discussion and shared knowledge with each other in a very democratic and responsible fashion. The second and third time I taught the course, however, I had twenty-three and twenty-five students, ranging from first-year students for whom this was a first literature course, to seniors with very specialized interests in various topics in American literature. These larger groups of students were motivated, but sometimes had difficulty sustaining independent discussions. They responded well to more formal classroom strategies such as oral reports and group work.

Interestingly enough, the second group of students to whom I taught this course had selected the class precisely because it was a survey course at a college (Swarthmore) where surveys are not generally taught. In the space of two years, then, my course went from being viewed as "radical" to quite conventional. Of course, this has something to do with the different institutions at which I taught, but there is also a larger lesson to be learned. When I first taught the course (in 1990), it was radical to include in a survey of American literature authors such as Du Bois, Silko, and Morrison, while excluding authors such as Fitzgerald, Williams, or Pound. By 1992, the canon has "opened up" and almost no one blinks an eye if we substitute Freeman and Jewett for James. Our most radical substitutions eventually become our canon. Or as one student at the University of Connecticut put it, "everyone keeps telling me that Charlotte Perkins Gilman is a noncanonical writer, but so far this is the third course in which I've read 'The Yellow Wallpaper'!" Gilman's text seems to have become part of the canon. I am not sure how we can escape this institutionalization of what we teach as the "canon," except to keep shifting what we teach and emphasizing that our choices are based on thematic usefulness and our own peculiar interests and idiosyncrasies, rather than on some inherent, transcendent, value-neutral standard.

In general, then, the class was structured to allow for as much autonomous discussion on the part of students as possible. With a larger and more heterogeneous group, of course, this was more difficult. The class's writing assignments, however, worked extremely well with both large and small groups of students. Many of the issues raised in the course are very difficult conceptually, so I rely on students coming to terms with issues in written work which is shared with the class. Following a model used in a graduate course taught by Scholes, my students write short (one-page, single- or double-spaced) "problem papers"— generally, but not always, in response to a question I have raised. Every week, one third of the class writes these papers, some of which I xerox and share with the class as a whole. (Paper writers must hand in their papers one day prior to the class's meeting; since the papers are short they can easily be read and discussed the next day in class, although I sometimes ask students to read them for the *following* class period). These problem papers allow students to work through difficult ideas, teach each other, and most importantly, feel "connected" with particular texts. This helps avoid the superficial understanding of texts which many survey courses promote, but it also disperses the authority of the classroom, focusing it on the paper writers rather than on the professor. In course evaluations students almost unanimously report that they learned a great deal from writing these papers, found class discussions stimulating when they centered on papers, and felt that seeing other people's responses to texts was very useful. This is also a valuable strategy for allowing quieter students to be heard—those who have much to say but are intimidated by older or simply louder students.

In these papers, I also encourage students to undertake creative responses to the works; for example, I have asked students to retell a scene in a novel from a slightly different point of view, or to imagine conversations between various characters within texts or from different texts (appendix II contains some sample assignments). These creative assignments often produced excellent results, as when one student rewrote a scene in *The Bostonians* from the point of view of the clock in Olive Chancellor's drawing room. The clock was slightly partial to its owner, which allowed the class to discuss point of view in the novel as a whole; they reached a consensus that the novel's "objective" first-person narration is a façade. On another occasion, a student imagined a dialogue between James' Daisy Miller and Sarah Penn (of Freeman's "The Revolt of 'Mother'"). This allowed the class as a whole to understand the different options for women created by James and Freeman, as well as these authors' underlying ideas about female empowerment.

Finally, a student recently wrote a perceptive and very funny "ghost chapter" in Chopin's "Elizabeth Stock's One Story"; the student used the ghost chapter to make connections between the treatment of women by medical authorities in Chopin's text, Gilman's "The Yellow Wallpaper," and Freeman's "A Village Singer." In these assignments, I ask my students to "talk back" to the texts we are discussing. This encourages students to see the text as a construct, a marshalling of linguistic and discursive structures, rather than a sacred icon, an absolute authority.

Finally, I ask my students to reach their own conclusions about the course as a whole by reading Toni Morrison's *Beloved* during reading period and connecting it with other texts we have read during the semester. Although some students invariably comment that they wish we had discussed the text during the semester, I like to have a final exam in which students must grapple with a difficult text on their own. I also give them a series of questions to respond to, questions which ask them to make connections between divergent periods and texts. This open-book final exam again encourages students to come to terms with texts and ideas on their own. I do not provide the course's closure, but encourage them to reread texts in order to broaden their understandings of the course as a whole.

In retrospect, I wish I had made my pedagogy more radical; I wish I could be less constrained by traditional academic structures. On the whole, though, each time I have taught this course class dynamics were relaxed and cooperative. Dissension is produced, but students seem willing to argue cooperatively with each other, with me, and perhaps most importantly, with texts. A limited success. Yet I want to stress that I do not abandon authority entirely in the classroom, but rather attempt to use my authority to foster a critical search for meaning, as Giroux suggests:

> The democratization and humanization of power in the classroom should not suggest that radical educators retreat from positions of authority. What is suggested is that we should abandon authority roles that deny the subjectivity and power students have to create and generate their own meanings and visions. . . . For instance, students must learn the distinction between authority

which dictates meaning and authority which fosters a
critical search for meaning. (*Ideology* 84)

In the class as a whole, I tried to find pedagogical methods
which allowed my students to feel that they were empowered to
engage in "a critical search for meaning."

IV. Results and Conclusions

Thus, in terms of the texts I choose and the theoretical and
pedagogical apparatus I employ, I attempt to create a course
which encourages the radical questioning of authority. Does the
method succeed? In terms of the texts I choose, when I originally
designed this course I had two main goals. First, I hoped to
create a meaningful dialogue between canonical and
noncanonical texts, a dialogue which would avoid what Barbara
Ewell has called the "add and stir" mode of canon expansion
(51). Second, I wanted to design a survey course which would
create this dialogue without promoting the superficial
understandings and treatments of texts so common in most
survey courses. Although the course did set up an interesting
dialectic between the "canon" and "anticanon"—a dialectic
which undermined canonicity itself—I felt that, particularly with
the larger classes, the level of discussion and reading of texts was
somewhat superficial. In short, I did not entirely avoid the "If It's
Monday This Must Be Melville" syndrome. I needed to keep in
mind that, as Scholes says, "what a course accomplishes is not to
be found in what it has supposedly 'covered,' but in what its
students have done and can do as a result of having taken that
course" ("Toward a Curriculum" 100). Were I to teach the course
again to a large, mixed-level group of students, I would cut
down the number of texts. I would also spend more time with
historical materials; the course is meant to have a strong
interdisciplinary component, but I am limited by my own
knowledge. The third time I taught this course, I had students do
collaborative oral reports in which they collected information
about historical contexts and applied this information to the text
at hand. While some students had trouble applying their

research to the text and spent too much time on biographical materials, other students were able to create interesting intersections between the history and the literature, thereby enhancing the course's interdisciplinary components.

The course design can be adapted to any institution or time period; appendix III, for example, contains a version of the first half of an American literature survey course which uses a similar organization. However, the course design does have some theoretical limitations. As mentioned above, whatever we teach seems to become the canon, co-opting the radical challenge created by a group of noncanonical writers. It is therefore important to keep changing the texts we teach and expanding the boundaries of what "literature" is to include formats such as diaries, journals, and private poetry. It is important to emphasize that both the canon and the anticanon are human, cultural constructs. It is also important not to replicate the binarisms of the past in which some texts were canonized as classics while others were abandoned. Students sometimes lament the fact that I am not specific about "what the canon is and what the anticanon is," but my omissions are deliberate. I do not want merely to invert the hierarchy, creating a new set of binarisms, a new set of texts which are "in" or "out." In fact, the "canon, anticanon" label is meant not as a designation for particular texts, but for a particular way of thinking about texts and about the relationships *between* texts. What succeeded in the course was precisely the interrelationships developed between texts, the critiquing of dominant ideologies, the uncovering of the actual brutality and oppression of many of the dominant traditions and writers of the United States, and the understanding of alternative paradigms offered to these projects and texts by writers who operate on the periphery of culture.

The course also avoids "ghettoizing" noncanonical writers on the basis of race, gender, class, or ethnicity. I am not opposed to courses on specific groups of writers; indeed, such courses allow for the understanding of an alternative tradition, a "literature of their own," to use Elaine Showalter's phrase. Yet, it is also important to see that voices outside the mainstream are constructed by, and construct, the dominant tradition. To return to Benstock's analysis of the palimpsest, we can never completely lift the "subtext" from the "text," for text and subtext are not separate but always implicated in each other. The "canon, anticanon" course allows literature and culture to be viewed as a play of dominant and repressed voices, a structure of both oppression and liberation. In the end I think this is the strongest enabling device for students to become resistant readers of the world in which they live.

Since developing this approach, I cannot say that all the problems of the survey course have disappeared; I still often feel that I am doing too much in too little time. But my approach does give me a sense that the survey itself is not inherently bad. We must find ways to redefine the survey course, making it responsive to the changed and changing literary and cultural landscape in which we live. The "canon, anticanon" approach is one such redefinition of the survey, and in my experience it has been a responsive and responsible pedagogical method for confronting the widening horizons of our canon, and of our world.

NOTES

1. For an analysis of the different views of culture embedded in Bloom and Bennett's texts, see Henry Giroux, "Liberal Arts Education and the Struggle for Public Life." For a broad discussion of the contrasting poles of pluralism versus educational fundamentalism, see Harold Kolb.

2. Charles Altieri makes a similar point, stating that "canons serve as dialectical resources, at once articulating the differences we need for a rich contrastive language and constituting models of what we can make of ourselves as we employ that language" (33).

3. By "ideology " I mean not "false consciousness," but rather an unconscious or semiconscious system of cultural representation. See Guillory for a useful discussion of different definitions of ideology.

4. Eve Kosofsky Sedgwick also notes the polarization of contemporary discussions of the canon and calls for an "interaction

between these two models of the canon" which would challenge "the conceptual *anonymity* of the master canon" (140).

5. Both Herrnstein Smith (34) and Lauter ("The Literature of America" 10) argue that texts which support dominant ideologies tend to be preserved as the canon.

6. Throwing out the canon may even make our task more difficult, as Elizabeth Fox-Genovese points out. See also Fox-Genovese's perceptive comments on ways of broadening the survey course.

7. As Heather Murray points out, there has been a great deal of theorizing about a postmodern pedagogy, but very little discussion of actual practices (197). One noted exception to the general paradigm of theory without classroom application is Scholes' *Textual Power*.

WORKS CITED

Altieri, Charles. *Canons and Consequences: Reflections on the Ethical Force of Imaginative Ideals.* Evanston: Northwestern UP, 1990.

Bennett, William. "'To Reclaim a Legacy': Text of Report on Humanities in Education." *Chronicle of Higher Education,* 28 Nov. 1984: 16–21.

Benstock, Shari. *Women of the Left Bank: Paris 1900–1940.* Austin: U of Texas P, 1986.

Bloom, Allan. *The Closing of the American Mind.* NY: Simon and Schuster, 1987.

Dasenbrock, Reed Way. "What to Teach When the Canon Closes Down: Toward a New Essentialism." *Reorientations.* Ed. Bruce Henricksen and Thaïs Morgan. 63–76.

Du Bois, W. E. B. *The Souls of Black Folk.* NY: New American Library, 1969.

Ewell, Barbara. "Empowering Otherness: Feminist Criticism and the Academy." *Reorientations.* Ed. Bruce Henricksen and Thaïs Morgan. 43–62.

Fox-Genovese, Elizabeth. "The Claims of a Common Culture: Gender, Race, Class and The Canon." *Salmagundi* 72 (1986): 131–43.

Freeman, Mary Wilkins. "A Village Singer." *Short Fiction of Sarah Orne Jewett and Mary Wilkins Freeman*. Ed. Barbara Solomon. NY: New American Library, 1979. 361–73.

Froula, Christine. "When Eve Reads Milton: Undoing the Canonical Economy." *Canons*. Ed. Robert Von Hallberg. 149–175.

Giroux, Henry. *Ideology Culture & The Process of Schooling*. Philadelphia: Temple UP, 1981.

———. "Liberal Arts Education and the Struggle for Public Life: Dreaming about Democracy." *South Atlantic Quarterly* 89 (1990): 113–138.

Graff, Gerald. "Teach the Conflicts: An Alternative to Educational Fundamentalism." *Literature, Language, and Politics*. Ed. Betty Jean Craige. Athens: U of Georgia P, 1988. 99–109.

Guillory, John. "The Ideology of Canon-Formation: T.S. Eliot and Cleanth Brooks." *Canons*. Ed. Robert Von Hallberg. 337–362.

Henricksen, Bruce, and Thaïs E. Morgan, eds. *Reorientations: Critical Theories and Pedagogies*. Urbana: U of Illinois P, 1990.

Horton, Susan. Response to Robert Scholes' "Interpretation and Criticism in the Classroom." *Critical Theory and the Teaching of Literature*. Ed. Stuart Peterfreund. Boston: Northeastern UP, 1985. 51–57.

Kermode, Frank. *Forms of Attention*. Chicago: U of Chicago P, 1985.

Kolb, Harold H. "Defining the Canon." *Redefining American Literary History*. Ed. A. LaVonne Ruoff and Jerry Ward. NY: MLA, 1990. 35–51.

Lauter, Paul. *Canons and Contexts*. NY: Oxford UP, 1991.

———. "The Literature of America: A Comparative Discipline." *Redefining American Literary History*. Ed. A. LaVonne Ruoff and Jerry Ward. NY: MLA, 1990. 9–34.

Morton, Donald, and Mas'ud Zavarzadeh, eds. *Theory/Pedagogy/ Politics*. Urbana: U of Illinois P, 1991.

Murray, Heather. "Charisma and Authority in Literary Study and Theory Study." *Theory/Pedagogy/Politics*. Ed. Donald Morton and Mas'ud Zavarzadeh. 187–199.

Ohmann, Richard. "The Shaping of a Canon: U.S. Fiction, 1960–1975." *Canons*. Ed. Robert Von Hallberg. 377–401.

Radhakrishnan, R. "Canonicity and Theory: Toward a Post-structuralist Pedagogy." *Theory/Pedagogy/Politics*. Ed. Donald Morton and Mas'ud Zavarzadeh. 112–135.

Scholes, Robert. *Textual Power: Literary Theory and the Teaching of English.* New Haven: Yale UP, 1985.

——. "Toward a Curriculum in Textual Studies." Reorientations. Ed. Bruce Henricksen and Thaïs Morgan. 95–112.

Sedgwick, Eve Kosofsky. "Pedagogy in the Context of an Antihomophobic Project." *South Atlantic Quarterly.* 89 (1990): 139–151.

Smith, Barbara Herrnstein. "Contingencies of Value." *Canons.* Ed. Robert Von Hallberg. 5–39.

Von Hallberg, Robert, ed. *Canons.* Chicago: U of Chicago P, 1984.

Washington, Booker T. *Up From Slavery.* NY: Airmont Books, 1967.

Canon, AntiCanon:
American Ideology, 1865–1945

Books:

Mark Twain, *Pudd'nhead Wilson* (1893)
Booker T. Washington, *Up From Slavery* (1901)
W. E. B. Du Bois, *The Souls of Black Folk* (1903)
Henry James, *The Bostonians* (1886)
Kate Chopin, *The Awakening and Other Stories* (1899)
Jean Toomer, *Cane* (1923)
Zora Neale Hurston, *Their Eyes Were Watching God* (1932)
Ernest Hemingway, *In Our Time* (1925)
William Faulkner, *Three Famous Short Novels* (1942)
Leslie Marmon Silko, *Ceremony* (1977)
Toni Morrison, *Beloved* (1987)

Additional Reading Materials (General Reserve; referred to in the syllabus as "GR")

Mary Wilkins Freeman, "A New England Nun," "Louisa," "The Revolt of 'Mother,'" "A Village Singer," and "A Church Mouse"
Sarah Orne Jewett, "A White Heron" and "The Foreigner"
Charlotte Perkins Gilman, "The Yellow Wallpaper," "Lost Women," "Old Water," "The Cottagette," "Making a Change," "Spoken To"
Willa Cather, "Lou The Prophet" and "Neighbor Rosicky"

Stephen Crane, "The Bride Comes to Yellow Sky" and "The Blue Hotel"

Standing Bear, "What I Am Going to Tell You Here Will Take Me Until Dark"

Gertrude Simmons Bonnin (Zitkala-Sä), "Impressions of an Indian Childhood," "The School Days of an Indian Girl," and "An Indian Teacher among Indians"

John G. Niedhardt, selections from *Black Elk Speaks*

John Steinbeck, "The Leader of the People"

Robert Frost, "The Gift Outright," "Mending Wall," "The Pasture"

Rolla Lynn Riggs, "The Arid Land," "Santo Domingo Corn Dance," "Shadow on Snow," "Always the Gulls"

Countee Cullen, "Incident," "From the Dark Tower," "Simon the Cyrenian Speaks," "Yet Do I Marvel," "Pagan Prayer," "Scottsboro, Too, Is Worth Its Song"

Gwendolyn Brooks, "The Sundays of Satin-Legs Smith," "We Real Cool," "A Bronzeville Mother . . .," and "The Last Quatrain of the Ballad of Emmett Till"

T. S. Eliot, "The Waste Land"

H. D., "The Walls Do Not Fall"

I. Course Outline

Unit One: Slavery and Freedom (Three Weeks)

Week One

The "Joke" of Race: Mark Twain's Sardonic Treatment of Race and Racism
Twain, *Pudd'nhead Wilson*

Week Two

Booker T. Washington and the Politics of Appeasement
Washington, *Up From Slavery*

Week Three

Du Bois and Washington: The Politics of Conflict
W. E. B. Du Bois: *The Souls of Black Folks* (selections)

Unit Two: "The Woman Question" (Three Weeks)

Week Four
Canonical Perspectives on "The Woman Question"
   Henry James, *The Bostonians*

Week Five
The Regionalist Critique of the Construction of "Woman"
   Stories by Freeman and Jewett (GR)

Sabotaging Scientific Theories of "Woman"
   Stories by Gilman (GR)

Week Six
Self-Possession, Self-Expression, and the Female Artist
   Kate Chopin, *The Awakening*; "Elizabeth Stock's One Story,"
   "Désirée's Baby," "Athenäise"

Unit Three: Conquest, Colonization, and the American Frontier (Four Weeks)

Week Seven
The Conquest of the Western Frontier
   Stories by Cather and Crane (GR)

Poetic Reflections on the Conquest of the Western Frontier
   Poems by Robert Frost and Rolla Lynn Riggs (GR)

Week Eight
Native American Views of the Conquest of the Frontier
   Stories and Speeches by Gertrude Simmons Bonnin (Zitkala-
   Sä), Standing Bear, and John G. Niedhardt/Black Elk (GR)

Week Nine
Later Reflections on the American Frontier
   Faulkner, *The Bear* (in *Three Short Novels*); Steinbeck, "The
   Leader of the People" (GR)

Week Ten
Revising Frontier Ideology in the Nuclear Age
   Silko, *Ceremony*

Unit Four:
Race and the Harlem Renaissance *(Three Weeks)*

Week Eleven
Blurring the Boundaries: Jean Toomer
    Jean Toomer, *Cane* (Parts One and Two)

Week Twelve
Poetic Reflections on Racial Identity:
    Poems by Cullen and Brooks

Week Thirteen
Telling a Tale of the Folk
    Hurston,*Their Eyes Were Watching God*

Unit Five: War and Modernism *(Two Weeks)*

Week Fourteen
Canonical Perspectives on War
    Hemingway, *In Our Time* (Selections)

Poetic Treatments of War and the Fall of "Civilization"
    Eliot, "The Waste Land" (GR)

Week Fifteen
Alternative Perspectives on War
    H. D., "The Walls Do Not Fall" (GR)

Unit Six: Final Exam Assignment

Toni Morrison, *Beloved*

II. Course Requirements

A.) Reading and Class Participation

This class is designed as a reading course. There is a great deal of assigned material in this course, and much of the reading is difficult. I will, nonetheless, expect that students carefully and thoroughly read all of the assigned material. This class will also be conducted as a discussion group, and as such it necessitates that students participate vigorously on a regular basis.

B.) Four One-Page Papers

These one page (single- or double-spaced) "problem papers" will address a particular issue regarding the work we will be discussing, and will be due on Monday by 1:00 P.M. in my mailbox. There will be no extensions for these papers; late papers will not be counted for credit. If appropriate, the instructor may xerox some of these papers for discussion in class on Tuesday. Students will be responsible for one of these short papers approximately every third week during the semester.

C.) A Fifteen-Minute Oral Report Which Will Become a Short (Four- to Five- Page) Paper

Each student will be responsible once during the course of the semester for presenting his/her ideas and thoughts about one of the works we have been reading. One week in advance of the presentation, I must receive a written description of the report. The student giving the oral report should allow adequate time for class discussion of his/her ideas. The student will then use these ideas and thoughts, as well as the class's reactions to these ideas and thoughts, to write a short paper.

D.) A Final Exam (Take-Home)

The final exam will include an analysis of the exam assignment—*Beloved*, by Toni Morrison—in terms of the overall themes and literature of the course as a whole. You will also be asked two or three other questions encouraging you to make connections between diverse units and issues.

APPENDIX II

Sample Problem Papers

Problem Paper #3: *The Bostonians*

Option A: Prediction

Are the fates of Verena, Olive, and Basil spelled out from the beginning of the novel? Or would you agree with Charles Anderson that (at least in the case of Verena) the novel's conclusion presents a diametrically opposite destiny for the characters from what we would expect, based on their heredity and environment (see Intro., p. 16)? Read Book First of *The Bostonians*, and then write the novel's final scene. Try to work with the information presented about each character's character in Book First in order to predict the novel's conclusion. And, as much as possible, try to adopt James' style, tone, language, humor, satire, etc. (A related question: if we can predict the novel's conclusion from its start, why do we read it?)

Option B: Talk Back

A contemporary review in the *Woman's Journal* had this to say about *The Bostonians*: "The book is evidently intended as a tremendous satire on the whole 'woman question,' though we believe no direct allusion whatever is made to women's suffrage. . . . Mr. James is by no means true to nature, and merely conveys the idea which he assumes the leaders of the 'woman's movement' to hold. It seems hardly worth while to take the trouble to issue a protest against this caricature." What do you think—is it worthwhile to issue a protest against James' caricatures—of both his male and female characters? Choose one character and have him or her "talk back" to James; take issue with his or her characterization. Trying to use the character's own idiom (or way of speaking), have the character criticize James' portrait. How do you suppose James would respond to his characters' criticisms? (You can also answer this question by creating a dialogue between James and a character; in other words, if you want to give James a chance to respond—and have the last word—you can have James "talk back" to his character).

Option C: If the Walls Could Speak

The Bostonians is told from a first-person point of view—by a narrator who may (or may not) represent Basil Ransom himself. But how would the novel be different if the narrative point of view was different? Pick a scene in which you think the narrative point of view plays a crucial role, and then rewrite this scene from the point of view of an object: a fly on the wall, a podium, a notebook, Miss Birdseye's spectacles, etc. Try to emphasize how changes in narrative point of view might radically alter a reader's interpretation of the meaning of a given scene. (Please indicate, by page numbers, which scene in the novel you are rewriting; but you don't have to specify what point of view you have chosen to write from—you can let us guess.)

Problem Paper #4: Kate Chopin's Fiction

As Susan Gubar has explained, within a patriarchal culture women are not supposed to be active creators: "If we think in terms of the production of culture, [woman] is an art object: she is the ivory carving or mud replica, and icon or doll, but she is not the sculptor" ("'The Blank Page' and the Issues of Female Creativity"). Thus a writer like Henry James presents Verena as being a spectacle, something to watch and gape at, rather than a creator of any form of expressive activity in her own right. But what of Kate Chopin? Consider her portrayals of the female artist in *The Awakening* and/or "Elizabeth Stock's One Story." Do you see any kind of progression in Chopin's thinking about how a woman can overcome the dictates of patriarchal society and achieve "expression"? How can nineteenth-century women move from being passive creations to active creators?

[Again: creative responses to the assignment are encouraged; a dialogue between Elizabeth Stock and Henry James? An interview of Mlle. Reisz by *People Magazine*? The ocean's response to Edna's final swim?]

APPENDIX III

Issues and Themes in Early American Literature:
The Moral, Political, and Literary Construction of a Nation, 1620–1865

I. Religious Constructions:
Puritanism and Its Discontents

A. *The Puritan Project and Its Critiques*
>   William Bradford, selections from *Of Plymouth Plantation* (1630–1650)
>   Jonathan Edwards, "Personal Narrative" and "Sinners . . . " (1740, 1741)
>   Anne Bradstreet, poems
>   Catharine Sedgwick, *Hope Leslie* (1820)
>   Hawthorne, *The Scarlet Letter* (1850)

B. *Those Left Out: Visions of Native Americans*
>   Mary Rowlandson, *A Narrative of The Captivity and Restoration . . .* (1682)
>   Roger Williams, selections from *A Key into the Native Language of America* (1643)

II. Political Constructions: Revolution and the Word

A. *American Revolutionaries Gaining Power*
>   Franklin, *The Autobiography* (1771); "Remarks Concerning the Savages of North America" (1784)

Paine, *Common Sense* (1776) (excerpts)
Jefferson, *Notes on the State of Virginia* (1780–1)(excerpts)

B. *Losing Battles: Race and Gender at the end of the century*
Hannah Foster, *The Coquette* (1798)
Crèvecoeur, *Letters From An American Farmer* (1782) (selections)

III. Moral Constructions: Race and the Civil War

A. *Working within the Tradition*
Ouladah Equiano, *The Interesting Narrative* (1814)
Stowe, Excerpts from *Uncle Tom's Cabin* (1852)

B. *Subversions of the Construction of Race*
Frederick Douglass, *The Narrative . . .* (1845)
Harriet Jacobs, *Incidents in the Life of a Slave Girl* (1861)

IV. Literary Constructions:
The Emergence of a "National" Literature

A. *Creating an "American" Literature*
Emerson, "Nature" (1836); "The American Scholar" (1837)
Thoreau, *Walden* (1846)
Fuller, *Summer on the Lakes* (1843)
Whitman, "Song of Myself" (1855) and other poems

B. *Deconstructing "American" Literature*
Fanny Fern, *Ruth Hall* (1855)
Dickinson, poems
Melville, *Billy Budd* (1891); "Bartleby"(1856) and "Benito Cereno"(1855)
Rebecca Harding Davis, *Life in the Iron Mills* (1861)

Conversing Texts
The Disinvention of American Modernism

Anne Stavney

It has become a commonplace that the subject matter of our college literature courses must be broadened to give voice to texts by women, black American, and immigrant writers. Yet simply dropping a less familiar text into a previous aesthetic framework—that is, trying to integrate new literature into old categories and old critical paradigms—results in a fundamental distortion of such texts and collapses the differences between them by forcing various literary traditions into one. With the broadening of our teaching canon, pedagogical changes are necessary. These changes must reflect the fact that texts recently added to the teaching canon defy inherited categories of discourse and evaluation. They must involve a revision of traditional categories and must invent new paradigms for literary study that constantly question themselves. In this essay I discuss some of the issues surrounding the canon and the classroom and suggest several of the pedagogical changes that are necessitated by the broadening of our teaching canon. I propose, by way of example, a course entitled "Conversing Texts: American Modernisms" in which the organizing principles acknowledge and seek to rectify the fact that traditional definitions of modernism are inadequate in their attempts to explain many of the formal and thematic innovations of newly "discovered" modernist texts.

With the many texts added to our teaching canon, the abundance of articles and books on the subject of canonization, and the increasing number of literary histories that take up the issue of the canon and the politics of publication, I see a central misconception that has begun to affect the books that we choose to teach and the ways in which they get taught. Frequently, in the effort to recognize and assert the value of a traditionally marginalized literary tradition, critics and teachers have created a false distinction between canonical and noncanonical texts. Jane Tompkins is one such critic who calls for a reconsideration of what she perceives as a male-dominated scholarly tradition in her book *Sensational Designs*. She argues that the popular domestic novel of the nineteenth century—while ignored by generations of literary scholars—in fact "represents a monumental effort to reorganize culture from the woman's point of view" and that it offers a "critique of American society far more devastating than any delivered by better-known critics such as Hawthorne and Melville" (124).

While Tompkins's efforts to reconsider the domestic novel and to question traditional definitions of literary "merit" are valuable, what is objectionable about her argument is that she sets up an artificial dichotomy between women's sentimental fiction that does cultural work and "turn[s] the socio-political order upside down" (139), and those white, male texts that she asserts share transhistorical male values, that have been praised for their "timeless" and "universal" elements, that are ahistorical, conspiratorial, and claim to be independent of social and political processes. In Tompkins's argument, Hawthorne becomes the equivalent of Melville, Emerson the equivalent of Thoreau: these writers and the male-dominated scholarly tradition which has asserted the value of these writers' works have served to implant and perpetuate the notion of "womanly inferiority" (123). In short, Tompkins essentializes canonical texts, suggesting that they share some intrinsic property.

In many course descriptions and classrooms, then, literary scholars such as Tompkins perpetuate this mistaken notion that noncanonical works provide the same message of emancipation and canonical works the same evidence of collaboration. Texts that have been considered "classic" in the past are set against those which "really" speak about and to the human condition.

Or, as a result of this essentializing of canonical texts, such texts are omitted from the classroom altogether.

But as John Guillory rightly argues in his piece titled "Canon," it is no longer desirable or necessary to characterize the literary curriculum in any one way. To characterize literary texts as either emancipatory or oppressive is to "mistake the social effects of the canonical form—the syllabus, the curriculum, the classroom itself—for the effects of individual works. The reading of 'great works' is not in itself liberating, nor does it necessarily immerse one in the illusions of ideology" (243). In other words, it's unlikely that the social effects of individual works can be simply established as progressive or regressive. Texts say many different and contradictory things relating to many different social issues. And I believe that it is this sense of contradiction— or in Bahktinian terms, this multivocality—that is one of the central aspects of fiction that must be foregrounded in the classroom. As well, the project of reading new works or noncanonical works is only one part of revising the curriculum of literature. In our critical work and in the classroom, we should also rethink how we read "old" or "canonical" works for what they said and did in their place and time.

Much of the impetus behind broadening the subject matter of our literary curriculum has resulted from the desire to expose students to more diverse human experiences. By teaching less familiar texts and texts written by authors of various races, classes, genders, and sexual preferences, most of us contend that students will learn of experiences and cultures that are not their own and will encounter differing values. And from my own experience in the classroom, some students also have the chance to learn more about their own traditionally marginalized culture and traditions.

Yet in addition to the problematics of essentializing canonical texts is the mistaken assumption that marginalized groups are "representable" through their fictional work. In his recent article "New Americanists: Revisionist Interventions into the Canon," Donald Pease suggests that new historicists, by foregrounding the relationship between the literary and the political, can include disenfranchised groups which have been previously unrepresentable in this relationship. That is, argues

Pease, the New Americanist critique allows for the linkage between repressed sociopolitical contexts and the sociopolitical issue external to the academic field. The language of Pease's discussion—the use of his terms "representable" and "unrepresentable" in his comments on texts new to the field of academic studies—reveals what I perceive to be a misconception that informs many of the calls to open the canon. When proponents for change in syllabi are forced to act as if the inclusion of texts will represent and make *accessible* the experience of women and minorities as generic types, then we are allowing texts not only to represent marginalized cultures, but to be *representative* of these cultures. Those same people who would argue in sophisticated terms that literary texts do not mirror reality but reconstruct particular historical realities are now finding themselves arguing that the identity of a social group can be represented by a single novel. Indeed, the complex relationship between text and context, between literature and history, often becomes oversimplified when critics and teachers of literature propose additions to the canon. As well, the mediated relation between author and text is neglected as scruples about authorial intentionality are put aside.

One of the ways to avoid what Mary Helen Washington has called the "crayon-box" approach to the literary curriculum—where there is an array of colors and each crayon is supposed to stand in and for a given social group—is to make certain that in our classrooms we present students with several texts written by women, by black Americans, by white males. Students will hear more than one voice, then, out of a given literary tradition and can examine the ways in which such texts both share common features and also exhibit their own origins, functions, and preoccupations. In a course on modern American literature, for example, Jean Toomer's *Cane* is not framed in such a way that students are likely to understand it as *the* black American voice of the early part of the century if it is read alongside Langston Hughes's *Weary Blues*, Du Bois's *Souls of Black Folk*, Jessie Fauset's *There is Confusion*, and Zora Neale Hurston's *Their Eyes Were Watching God*. Connections can be made between these texts by focusing on images of the South, images of the urban landscape, the influence of the spirituals and the sorrow songs, representations of women and women's experience, the color line, double-consciousness, blues ideology, and the myth of the American Dream. Toomer's *Cane*, then, is part of a larger conversation among texts written by black men and women and thus provides one representation of black experience, rather than being representative of it.

This notion of a conversation among texts is one that can function as a useful metaphor for the relation between familiar and less familiar texts, between texts written by blacks and whites, women and men, upper-class and working-class writers. If, as Alice Walker suggests, we can "never be satisfied with a segregated literature. [We] . . . have to read Zora Neale Hurston *and* Flannery O'Connor, Nella Larsen *and* Carson McCullers, Jean Toomer *and* William Faulkner, before [we can] begin to feel well read at all" (43), then a way of thinking about the relation between such texts as we bring them into the classroom is in terms of a range of voices conversing with each other—voices which are also part of a larger conversation of the literary-historical period being studied. Given this metaphor of conversing texts, literary works are then related in such a way that they are mutually informing. They complement, contrast, speak to one another, ask and answer questions of each other, and say what other texts cannot.

In my course titled "Conversing Texts: American Modernisms," I have paired ten texts that I perceive as speaking to each other in instructive ways: I have paired familiar texts with less familiar texts, allowing for fresh perceptions of new works and renewed access to familiar texts. As well, I have attempted to reflect a diversity of voices and traditions within what can be called modernism, to provide a fuller, more accurate description of the historical period and to open up the period to its greater complexity. And with each pair, an African American writer and a white American writer have been paired so that the similarities between these texts in terms of the cultural, social, and historic contexts out of which they arise can be studied, as well as their differences. In addition, students can come to understand the historical, cultural, and literary imperatives that might be common to African American texts that are not shared by texts by white authors, and vice versa. In other words, this pairing of texts does not bracket off black voices into a separate canon and by extension a separate literature course, but it also does not prohibit the tracing of influences within black letters. Literary influences can be interrogated as they move *along* and move *across* race lines.

Although each pairing allows for the creation of new and multiple connections that are not immediately apparent, the texts have been organized in terms of a single trope that serves as a point of departure for our classroom discussions. For example, Nathaniel West's *Miss Lonelyhearts* and Langston Hughes's *Weary Blues* have been paired by the trope "New York and Harlem: Deprivation and Redemption in the City"; and images of the urban landscape, the perpetuation or dissolution of spirituality in the city, New York and Harlem as sites of cultural renewal or alienation are the focus of our early discussions. The notion of "Fragments and (W)holes" is our point of departure for considering Toomer's *Cane* and Eliot's *The Waste Land*, while the tension between "Private Dreams and Social Realities" informs our early discussions of Fitzgerald's *The Great Gatsby* and Fauset's *There Is Confusion*. Such tropes provide ways for rethinking and revising traditional definitions of modernism. And these various tropes are generated out of and by the literature itself, thus avoiding a singular, monolithic definition of modernism into which the texts must "fit." Finally, the pairing of texts is intended to promote an interplay between literary works: a simultaneous putting together and taking apart of texts, a "disinventing," if you will, of literary modernism.

In the last few weeks of the course, Faulkner's *Absalom, Absalom!* and Hurston's *Their Eyes Were Watching God* are paired under the trope "Confronting the Past through Narrative Performance," and I would like to discuss some of the ways these two texts speak to each other (ask and answer questions of one another) in order to provide an example of a conversation between texts that can be brought into the classroom. *Absalom* and *Their Eyes* are both texts that possess a performative dimension; they enact as well as mean. Narrative is shown to have a transformative capacity in these literary works—for both Quentin Compson and Janie Crawford find meaning in the present by telling, remembering, their past. Yet the pasts that

Quentin and Janie probe, the layers of experience that inform their present lives, and the knowledge and insight that they achieve are considerably different.

Through telling their own stories, the characters in *Absalom* try to reconstruct and explain their white, Southern, racist past. They attempt to place themselves in this Southern past, to make sense of this cultural history, and thereby make sense of the personal present. One character, Quentin Compson, feels a deep shame for the South's slave past, but also has a strong love for the romantic myth of the South. Tormented by this ambivalence—this hatred and love—Quentin probes the past for self-knowledge. In his collective tale with Shreve, Quentin explains Charles Bon's murder through miscegenation and in so doing identifies the racist past of the South, the racist past of his *own* ancestors, and his own complicity in that racism. Through his interpretive narrative, Quentin transforms himself from a paralyzed inheritor of the past—to which he can add nothing— into a creator of that past. He becomes the namer of the past and the bearer of its consequences, a process which culminates in Quentin's identity.

Importantly, in the process of remembering his past, Quentin is not confined to his own telling. A Southerner, the "offspring of rain and steamy heat," Quentin tells a collective tale with Shreve, a Northerner, a "child of blizzards and of cold." Through their shared fiction, the opposites Quentin and Shreve go beyond their own myopic visions and personal isolation and momentarily become one, "neither of them conscious of the distinction . . . [of] which one had been doing the talking" (417). Although one with each other as they seek meaning from the past, *Absalom* suggests that, ultimately, private personalities and frustrations must return. As Quentin insists to Shreve that Shreve can never really understand the South for he's an outsider—thus breaking the bond between the two young men— so the community that *Absalom* suggests is possible through stories told by a collective imagination proves to be fragile and momentary.

While the black characters Jim Bond, Clytie, and Wash Jones symbolize the reasons for Quentin's ambivalence toward the South in *Absalom* and his rediscovery of racism in its cultural history, nevertheless the voices of these black characters are unheard and suppressed in the novel. Clytie is just a "nigger" that Rosa does not want to touch; blacks are Sutpen's "wild men" with which he builds his mansion; Jim Bond's anguished cry is outside the language of the novel. Confronting and describing the shameful racism of the South, *Absalom, Absalom!* nevertheless renders African-Americans themselves silent and inarticulate. Hurston's *Their Eyes Were Watching God* speaks what is silent in *Absalom*. It tells a different story of the South and probes a different past.

An oppressed raced and gendered subject, Janie Crawford is nevertheless like Quentin Compson in that through narrative she too attempts to make sense of her cultural history and thereby make sense of the personal present. And also similar to Quentin, as Janie speaks her history—in the very process of finding the words to tell her story—she locates a voice and a self. Yet unlike the history of the white, racist South that concerns Quentin Compson, what Janie confronts is the historical memory of her black, slave past and the black woman's role as beast of burden. She also attempts to explain the personal memory of her Nanny's slave experience and Nanny's advice to her. Janie's struggle throughout the novel, like Quentin's, is to rectify an ambivalence: she both loves her Nanny, her ancestral past, for it is necessarily a part of her. But she also hates her Nanny, again, representative of her ancestral past, because the white racism embedded in the institution of slavery has taught Nanny to hate her own people, her own black culture. Janie feels as if Nanny has "taken the biggest thing God ever made, the horizon . . . and pinched it in to such a little bit of a thing that [Nanny] could tie it about her . . . neck tight enough to choke her" (138).

But as Janie learns that it is her own historical and personal past that makes her who she is in the present, so she comes to understand that many layers of experience inform Nanny's present life. That is, Janie comes to realize that although it does not speak to her life, Nanny's advice that the black woman should aspire to be like white folks and "sit on the porch" above the other black women around her is the result of Nanny's own slave experiences and belief that in order to move up, a black woman must leave behind her people. But what Janie learns from her layers of experience (her unhappy marriages to Killicks and Starks, her ownership of material things but her personal isolation) is that it is through celebrating the black community and by living in the "muck" among her people that she is able to become whole.

Janie's story, then, as she tells it to her friend Phoeby Watson, records and enacts her passage from a voiceless, repressed girl to a woman who can tell tales about and to the folk community, a woman who is not above or apart from other blacks but who has become their "delegate to de big 'ssociation of life" (18). It also records Janie's gradual acceptance of her Nanny, but her simultaneous rejection of the black self-hatred that Nanny represents. Indeed, Janie's formation of self in *Their Eyes* is not resolved in individualistic terms but by Janie's identification with blackness and black culture. Unlike the final vision of isolation and fragmentation that we are left with in *Absalom* and the suggestion that shared meaning can be only momentary, Hurston's text suggests that shared meaning can be *sustained* within and by the black community.

In addition, we see that Quentin's ambivalence, the white Southerner's ambivalence, about the racist past can be acknowledged but not resolved. Faulkner's own focus on his Southern past with *Absalom, Absalom!* suggests that he too is attempting to remember and make sense of his cultural history through narrative performance. In contrast, Janie's conflict about her slave past and the self-hatred it has generated in her people is resolved in *Their Eyes* by a turning inward, a celebration of the black community by the community itself. Hurston, too, turns "inward" with *Their Eyes*, writing a text out of and exclusively about African American experience.

Given these important contrasts, the texts also echo each other by foregrounding the dimension of exchange between someone telling a story and someone listening to it. By speaking about the past, the speaker and listener (Quentin and Shreve in *Absalom* and Janie and Phoeby in *Their Eyes*) form a relationship in the present and establish a bond that does not necessarily exist prior to the exchange. Thus, in both novels, even more important than the event recounted is the act of recounting itself. As Phoeby Watson tells Janie in *Their Eyes*, "Ah done growed ten feet higher from jus' listenin' tuh you, Janie" (284), so both texts suggest that speaking about the past heals the individual and creates community in the present. And the reader becomes part of this circle of communication, an active participant in reconstructing the fragmented narrative of *Absalom* and in sounding out the black vernacular and idiom in *Their Eyes*. As readers, we are placed within the process of formation, too, creating meaning that the narratives themselves enact.

After Katherine Mansfield's death, Virginia Woolf made a diary entry: "Though I can do this better than she could, where is she, who can do what I can't." By pairing texts such as Faulkner's *Absalom, Absalom!* and Hurston's *Their Eyes Were Watching God* as pedagogical practice, we can consider with our students what texts "can" and "can't" do, and examine what certain texts "do better" than others. Faulkner's and Hurston's texts, for example, speak what is unspoken, implied, elided in the other. Each articulates what the other does not, and what the other cannot. Constantly putting together and taking apart such pairs of texts and encouraging students to create their own "conversing texts" foregrounds the fact that a definition of modernism or realism or romanticism is never single, static, or complete. Each new pair converses in multiple and often unexpected ways and generates new topics of conversation. As we look at what texts have to say to one another, we will also find that they speak new things to us.

WORKS CITED

Faulkner, William. *Absalom, Absalom!* NY: Random, 1986.

Guillory, John. "Canon." *Critical Terms for Literary Study.* Ed. Frank Lentricchia and Thomas McLaughlin. Chicago: U of Chicago P, 1990. 233–249.

Hurston, Zora Neale. *Their Eyes Were Watching God.* Chicago: U of Illinois P, 1978.

Pease, Donald. "New Americanists: Revisionist Interventions into the Canon." *Boundary* 2 17 (1990): 1–37.

Tompkins, Jane. *Sensational Designs: The Cultural Work of American Fiction 1790–1860*. NY: Oxford UP, 1985.

Walker, Alice. "Beyond the Peacock: The Reconstruction of Flannery O'Connor." *In Search of Our Mother's Gardens: Womanist Prose By Alice Walker*. Orlando: Harcourt, 1984. 42–59.

APPENDIX I

Syllabus

Course Title: "Conversing Texts: American Modernisms"

Wks. 1–2: "Looking at One's Self through the Eyes of Others": Constructions of Femininity and Race
    Edith Wharton, *The House of Mirth*
    W. E. B. Du Bois, *The Souls of Black Folk*

Wks. 3–4: Fragments and (W)holes
    Jean Toomer, *Cane*
    T. S. Eliot, *The Waste Land*

Wks. 5–6: Private Dreams and Social Realities
    F. Scott Fitzgerald, *The Great Gatsby*
    Jessie Fauset, *There is Confusion*

Wks. 7–8: New York and Harlem: Deprivation and Redemption in the City
    Nathaniel West, *Miss Lonelyhearts*
    Langston Hughes, *The Weary Blues*

Wks. 9–10: Confronting the Past Through Narrative Performance
    Zora Neale Hurston, *Their Eyes Were Watching God*
    William Faulkner, *Absalom, Absalom!*

Problems and Opportunities in Teaching Native American Literature from *The Heath Anthology of American Literature*

Jeanne Holland

> People and their cultures perish in isolation, but they are
> born or reborn in contact with other men and women,
> with men and women of another culture, another creed,
> another race. If we do not recognize our humanity in
> others, we shall not recognize it in ourselves.
> —*Carlos Fuentes*, The Buried Mirror

In 1981 as an instructor at the University of Alabama, I began teaching the sophomore American literature survey. Until recently, I have almost always used *The Norton Anthology of American Literature* for this course, although I grew increasingly disenchanted with its narrow canon of American literature. When *The Heath Anthology of American Literature* appeared in 1990, I was thrilled. As Paula Bennett notes, "Whatever its limitations, *The Heath Anthology of Literature* is the first sustained effort on the part of America's scholarly community to come to terms with the vast wealth of our multiracial, multiethnic literary inheritance" (15). The *Heath* includes Native American, black, Hispanic, Chicânola, and women's voices that the *Norton* for years silently omitted and ignored. This absence helped maintain a literary canon which was not only sociopolitically inaccurate and unjust, but aesthetically constrained as well. Given the slowness of the *Norton's* response to the epistemic shifts occurring in American literature since 1970, I cannot imagine using it again.

Yet in the demands it places upon the instructor who is a novice at teaching minority literatures, the *Heath* presents its own host of pedagogical problems and opportunities. Like many who teach from the *Heath*, I am a white, middle-class academic whose politics are liberal, but whose graduate school training was largely traditional. Yet as a feminist, I gradually became (and am still becoming) attuned to the urgent problems faced by the Other as she struggles to find a voice in the "malestream" literary tradition. Feminism raised my intellectual awareness of the doubled injustice of gender and race, and I eagerly read the novels of Toni Morrison, Alice Walker, and Ntozake Shange which eloquently expressed the anger, sadness, but also resilience of black women. These novelists fostered my desire to study more minority works. Rapidly I grew to love the novels of Leslie Marmon Silko and Louise Erdrich.

But not surprisingly, reading contemporary Native American writers and teaching centuries-old Native American oral myths prove to be quite different enterprises. After I moved from Buffalo, New York to Laramie, Wyoming to become an assistant professor of English at the University of Wyoming, the presence of Native American students in some of my classes and the proximity of the Shoshone-Arapahoe reservation convinced me to begin my sophomore literature survey with Native American literature. As soon as the *Heath* appeared, I decided to adopt it for my fall 1990 class.

However as a new assistant professor—teaching three unfamiliar courses, participating on departmental committees, running an independent study, directing theses, turning my own dissertation into a book—I had little time to teach myself the particular histories of the Zuni, Hopi, Navajo, and Tlingit peoples before I taught their oral traditions to my class. Furthermore, I understood only superficially the differences between art produced by oral and by written cultures. For faculty in similar situations, the pedagogical question becomes, "Given that I am not a Native Americanist, that I am loaded with academic responsibilities, and that the survey class allots only a small amount of time for Native American literature, how may I teach this literature responsibly?" More crucial are the ethical questions which underlie this project: "Why am I reading and teaching Native American literature? Who profits when I teach these works?" What makes these questions difficult to consider forthrightly is the conservative backlash over expanding the canon. The silliness, hysteria, and misinformation which comprise most of the outcry against political correctness and multiculturalism make many of us ignore the thoughtful questions raised by a few critics.

After two years of wrestling with these problems, I now realize that I will be struggling with them for the rest of my life. As of this writing, I have taught Native American literature from the *Heath* twice—in the fall 1990 and spring 1992 semesters. Since I am discovering how to teach minority literatures and analyzing my own motivations for doing so, this essay reflects that process. I have retained sections from the original version of this essay written in late December 1990 for the CEA Convention. The essay is now constructed as criss-crossing dialogues: between its earlier and later versions, between Paul Lauter (who kindly responded to a version of the essay I mailed him in fall 1991) and myself, between my students and myself, and between me and my lingering concerns. Lest this mea culpa reek of a smug "I was blind and now I see" chorus, as I write I remember the trenchant warning Gregory Jay issues to all of us new multiculturalists:

> Before we get too busy celebrating our position at the forefront of the liberation of the culture, we must recognize that we are often the problem. It is our racism, our sexual prejudices, our class anxieties, our empowered desires that we must confront and resist. The unconscious character of these biases means that we cannot be complacent or comfortable even with the conscious avowal of our positions (as in this essay) for that can always be a defensive reassertion of our own authority. (265)

Throughout this essay, I will give advice but simultaneously wonder what I have left out, what I can't see, what's in it for me to interpret this way. What I have recently learned about reading and teaching Native American literature leaves me all the more embarrassed at what I didn't know. But with the constructive criticism of Andrea Lerner (a Native Americanist at California State University at Chico), hindsight, and further study, I do understand a few of the basic mistakes I made.

In fall 1990, most of my pedagogical problems resulted because I was so comfortable in my own skin. Then, as a white liberal female university professor new to Wyoming, I was hell-bent to dispel the demonic stereotyping of the Indian by white America. So I unconsciously overcompensated, constructing a romanticized picture of Native Americans and their cultures. Because I found plenty of textual evidence in the *Heath* to support my ideas about Native Americans' ecological awareness, matriarchy, holistic life-styles, and sensitive parenting, I thought I was being objective by emphasizing these traits. Only later have I come to understand how Edward Said's words illuminate my misreading of the Other:

> The difficulty of the question [of our relationship to others] is that there is no vantage outside the actuality of relationships between cultures, between unequal imperial and nonimperial powers, between different Others, a vantage that might allow one the epistemological privilege of somehow judging, evaluating, and interpreting free of the encumbering interests, emotions, and engagements of the ongoing relationships themselves. When we consider the connections between the United States and the rest of the world, we are so to speak of the connections, not outside and beyond them. ("Representing" 216–17)

Being caught up in the encumbering interests of my race, class, and gender, I unwittingly mythologized the Native American to reflect my own wishes for a kinder, gentler America. While instructors can never completely escape their cultural positioning, they must become more aware of what that position encourages in terms of misconstruing the Other. I hope this essay will help many perceive their own socialized blindnesses. But for me, only by making mistakes which I will discuss in the next section did I belatedly realize that "pedagogy is itself part of the production of knowledge, a deliberate and critical attempt to influence the ways in which knowledge and identities are produced within and among particular sets of social relations" (Giroux 119).

My early efforts to teach Native American literature were hampered by the binary logic of racism I unconsciously adopted. By "binary logic of racism," I mean that in trying to dispel the historic hatred which portrays Native Americans as savages, I naively reacted against this attitude by depicting them as noble savages. I didn't realize that this paternalism derives from a racist epistemology which can define "Native American" only as demonic or—the option I chose—angelic.

For the greatest part, my misinterpretations arose from my own ignorance. But they were also more subtly encouraged, I believe, through the construction of the *Heath* and the pedagogy its instructor's manual recommends. Consequently, this essay is intended to provide pedagogical suggestions and bibliographical information for novice instructors in Native American literature, as well as to issue a caveat emptor about the "Native American Traditions" section (3–9) of the instructor's manual. A retrospective analysis—of my subject, my pedagogy, and myself—has led me to reconsider what happens, and what I want to happen, when I teach Native American literatures in the fast-paced sophomore survey.

I

One of the main reasons I adopted the *Heath* in Fall 1990 was to help my students grasp that what has been enshrined as "classic" literature not coincidentally teaches, and reaffirms, dominant cultural values. Although many of these values are admirable, the standard canon implicitly reflects an ideology which ranks differences in literary production to the detriment of those groups who do not possess significant economic, political, and social power. White males with access to money, classical education, and the leisure to produce polished, allusive works have most often been praised. Since the New Criticism, other didactic modes which reflect the political desires of working classes and the powerless have been derided.

Thus I began my survey with a discussion of which authors and works constituted "classic" American literature. My students initially countered with the usual American

Renaissance lineup: Hawthorne, Melville, Emerson, Thoreau. Poe, Fitzgerald (*The Great Gatsby* as "the great American novel"), and Hemingway were also named. Sensing what I was leading up to with all these white male authors, one male student mentioned Frederick Douglass; "Harriet Beecher Stowe," a woman called out.

"Why weren't these last two authors named at the top of the list? Why did it take us awhile to think of them?" I wanted to know. "What has lately caused us to become more aware of women's and minority writings? And by omitting women and minority writers from the old list of 'classic' American literature, what message did that omission convey about the quality of these peoples' works?"

Calling students' attention to the fact that most other American literature anthologies begin with John Smith, I asked students how their perceptions might be different if we started the course with Native American literature. "They were here first," one student noted, "although we usually don't think of them as producing 'literature.' I think of their chants as being sort of primitive and quaint."

"So what idea does this give us of their cultures?"

"They aren't as civilized, as advanced as we are," another student figured out. "When you find their works in a college literature book, it makes us take those works and the people more seriously."

At the next class meeting I led my class into an analysis of the Winnebago origin poem, "This Newly Created World":

> Pleasant it looked,
> this newly created world.
> Along the entire length and breadth
> of the earth, our grandmother,
> extended the green reflection
> of her covering
> and the escaping odors
> were pleasant to inhale. (Lauter et al. 25)

Predictably (especially with my questioning) students seized upon "the earth, our grandmother" imagery. Many students recalled the Native American reverence for nature and respect for the earth, a much different attitude from what we saw displayed by strip-mining operations and toxic waste dumps. One student remembered a TV commercial which showed an old Indian chief crying at a polluted stream. "It's awful that we've lost that kind of feeling, if we ever had it," she observed. Another student stated, "There's a bumper sticker with a picture of the earth, and 'Love Your Mother' is the motto. That's a cliché, but this poem makes it a bit more real. When you stop to think that the earth really is your mother, that she feeds you and keeps you alive, that changes your view of it. You feel connected to, indebted to her." Although some students may have been turned off by this kind of talk, the general feeling I got from the class was one of sadness and yearning.

While "This Newly Created World" certainly authorizes such a reading, unfortunately our discussion largely stopped here. Having addressed my students' (and my own) complaints against our ecologically insensitive culture, I felt I had taught the poem. I did not wonder why I and my students were so eager to find these values in another culture. With this poem, we did not engage in the sort of aesthetic analysis I usually require. Furthermore, I did not question why the *Heath*'s version of this poem lists "1978" after it. I presume the poem was published somewhere in 1978. But what is a 1978 poem doing in the "Colonial Period: to 1700" section? Who recited the poem? Who made the translation? What material conditions influenced the translation?

Thus my first methodological mistake was I taught as if there existed one entity called "Native American culture" and as if it possessed all that was missing in the modernized white man's world. This predilection caused me to misread texts in that I stopped too soon in my examinations and was too easily satisfied that I had done justice to the work once I had unearthed the desired values. In fall 1990, I did not push my discussion into more complicated, less reassuring areas.

My second mistake was that I contrasted a reductive "Native American worldview" with a simplistic "Eurocentric" worldview. When teaching the standard canon of American literature in the past, I never used instructor's manuals. But with the *Heath*, I found myself turning to it (as I would imagine other novices do) whenever I felt on shaky ground, especially in teaching Native American literature. In "Major Themes, Historical Perspectives, and Personal Issues," Native Americanist Andrew Wiget recommends emphasizing the stark contrast between two monolithic cultures:

> Native American views of the world as represented in these mythologies contrast strongly with Euro-American perspectives. Recognizing this is absolutely essential for a later discussion of differences between Anglo-Americans and Native Americans over questions of land, social organization, religion, and so on. In other words, if one can identify these fundamental differences through the literature very early on, then later it becomes easier to explain the differences in outlook between Native American peoples and Anglo-American peoples that often led to tragic consequences. (Stanford 4–5)

Undeniably, history has proven the vast, tragic differences between many Native American views and those of many Europeans. Framing the collision of ideologies between Native American and Europeans prepares students for why and how indigenous people were ruthlessly exploited and exterminated. Wiget's methodology is important in providing a view of what America became. But in the *Heath's* current form, his suggestion that we can grasp something as global, complex, and contradictory as the "Native American views of the world . . . very early on" may lead to arrogant oversimplification.

The *Heath's* current form, I would stress, obviates much of Wiget's well-intentioned advice. He rightly emphasizes, for example, that "the most important teaching strategy for Native American literature is to single out one text and embed it richly in its cultural and historical context" (4). Yet the anthology's opening "Native American Traditions" section—which includes one work each from the Winnebago, Pima, Zuni, Navajo, Hopi, Iroquois, Tlingit, and Tsimshian peoples—provides little of this context. For the most part, brief footnotes explain the geographical location and means of subsistence of each tribe. Furthermore, the one-text-per-tribe plus tribal-footnote package situates instructors to make assumptions about each culture based on that one "representative" work.

To be fair, I must quote from Paul Lauter, who read an earlier version of this article. Answering my objection that reading one or two poems, then generalizing about an entire culture, is misleading, Lauter responds:

> I don't think you can, from an ethnographic viewpoint, say much about a culture from a single brief poem. But I do think that a comparison between the Zuni and Tlingit and Tsimshian narratives can suggest very interesting differences between their cultures—about conceptions of wealth, for example, or behavioral norms. And if you extend that kind of ethnographic reading to later Spanish and English narratives like Bradford's or Villagra's (rather than reproducing the notion that only "primitive" texts bear ethnographic scrutiny), the comparisons are, at least to me, quite enlightening. Further, if you also use comparative techniques to look at formal tactics in the same texts, you establish a kind of textual equality that has interesting extensions. (Letter)

Yet I would still quibble with Lauter: if you cannot, from an ethnographic viewpoint, "say much about a culture from a single brief poem," doesn't that invalidate making comparisons between cultures? How can you know what a culture's concept of wealth or behavior is from a single text? I can't help imagining an analogous scene where someone reads *The Journal of John Woolman* and contrasts it with Lenin's *What Is to Be Done?* to understand American and Soviet conceptions of wealth. While some aspects of the comparison may be accurate, too much is left out of the schema and a misleading sense that we gained knowledge may occur.

As it stands, the *Heath*'s brevity of contextual information, the lack of other works from the same tribes to make comparisons, and the omission of justification as to why texts were chosen make for trouble. As Native Americanist Larry Evers asserts:

> The Whitman's Sampler solution used by nearly all anthologists is clearly unsatisfactory. It begs us to wrench songs and narratives from their cultural contexts and leaves us without enough time and space to develop the cultural understandings necessary to allow responsible

appreciation of the material. The experience of the anthologists suggests that we should attempt to be less extensive and more intensive in our treatment of oral literatures. (27)

Evers suggests adopting either a regional approach or a masterworks approach (27). I hope that the future editions of the *Heath* will choose the masterworks option, giving readers the rationale to explain why each text may be seen as a masterwork.

In his letter Lauter also replied to my criticism that the *Heath* and the instructor's manual encourage instructors to draw reductive differences between Eurocentric and Native American cultures, ignoring the complexity of each:

> Yes, "the establishment of a clear difference between two entities is often achieved at the expense of ignoring difference within each entity." But it doesn't follow that establishing (relatively) clear differences isn't a useful or legitimate enterprise, even if such differences then need to be complicated, nuanced, and made open to denial. Yes, it is perhaps easy to amalgamate the enormous diversity of American Indian tribes (which Wiget strongly points out in the text) into a simplistic "other" constructed from Euro-American consciousness. On the other hand, perhaps it's useful to begin from students' desires to find an alternative to Euro-American ideology, including its religions, to validate that desire, before one goes on to deconstruct the Other produced in that process. (Letter)

This two-step approach, which Lauter explains, of (1) tentatively establishing cultural difference but then (2) complicating or even denying that difference is useful. As I will discuss in the next section, I emphasized this self-reflexivity throughout my spring 1992 class's discussion of Native American literature. Our cultural critique was still intense, but less complacent. We had a less reassuring, but more productively uncomfortable look at ourselves while developing a more complex awareness of how we relate to Native Americans.

While I value Lauter's helpful suggestion, I would still insist that if the *Heath* is to do justice to the Native American works it includes, it must furnish much more information about each culture, if not in the anthology then in the instructor's manual. Meanwhile, responsible instructors must make sure their classes get detailed information to distinguish one tribe from the other, such as the nomadic Navajo from the sedentary, peace-loving Hopi. Through oral reports, students may present a detailed look at one culture as well as at least one other work from that tribe.

My third fundamental mistake was that my stereotyping of a "Eurocentric" culture extended to stereotyping my class. Looking out at all those white faces, I inadvertently took a racist view of my class, casting all of us as the "bland across which the exotic would dance." In the December 1990 version of this essay, I wondered about my Wyoming students: "How did they react when their American literature was estranged?" Now I would ask, "Who is this 'they' whose American literature was estranged?" In fall 1990, I was too quick to limit my vision merely to my class's racial homogeneity. Faced by that wonderful rainbow coalition of voices in the *Heath* (and having moved away only a year earlier from a more ethnically diverse community in Buffalo, New York), all I could see when I looked out on my Wyoming students was the whiteness of my class.

To wit, I wrote at the end of that semester:

> "To understand fully the impact of the *Heath*, it's important to know something of the ethnic make-up of the University of Wyoming's student body. In Laramie, the student population is overwhelmingly homogeneous. About 80% of the students are in-state; most of the other 20% of out-of-state students come from either Montana or Colorado. Only 5.92% of the student body may be classified as "minorities": 2.55% Hispanic, 1.32% Native American, 1.01% black, .62% Asian, and .42% others. My fall 1990 survey class reflected the above percentages: of 20 students, only one was not a white Anglo-American. As such, my experience teaching a text which challenged white, Anglo-American, Protestant patriarchal discourse to students who, one would presume [and I did presume], largely accepted this discourse as transparent should prove illuminating for students, myself, and other instructors considering the *Heath* for their classes."

One result of my racist assumptions about my students was that I did not attend to, or marshal pedagogically, the significant differences among them in terms of gender, class, or experience. This approach would have enabled my students to identify a bit with certain experiences dramatized in Native American literature. For example, in later reader-response papers on Transcendentalism, I learned that many of my Fall 1990 students had had the sort of outdoor experiences which would have provided a common ground for them to empathize with the reverence for nature we discovered in many Native American texts. Several of my students, having grown up on ranches, were proficient horseback riders. One woman discussed the peace she felt riding alone across the vast plains. Others were backpackers or mountain climbers who had explored the beautiful area around the Wind River Mountains, near the reservation. But it was a year later, as I was rethinking my assumptions about my students and what understanding I wanted all of us to have about Native American literature, that I realized how I might have facilitated a more personal, less strange and exotic, reading.

The next three paragraphs recount my breathless report after first teaching the Zuni emergence tale, "Talk Concerning the First Beginning." This account reflects my portrayal of Native America as the Edenic repository for values denigrated in my civilization, my knocking down the construction of Eurocentrism, and my patronizing my white Christian students. In this present essay, it exemplifies a well-intentioned, but obtuse and condescending approach to Native American literature.

In December 1990, I wrote:

> My fall 1990 students responded overwhelmingly positively to "Talk Concerning the First Beginning," which explains the Zuni people's journey up from the dark underground of the fourth world, to the light and knowledge of our world. Andrew Wiget suggests that this myth be taught alongside the Genesis version of creation (Instructor's Manual 7). In contrasting the opening of the Zuni tale, "Yes, indeed. In this world there was no one at all. Always the sun came up; always he went in. No one in the morning gave him sacred meal; no one gave him prayer sticks; it was very lonely" (26), with the beginning of Genesis, "In the beginning, God created the heavens

and the earth," most students immediately commented upon the "humanizing" of the Zuni sun god, who desires the people's company because of his loneliness, and the austere inscrutability of the Christian God, whose motives for creation remain hidden.

This origin myth became the paradigm as my fall 1990 students and I approached texts from a minority subculture's traditions. Throughout the semester, my students eagerly turned to those voices to learn what they had to teach us, what values we might find that had been excluded from "mainstream" culture for one reason or another. Continuing the contrast between Zuni mythology and Christianity, for example, students quickly perceived that in the Zuni worldview, there is no such thing as sin and damnation. When a young boy desires his sister and copulates with her, this inversion of the natural order causes both of them to speak gibberish. The parents say, "'Oh alas, alas! Our children have become different beings!'" The boy draws a line in the sand, which becomes a river, and orders the people, who are journeying to the special place which will be their Center, to cross. As they cross, the boy warns the older folks that some of their children will be turned into snakes, turtles, and frogs. These children will bite their parents, but the parents must hold onto them and carry them out on the other side. If the children are not transformed back into humans, parents are instructed to throw them into the river. Most children are returned to their normal states. But the ones who aren't, who are tossed back into the water, become kachinas. These are the spirits of transformation which work to bring the rain to the people later when they grow corn. The kachinas spend most of their time frolicking beneath the waves as they wait for the people to summon them.

My fall 1990 students compared this scene of transgression with the temptation, fall, and expulsion of Adam and Eve from Eden. "It's as if the brother and sister just made a mistake," one said. Another noted that the mistake turns out to be fortunate since it provides for the people's future survival. One student noted that even in the midst of crisis, the sanctity of the family is upheld in this scene; parents, we learn, should hold onto their children during rough times. And if children hurt them, the hurt is unintentional. Still another commented that in Genesis, we are told of the Fall of man, his transgression and subsequent punishment by a wrathful God the Father. But in the Zuni tale, the people move upward from the underworld, and move forward toward their Center. Quite literally, "Talk Concerning the First Beginning" is positive, uplifting.

When I now read this previous section, I cringe. In our craving to find in another culture relief from an omnipresent Calvinist awareness of sin and a longing for supportive parents, my class and I turned this reading into nostalgic projection. While studying the Zuni's mythology is important, a pedagogical approach which totally erases its strangeness is insulting. If my students had doubts, they kept them quiet. My evaluations from this course were enthusiastic, the sort of rave reviews Kevin Costner earned from Hollywood for *Dances With Wolves*. I felt great.

II

Over the course of the past two years, I've learned a bit more about how to teach Native American literature. Although, given time constraints, implementing all the following suggestions may be impossible, it is imperative to address each concern in some way. Only for organization's sake have I numbered these suggestions. They are in no way ranked in importance; nor are they mutually exclusive. Numbers 1–5 represent ideas which orient the instructor and the class to the potential pitfalls which often occur when novices study Native America. Numbers 6–9 focus on the challenges involved in effectively teaching oral texts. Numbers 10–15, however, should be used simultaneously with 6–9 to prevent sentimental, oversimplified interpretations. In keeping with the dialogic construction of this essay, number 16 should probably be read first.

1. Recognize that especially with teaching Native American texts, it is essential to pay attention to critical pedagogy. As Henry Giroux defines the term,

> [i]f liberal arts education is to be developed in relation to
> principles consistent with a democratic public philosophy,
> it is equally important to develop forms of critical
> pedagogy that embody these principles and practices, a
> pedagogy in which such practices are understood in
> relation to rather than in isolation from those economies of
> power and privilege at work in wider social and political
> formations. (122)

Especially with Native American literature, where pedagogy can go so wrong and seem so right, instructors must scrupulously examine how their approaches may be reifying existing modes of misunderstanding and oppression. In introducing students to Native American literature, the ethical instructor walks a tightrope. Criticizing their own culture is one of the first things students do when they read Native American literatures. As Lauter recommends, the instructor should encourage students' need to examine their own culture through positing an Other that they construct. Yet the instructor must then portray that Other in its strangeness, its resistance to being co-opted.

In teaching Native American literature, then, we should orient ourselves toward it not just in terms of instrumentality— what content, wisdom can we raid from it, as the colonizer takes raw materials from the colonized? Instead establish a dialogue— how do our desires reflect on us? Every step of the way, be self-reflexive. Ask yourself and your class, "As amateur anthropologists, why are we so primed to look for certain elements? What does this tell us about the shortcomings in our own culture?"

In spring 1992, we discussed "Talk Concerning the First Beginning," but with more self-reflexivity. While we still noted the lack of sin and damnation, the emphasis on progress and hope, the parents' love for children, we then stopped and wondered why these themes seemed to leap out at us.

"I feel like there's so much guilt in my culture. It's been drummed into my head ever since Sunday school," one older woman offered with remarkable candor. "I'm sick of feeling sorry that I'm not perfect." Many students nodded their heads.

"This seems to be a powerful feeling, right?" I asked. More nods. "How might it set us up to misread a Native American story?"

Silence, and then one student hesitatingly said, "Well, you feel so good when you find another understanding about sin that you'd just want to linger over that."

"What are we missing in this tale if we do that?" I prodded.

"Everything else," several said, "how it's written, what it sounds like, what's not so reassuring about it." While this isn't the perfect class discussion of "Talk Concerning the First Beginning," I'm happier with what my students are now learning about the difficulties of studying the Other.

2. On the first day, have students write about their knowledge/impressions of (a) early America and (b) Native Americans. Explain Said's idea about orientalism: Hollywood movies, tourism, children's games, myths of Pocahontas, early anthropology.

To continue the analysis of cutting through what we think we know but really don't, have students examine their preconceptions, attitudes, and experiences regarding the relation between Native Americans and early American history. In spring 1992, their papers provoked a thoughtful discussion of the accreted attitudes most of us possessed about Indians. We uncovered and began to grapple with the difficulty of escaping the cluster of attitudes we called "Indianism" which resemble Said's definition of orientalism.

For example, one student mentioned the Hollywood image of Indians: "I don't want to sound racist," she hesitated, "but to me, all Indians looked the same in those cowboy-and-Indian movies." We talked about the "facelessness" of the Other, how often in movies Indians appeared as hordes or howling mobs, riding down on hapless settlers from the hilltops. "They didn't really seem human," another student observed.

Another student wrote about how she grew up thinking that "all Indians were stupid." This idea came from her seeing Indians on Saturday afternoon television, where their dialogue consisted of variations on, "Ugh! White man speak with forked tongue." Her observation led us to speculate on the effect *Dances With Wolves* might have upon audiences, many of whom heard for the first time Sioux speaking in their own language (for the more critical part of this discussion, see #5 below).

Keep these papers and discuss them again after your class has read more widely in Native American literature. How have their earlier attitudes changed? What resistance do they still have?

3. Have students tell stories from their own international travels overseas of how others view Americans. This discussion gives the class a sense of being the Other in someone else's culture. In fall 1992, Kerry McFarland told us about traveling to Mexico with her family, her father screaming at a taxi driver because of the language barrier. "My dad assumed that everyone should know how to speak English. As an American he expected it." How did she feel during this scene? "We were laughing, embarrassed, and a little bit worried. We didn't know if we could get where we wanted to go. It really dawned on us that this was a foreign country."

Another student, Roberto Proal, spoke to the other side about how he felt when his hometown in Mexico was invaded each year by American tourists. With good-natured exasperation, he discussed American tourists. "Nearly all of them wear running shoes and complain about the heat," he stated. "You can see them coming from a mile away."

Whether narrating personal stories or repeating Native American tales, storytelling can become a dynamic means through which to involve students.

4. Talk to colleagues in English as a Second Language and in anthropology to discover their pedagogical strategies for teaching about the Other.

Those of us teaching multicultural American literature should discuss the challenges inherent in this activity with faculty teaching English as a Second Language. My ESL colleagues Joy Reid and Janet Constantinides have been wonderfully enlightening on this subject, suggesting the storytelling exercise above. Among the sources they have recommended is Margaret Pusch's *Multicultural Education*, which contains essays on intercultural pedagogy as well as exercises to aid students in perceiving cultural blindnesses and difference. One of the most dramatic classroom activities is the "Ambiguous Lady" perception picture (Pusch 110–11). Looked at one way, the drawing reveals a young woman; from another angle, it shows a crone. Students learn to see the image in its complexity and realize that there is more than one proper way to view it. Although I can imagine someone might criticize this exercise as "gimmicky," I have found that it engages students and produces discussion regarding their feelings of disorientation and early anxiety to see it the "right" way. Students may begin to understand the experiences of a minority member who, entering the dominant culture, must learn to read the signs "rightly" and may find his way of seeing, although justifiable, not affirmed.

Of course, anthropology provides an invaluable resource in helping the observer understand his/her own projected desires. In talking with the anthropologist Audrey Shalinsky, I came to realize that the *Heath*, in its minority literature sections, implicitly situates the reader in the position of "amateur anthropologist/ethnographer." So perhaps it is not surprising that traditional readers new to Native American literature may make the same mistakes as did early anthropologists. As Marcus and Fischer explain:

> In the 1920s and 1930s, anthropology developed the ethnographic paradigm, which entailed a submerged, unrelenting critique of Western civilization as capitalism. The idea was that we in the West have lost what they—the cultural other—still have, and that we can learn basic moral and practical lessons from ethnographic representations. Generally and simplistically, ethnography has offered three broad criticisms. They—primitive man— have retained a respect for nature, and we have lost it [the ecological Eden]; they have sustained close, intimate, satisfying communal lives, and we have lost this way of life [the experience of community]; and they have retained a sense of the sacred in everyday life, and we have lost this [spiritual vision]. (129)

Consider these issues with your class.

5. To critique how the dominant culture accesses the minority culture, show *Hopi: Songs of the Fourth World* and analyze it. What seems desirable? What is left out of the film? What is the film's purpose? Critique the runaway romanticism.

Wiget recommends showing this film (Instructor's Manual 4). Overall it is an educational, poignant film, important for a class to see. But it must be shown with a note of caution. One scene depicts several Hopi women and children shucking corn together. Soothing flute music plays in the background. The narrator tells us about the Hopis' communal ideal of "cooperation without submission" and their respect for children.

The visually stunning film depicts gorgeous scenes of fluffy white clouds rolling in which the Hopis believe are their ancestors. (Rain is crucial in the desert area where the Hopis live.) Tall green corn then wave in the breeze. Traditional Hopis raise corn without using any modern farm machinery; they plant the seeds individually, singing and chanting, in Mother Earth.

In fall 1992, my students noticed that nearly all of the Hopis filmed were middle-aged or elderly: a grandmother tells stories about the courtship customs, a fortyish man discusses how to raise corn without machinery or artificial technology, a fortyish woman potter discusses her dream visions for her works. "Where are the young people? Why aren't they being interviewed?" students asked. These questions led to a more complex interrogation regarding generational differences among the Hopi. This kind of skepticism prevents too facile an identification with Native Americans and helps appreciate how history has created problems which still plague them.

Another film, *Dances With Wolves*, which all of my students had seen, was a prime candidate for the runaway romanticism award. It enabled us to see "savagism/primitivism" as two sides of the same coin. Students criticized the film's racism and oversimplifications: Kevin Costner as John Dunbar who happens to find a white woman among the Sioux he can marry. The Sioux are good, the Pawnee are evil. The U.S. Calvary are evil.

6. Ideally, bring in a Native American speaker. Having a Native American speaker address your class shows your students that the culture has not utterly died out. When students have the opportunity to ask questions of someone who grew up in an Indian culture, this occasion unsettles preexisting assumptions about Indians. If the speaker is another university student, students realize how much they share in common with that speaker in terms of tastes and attitudes. Yet, as when one young Blackfoot woman spoke to my class about their sweat

lodge, and the spiritualism involved in the practice, students could measure the difference from just going to a sauna.

Ideally, you will be able to procure a Native American storyteller who will perform a tale for your class. Hearing a speaker who is also a performer will dramatize the difference between oral and written artifacts. Being part of a listening audience dramatizes what gets lost from performance to transcription. As A. LaVonne Brown Ruoff explains, the audience frequently has a dynamic role to play with the storyteller: "Often the audience is expected to give a ritual response during the course of the story, to encourage the storyteller either to begin or to continue. If such encouragement is not forthcoming, the storyteller may stop" (15). "Wouldn't this interaction be expected when the tales we read are performed?" we may speculate when teaching oral literature.

Before the semester begins, contact your state or local governments to discover what information on Indian affairs your region provides. Instructors located near reservations should contact the reservation directly to see whether the local indigenous communities have tribal projects to share or lectures to give. At the University of Wyoming, Project Native, a division of the Indian Educational Office and a liaison between the university and state government, puts instructors in touch with students from the Shoshone-Arapahoe reservation who will address a class. If you come up empty-handed, several mail-order businesses provide videotapes or recordings of Native Americans telling stories, reading poetry, or playing music.

7. Have students read aloud excerpts from Native American literature. A Native American oral tale may call us to reexamine conventional aesthetic dictates through its use of repetition. As the people struggle upward in "Talk Concerning the First Beginning," one refrain is, "Now that you have come to us here inside where we just trample on one another, where we just spit on one another, where we just urinate on one another, where we just befoul each other, where we just follow one another about, how should I speak against it?" (Lauter, et al., 28). Many students, trained to read silently and efficiently, find repetition superfluous, disruptive, and irritating.

Yet having students read these passages aloud demonstrates how they may function performatively. In "Talk Concerning the First Beginning," the refrain provides a sense of despair and heaviness, of longing to escape from the dark underworld but feeling it is too powerful and constraining.

In other poems and ceremonies, repetition may work as a kind of mantra to subvert the individualism members of white, Western culture are taught to prize. Paula Gunn Allen explains:

> Repetition has an entrancing effect. Its regular recurrence creates a state of consciousness best described as "oceanic," but without the hypersentimental side effects implied by that term. It is hypnotic, and a hypnotic state of consciousness is the aim of the ceremony. The participant's attention must become diffused. The distractions of ordinary life must be put to rest and emotions redirected and integrated into a ceremonial context, so that the greater awareness can come into full consciousness and functioning. In this way the person becomes literally one with the universe, for he or she loses consciousness of mere individuality and shares the consciousness that characterizes most orders of being. (11)

8. Discuss the specificities of "oral" literature. One of the things I would hope to see happen is that future editions of the *Heath* would reprint at least one Zuni oral tale following the typography that Dennis Tedlock adopts in *Finding the Center: Narrative Poetry of the Zuni Indians*. In his Introduction and "Guide to Reading Aloud," Tedlock explains why and how he has broken up the rules of conventional typography in order to convey some sense of the text as orally performed. For instance, he prints: "Up on the hills/ HE SAW A HERD OF DEER." Tedlock instructs the reader, "Use a soft voice for words in small type and a loud one for words in capitals" (xxxiii). With "O------n he went," Tedlock explains, "Hold the vowels followed by dashes for about two seconds" (xxxiii). On the printed page, the Zuni poems Tedlock has transcribed often appear to be jagged, unevenly spaced, broken up by gaps and dashes. The typographical peculiarities, the strange appearance of the poem on the page, exemplify that the poems are properly oral.

The *Heath* needs to make much of the Native American literature it includes more "alien," more challenging to read, to represent its difference appropriately. Not despite but because of the increased difficulty Tedlock's typography would present, the *Heath* should adopt this method.

9. Discuss the mode of production of the text. Ask questions about translation. Discuss the possible styles of performance and occasions for performance of certain texts. The *Heath*'s introduction to "Native American Traditions" (22–25) says nothing about how these oral tales were transcribed. It is crucial to consider the mode of production of Native American "texts," which, as Native Americanist Arnold Krupat notes:

> cannot even be thought of except as the products of a complex but historically specifiable division of labor. There simply were no Native American texts until whites decided to collaborate with Indians and make them . . . With a few exceptions, Indian texts did not begin to be produced until the 1830s, when the eastern tribes were forcibly removed west of the Mississippi . . . But most of what appears today in the anthologies as Indian literature—poems, tales, stories—was collected after the Civil War, very roughly from 1887–1934, inscribed by anthropologists determined to preserve this vanishing heritage for science. (118–19)

Krupat provides a series of incisive questions to investigate, to determine when, how, and by whom transcriptions were made. Even if such questions cannot be answered within the limited scope of a survey class, it is vital to pose them, raising the class's consciousness regarding the provisionality of the text they are reading and the power at stake in who has access to representation and print technology.

10. As you study the poems and narratives, develop a broad but provisional overview of "Native American worldview." Ruoff also points out some perspectives that many Native American groups share:

> Among these are an emphasis on the importance of living in harmony with the physical and spiritual universe, the power of thought and word to maintain this balance, a

deep reverence for the land, and a strong sense of community. (2)

Paula Gunn Allen elaborates how an emphasis on growth and change permeates much Native American art.

Future editions of the *Heath* need to provide more complete information regarding the context of each tale. Eventually this expansion may cause fewer Native American oral literatures to be included, but those which are included will be more fully embodied.

11. After your overview, complicate that understanding by embedding each Native American text in its cultural and historical context. Better to teach fewer with deeper contextualization than many with little or no contextualization. Make up handouts and provide maps with locations.

To give a fuller background on the tribes whose works you choose to teach, consult the volumes in *The Handbook of North American Indians*. Many volumes are organized as to region such as "Southwest" (vol. 10) and "Northeast" (vol. 15).

12. To avoid the simplistic "Europeans" versus "Native American" dichotomy, use specific information about each tribe to contrast one from the other. From watching *Hopi: Songs of the Fourth World*, a few of my students assumed that "Native American" was synonymous with "pacifist." Thus they were surprised and a bit confused to read about Cabeza da Vaca's depiction of the vicious Indians in Terra Florida.

Not all Native American tribes are as peace-loving as the Hopi. Paula Gunn Allen notes differences:

> The purpose of ceremony is to integrate: to fuse the individual with his or her fellows, the community of people with that of the other kingdoms, and this larger communal group with the worlds beyond this one. A raising or expansion of individual consciousness naturally accompanies this process . . . . In addition to this general purpose, each ceremony has its own specific purpose. This purpose usually varies from tribe to tribe and may be culture-specific. For example, the rain dances of the Southwest are peculiar to certain groups, such as the Pueblos, and are not found among some other tribes, while war ceremonies, which make up a large part of

certain Plains tribes' ceremonial life, are unknown among
many tribes in California. (10)

Ruoff explains that some themes "are more culturally specific.
For example, the narratives of the pueblo-dwelling Hopis tend to
stress hard work, while those of the nomadic Navajos tend to
emphasize movement" (11).

13. To combat the perception that Native American
civilizations were simplistic, Edenic, and not technologically
advanced, discuss contributions Native American cultures have
made to mainstream American civilization.

Assign oral reports on Jack Weatherford's *Indian Givers:
How the Indians of the Americas Transformed the World.* "The
Founding Indian Fathers" further contextualizes developments
in Native American government raised in "Iroquois or
Confederacy of the Five Nations" (56–59). The chapters "Indian
Agricultural Technology" and "The Food Revolution" expand
the discussion regarding food and technologies (complicating
the stereotype of the First Thanksgiving, resulting from Squanto
teaching English colonists to plant fish with Indian corn).

These reports will prove Jay's statement regarding
heterogeneity: "Cultural education must aim to re-present
historically that ours has always been a multicultural society and
that the repression of this heterogeneity (usually in the service of
one group) ultimately threatens the cultural vitality and even
survival of every group within it" (267).

14. To make Native American stories seem less
"primitive," ask students about "fantastic" and "unrealistic"
elements they can cite in contemporary science-fiction stories, TV
shows, and movies. Use Tedlock's ideas explaining similarities
in popular media's uses of bizarre happenings.

Several of my students in fall 1990 and spring 1992 felt that
the Zuni tale was just too weird. "These people are covered with
scales and have webbed feet! Yuck!" one student cried.
Answering the criticism that the Zuni tales are too "strange,"
Tedlock compares the supernatural happenings in Zuni tales
with popular science fiction:

> It may be objected that some of the Zuni tale activities,
> unlike those in science fiction, involve a supernatural
> connection between cause and effect (as in the case of the

> restoration of a head to its body), but the mere fact that science fiction carries the science label does not make it science in fact: spaceships, for example, are constantly described as flying faster than the speed of light, which in a way is more fantastic than anything in a Zuni tale. Just as a Zuni tale-teller makes no distinction between what we would divide into technology and magic, so the writer of science fiction makes no distinction between plausible technology and impossible technology. (*Spoken Word* 176–77)

See Tedlock's discussion of the role technology plays in the construction of cultural fantasies.

15. As you're concluding this introduction to Native American literature, be aware that since the course begins with it, students may assume that these civilizations have long since died out. This misapprehension can make the conquest of indigenous peoples seem inevitable, part of America's necessary social progress. Thus do not leave your opening section on Native American literature without discussing some contemporary Native American literature.

For an excellent gathering of contemporary Native American poetry and prose, see *Dancing on the Rim of the World: An Anthology of Contemporary Northwest Native American Writing*, edited by Andrea Lerner. From this anthology, teach contemporary protest poems by Chrystos, such as "I Have Not Signed a Treaty with the United State Government" (33) or "Dear Mr. President" (35). The speaker is angry, the outlook is hopeless. Some students seem relieved to investigate issues of alcoholism, poverty, and the stereotypical "lazy Indians on welfare" they had heard about.

Teaching at least one contemporary work as you wrap up your introductory section realistically qualifies the cliché of the "vanishing red man." This final step precludes the easy nostalgia which may mark this section of the course. More significantly, it opens a difficult critique of current Native American problems, bringing us back to the question of why we are reading this literature in the first place.

16. Ironically, the instructor must get comfortable with being uncomfortable. Novice instructors must learn to accept their own status as student, with a lack of closure and mastery in

the class discussions they lead, with diminished comprehensibility and an increased awareness of the strangeness of the Other.

Near the beginning of this essay, I mentioned that I was "too comfortable in my own skin" as a new instructor. Yet this complacency does not tell the whole story. As a new assistant professor, recognizing my continuing status as student was probably the most personally unsettling business about teaching from the *Heath*. On the one hand, I was eager to teach Native American literature. But on the other, since I was teaching other new courses, I think I wanted the survey course to remain as familiar as I could make it. The *Heath* does require conventional scholars to teach unfamiliar texts.

I think that the way this sophomore literature class failed was not then apparent while its successes were. But now I'm wondering: how can a survey instructor highlight a class's internal differences in terms of race, class, gender to have students speak of their own experiences of discrimination? While more explosive, these stories may help students begin to understand the Other's problems. And as soon as I voice this concern, I immediately perceive the danger: how can an instructor prevent too facile or oversimplified an identification with the Other, so that the material conditions of the Other's oppression (i.e., statistics about economic deprivation, disease, alcoholism, lack of educational and vocational opportunity on a Navajo reservation, for example) are not glossed over? Teaching Native American literature in a survey class does afford us the opportunity of reading what our interpretations say about us. But isn't it narcissistic to use Native American texts as the excuse for probing the desires of the dominant class? While we must not generalize about a complex Indian culture based on a limited sample, how much time can we devote to Native American ethnography and literature?

Henry Giroux reminds us, "As an introduction to, preparation for, and legitimation of social life, a liberal arts education always presupposes a vision of the future" (115). By teaching from *The Heath Anthology of American Literature*, I hope we are preparing a new generation of students, citizens, and scholars to read and value Native American literature. The vision which the *Heath* rigorously demands from its readers is not merely generous; it is essential for America's survival and healthy growth as we approach the twenty-first century.

*   *   *

An earlier version of this essay was read at the 1991 CEA Convention in San Antonio, Texas. For their helpful advice with revision, I am especially grateful to Paul Lauter, Andrea Lerner, Audrey Shalinsky, Joy Reid, and Janet Constantinides.

WORKS CITED

Allen, Paula Gunn. "The Sacred Hoop: A Contemporary Perspective." *Studies in American Indian Literature*. Ed. Paula Gunn Allen. NY: MLA Press, 1983. 3–22.

——, ed. *Studies in American Indian Literature: Critical Essays and Course Designs*. NY: MLA Press, 1983.

Bennett, Paula. "Canons to the right of them . . ." Rev. of *The Heath Anthology of American Literature*, ed. Paul Lauter. *The Women's Review of Books* Sept. 1991: 15–16.

Evers, Larry. "Cycles of Appreciation." *Studies in American Indian Literature*. Ed. Paula Gunn Allen. NY: MLA Press, 1983. 23–32.

Giroux, Henry A. "Liberal Arts Education and the Struggle for Public Life: Dreaming About Democracy." *South Atlantic Quarterly* 89 (1990): 113–38.

Jay, Gregory S. "The End of 'American' Literature: Toward a Multicultural Practice." *College English* 53 (1991): 264–81.

Kincaid, James. "Who Gets to Tell Their Stories?" *New York Times Book Review*, 3 May 1992: 1, 24–29.

Krupat, Arnold. "An Approach to Native American Texts." *Critical Essays on Native American Literature*. Ed. Andrew Wiget. Boston: G.K. Hall, 1985. 116–31.

——. *The Voice in the Margin: Native American Literature and the Canon*. Berkeley: U of California P, 1989.

Lauter, Paul. *Canons and Contexts*. NY: Oxford, 1991.

————, Juan Bruce-Novoa, Jackson Bryer, et al. *The Heath Anthology of American Literature*. 1st ed. 2 vols. NY: D.C. Heath and Co., 1990.

————. Letter to the author. October 8, 1991.

————. "On the Implications of the *Heath Anthology*: Response to Ruland." *American Literary History* 4 (1992): 329–33.

Lerner, Andrea, ed. *Dancing on the Rim of the World: An Anthology of Contemporary Northwest Native American Writing*. Tucson: Sun Tracks and U of Arizona P, 1990.

Marcus, George E., and Michael M. J. Fischer. *Anthropology as Cultural Critique*. Chicago: U of Chicago P, 1986.

Pearce, Roy Harvey. *Savagism and Civilization: A Study of the Indian and the American Mind*. Berkeley: U of California P, 1988.

Pusch, Margaret D., ed. *Multicultural Education: A Cross Cultural Training Approach*. LaGrange Park, IL: Intercultural Network, 1979.

Ruland, Richard. "Art and a Better America." *American Literary History* 3 (1991): 337–59.

————. "A Reply to Paul Lauter." *American Literary History* 4 (1992): 334–36.

Ruoff, A. LaVonne Brown. *American Indian Literatures: An Introduction, Bibliographic Review, and Selected Bibliography*. NY: MLA Press, 1990.

Said, Edward W. *Orientalism*. NY: Pantheon, 1978.

————. "Representing the Colonized: Anthropology's Interlocutors." *Critical Inquiry* 15 (1989): 205–25.

Sarris, Greg. "Storytelling in the Classroom: Crossing Vexed Chasms." *College English* 52 (1990): 169–85.

Stanford, Judith, ed. *Instructor's Guide for The* Heath Anthology of American Literature. 1st ed. Lexington, MA: D.C. Heath and Co., 1990.

Tedlock, Dennis, trans. *Finding the Center: Narrative Poetry of the Zuni Indians*. NY: Dial Press, 1972.

————. *The Spoken Word and the Work of Interpretation*. Philadelphia: U of Pennsylvania P, 1983.

Weatherford, Jack. *Indian Givers: How the Indians of the Americas Transformed the World*. NY: Crown Publishers, 1988.

Entering the World
of American Literature
through the Discourse of Harmony

Irene Moser

At the 1993 Penn State Summer Seminar, "Multiculturalism in the United States: Putting Theory into Practice," Teresa McKenna challenged participants to engage students in the conceptual space between cultures that Gloria Anzaldúa names the "borderlands." Within the borderlands, we may glimpse "the other" (whether defined as culture, gender, class, or rhetoric) not solely as object but also, however momentarily, as lived experience. This essay responds to McKenna's challenge. The experience of teaching literature has shown me that the critical lens through which I introduce Native American literature makes all the difference in students' abilities to open their own perceptual boundaries in my class. To maximize those border crossings, I ask students to enter the world of American literature through an indigenous discourse and to reference that initial discourse throughout the course. This strategy allows the class to generate questions that can weaken conceptual and perceptual barriers between cultures and discourses.

In about 1890 James Mooney recorded a story about the creation of the world from the "aniyv'wiya" or "principal people," called Tsalaki by the Choctaw, and whom we know as the Cherokee. Mooney entitled this storytelling event "How the World Was Made." Along with Emory Elliott and the other editors of Prentice-Hall's American literature anthology, I place this example of the earliest southern Appalachian expressive culture at the very beginning of the study of American literature. The probability of parallels to the story in Native American performance tradition prior to European contact justifies this positioning. In order to lighten the cultural load that contemporary students—often relatively unsophisticated regarding Native peoples—bring to this storytelling event, I minimize my preliminary remarks about it and immediately immerse the class in a rhetorical reading that emphasizes image and form. A brief review of the pertinent ethnographic history and its consequences in the classroom will clarify the reasoning that underlies this approach.

I

One critical lens that inadvertently encourages stereotyping across cultures is the privileging of a representational function for myth. A representational warrant underpins the common anthropological reading of Native American mythic discourses as statements of belief or worldview. Bronislaw Malinowski articulated this perspective in his famous characterization of myth as a "charter for belief." It is in this framework of belief system that Charles Hudson, the anthropologist best known for work with southeastern Indians, reads the Cherokee "How the World Was Made."

This emphasis on belief as such makes it easy for some students to voice ethnocentric perspectives and stereotypes, e.g., the Indian as naive, superstitious, pagan. In one class, our examination of Cherokee narratives as imaginative expression was deflected into a discussion of whether the Cherokee's primordial watery world proves they knew about Noah's flood! In another, a student wanted to know, in reference to the cosmogonic story, whether Indians really believe a man can make his sister pregnant by hitting her with a fish. Asking students how many of their peers believe a woman could be made from a man's rib has helped to get such digressions back on track. Most students understand that while many Americans can tell stories about Noah or Adam and Eve, the degree to which storytellers conceive the story in literal or figurative terms varies considerably. Such unforeseen discussions have led me to seek an approach that discourages my literature class from becoming a class in comparative religion or a forum for ethnocentric speculation.

Reinforcement of the stereotype of the noble savage can also result from reading Native American myths as "charters for belief." Native worldviews are often presented as privileging cosmic order, harmony, and balance. Hudson characterizes the Cherokee belief system in this way. Direct testimony and observation of behavior based on such consensus strategies as the Cherokee Harmony Ethic support inferences about the mimetic nature of traditional discourses that privilege harmony.[1] These inferred beliefs in cosmic balance are often assumed to lead *necessarily* to individual environmental conscientiousness.

But conceiving of all Indians as homogeneously adhering to environmentally conscientious worldviews can conflict with the historical record and raise highly problematic issues in the literature class. As Christopher Vecsey and Robert Venables contend, Native habitation of the Americas, when compared with human habitation in other parts of the globe, has resulted in substantial preservation of natural resources; nevertheless, evidence of prehistoric environmental damage argues against a presumption that Native Americans have spiritual resources that guarantee *individual* environmental conscientiousness.[2] Well-known examples include soil depletion due to overcultivation of corn at what was to become Plymouth plantation, similar soil damage at Chaco Canyon in New Mexico and in Mesoamerica, and destruction of the sacred beaver in the Northeast in response to the fur trade.

This history of environmental damage can raise questions about the strength of belief systems supposedly "chartered" by such sacred stories as those of the Cherokee. To overgeneralize about a universal Native "belief" in cosmic harmony can be very disillusioning for Indian and non-Indian alike. Ruth Benedict's observation that myth "tallies" and *does not tally* with what actually happens in a given culture is pertinent in resolving this dilemma (Benedict 105). Clearly, *many* Indian persons have practiced ecological sensitivity and others have not. If one sees myth as representing belief, history can require the very complex explanation of failed belief systems in certain instances. I have found that time and subject constraints prevent adequate discussion in the *literature* classroom of the dynamics of failed belief.

Instead of providing a preliminary hermeneutic framework that encourages students to see the storytelling event as cultural "other," after a brief historical introduction I engage them in reading the narrative as argument. Reading this storytelling event as argument tends to postpone the calling forth of cross-culturally evaluative presuppositions that lead to stereotyping and disillusionment.[3] This focus on rhetorical and poetic strategies reveals a traditional discourse that models negotiation and adaptation between and among human and extrahuman forces in the interest of harmony and balance throughout the cosmic community. Within a rhetorical framework, the historical record may raise questions about why such ecologically sensitive *arguments* may have been ineffective in given instances, but the necessity of explaining the very complex issue of the failed worldview or belief system becomes less pressing for the unprepared instructor. Mooney's Cherokee myth offers an especially clear and efficiently presented example of such traditional argumentation.[4]

As we read this narrative together, I ask students to focus primarily on imagery and form and rarely on diction, a choice in emphasis that minimizes the complications inherent in Mooney's editing and translation. Mooney's text represents a storytelling performance that may have never actually occurred. Mooney compiled his material from two sources: the traditional eastern Cherokee storytellers Itagu`nuhi and A`yun`ini. Mooney, as translator as well as editor, becomes a third voice in the storytelling. Ideally, examination of his original records would clarify the import of his editorial choices. As Dennis Tedlock's retranslations of Zuni materials have shown, an earlier translator's usage and preconceptions can have a significant impact on the story we now read in English. Efforts to translate anew Mooney's original transcriptions, however, have been foiled by the loss of his manuscript.

The extent to which Mooney's editing may skew our current perceptions of this Cherokee narrative is unclear. For example, Mooney translates the name of his informant, the medicine man A`yun`ini, as "Swimmer." The linguist and native speaker Laura Hughes translates A`yun`ini as "the one who floats or moves on water." While this difference may seem minor, water was a source of spiritual wisdom for this medicine man, as the myth shows, and Hughes' translation emphasizes that connection. Mooney also uses "conjurors" and "underworld," the connotations of which may not coincide with original Cherokee usage. This storytelling event thus exemplifies what Stephen Greenblatt terms an "opaque" text. Its original interpreters and even its wording are lost; the "reality" of experience it references is only dimly glimpsed. However, significant parallels between this text and other American Indian discourses suggest ancient origins for its rhetorical and poetic strategies.

II

To discover that ancient rhetoric that privileges ecological sensitivity and negotiation across the cosmos, I ask students to examine specific images and event structures as we share in reading the story aloud, a process enhanced by the narrative's brevity and episodic structure. Our goal is to infer the argument's social, environmental, and poetic premises. As we read, we look at how the storyteller describes the making of a work of art (the world itself). Since art often exhibits balance and symmetry, we look for evidence of those values. We imagine drawing a picture of this world design and consider the shape of the cosmos, what categories of beings appear in it, which artists participate in its creation, and what design strategies they use. Some of these questions we ask of each work throughout our American literature survey—who and what are accepted into a given community? how is the community maintained? and how do its members resolve conflicts? In selectively reviewing the myth here, I call attention to images, characters, events, and structural features students notice as they answer these questions.

The opening scene foregrounds the concept of balance necessary to any work of art:

> The earth is a great island floating in a sea of water, and
> suspended at each of the four cardinal points by a cord
> hanging down from the sky vault, which is of solid rock.
> When the world grows old and worn out, the people will
> die and the cords will break and let the earth sink down
> into the ocean, and all will be water again. The Indians are
> afraid of this. (Mooney 239)

This image of balance—of the earth community suspended by
four cords, as is a scale—suggests a fragile, ongoing process,
emphasized by the participle "floating." In the first incident of
the narrative proper, the idea of environmental balance achieves
thematic significance. In Vladimir Propp's phrasing, the initial
situation "lacks" ecological balance, and "liquidating this lack"
motivates the characters.[5]

> When all was water, the animals were above, beyond the
> arch; but it was very crowded, and they were wanting
> more room. . . . Dayunisi, "Beaver's Grandchild," the little
> Water-beetle. . . . darted in every direction . . . but could
> find no firm place to rest. Then it dived to the bottom and
> came up with some soft mud, which began to grow and
> spread on every side until it became the island . . . we call
> the earth. It was afterward fastened to the sky with four
> cords, but no one remembers who did this. (239)

This first incident, which many readers will recognize as an
example of the "earth-diver" motif, focuses on achievement of a
demographic balance in the cosmos, a focus that will be
reiterated in the closing episode.

    Two artists, one known (the little Water-beetle) and one
unknown (the one who sets the cardinal points), have thus far
been involved in designing this work of art. In the next episode,
in which the expository mode is process analysis, another
creative force appears:

> At first the earth was flat and very soft and wet. The
> animals were anxious to get down. . . . They sent out the
> [Great Buzzard, the father of all the buzzards we see now]
> . . . to . . . make [it] ready for them. . . . He flew all over the
> earth, low down near the ground, and it was still soft.
> When he reached the Cherokee country, he was very tired,
> and his wings began to flap and strike the ground, and

> wherever they struck the earth there was a valley, and
> where they turned up again there was a mountain. When
> the animals . . . saw this, they were afraid that the whole
> world would become mountains, so they called him back,
> but the Cherokee country remains full of mountains to this
> day. (239)

The Great Buzzard's artistry requires containment to preserve
balance in the design. I discuss below the roles such anomalies as
the Great Buzzard play in this community. It is worth noting
here that the community deals with the Great Buzzard's loss of
control not by banishing him from the creation but by calling
him back to his *proper* place, the mythic sky world. This
etiological incident suggests negotiation is possible between
cosmic forces, a concept emphasized as the narrative continues.[6]

In the next section, several parties are needed to place the
sun, a key element in the cosmic design, into a balanced position.

> The earth was dry and . . . it was still dark, so [the animals]
> got the sun and set it in a track to go every day across the
> island from east to west, just overhead. It was too hot this
> way, and Tsiskagili, the Red Crawfish had his shell
> scorched a bright red, so that his meat was spoiled; and
> the Cherokee do not eat it. The conjurers put the sun
> another handbreadth higher in the air, but it was still too
> hot. They raised it [so] . . . , until it was seven
> handbreadths high and just under the sky arch. (239)

Like the animals who negotiate with the Great Buzzard, the
conjurors try different locations for the sun until a cosmic
balance is reached.

Having outlined two dimensions of the cosmology (the
sky vault and the earth surface), the storyteller then describes a
third dimension of experience below that of the ordinary surface
of the earth. This description again suggests balance and
symmetry on a cosmic scale: under this world is another, "like
ours in everything—animals, plants, and people—save that the
seasons are different." The streams lead to this world, but to
enter the springs which are its doorways, "one must fast and go
to water and have one of the underground people for a guide"
(240). Outright colonization of this symmetrically defined
underground territory is not a viable option. Proper cleansing

rituals must be performed and the traveler must negotiate with the underground people, a process with which the storyteller and medicine person, A`yun`ini, was presumably familiar.

The myth's concluding episodes return to the earth's surface to define the contemporary community. One of these episodes features anomalies—beings who cross boundaries between the categories of ordinary life as the Cherokee conceive it. These extraordinary beings' special powers help maintain the cosmic balancing process. The Great Buzzard, as noted, exemplifies such an anomaly. The buzzard, who physically crosses the boundaries between the living and the dead, can cleanse the environment—he is the original sanitation worker. In this episode other anomalous beings are revealed and their special roles defined as the animals and plants attempt a marathon vigil:

> [By] . . . the seventh night . . . only the owl, the panther, and one or two more [animals] were still awake. . . . These were given the power to see and to go about in the dark, and to make prey of the birds and animals which must sleep at night. . . . [To] the cedar, the pine, the spruce, the holly, and the laurel . . . it was given to be always green and to be greatest for medicine. (240)

Students readily note that the animals that prey on others are significant characters in the myth because they help control overpopulation. Understanding the ecological significance of the medicine plants may require an ethnographic reference. Another myth documented by Mooney, and also by Sharlotte Neely among present-day Snowbird Cherokee, tells how the animals bring disease to humans to protest abusive overhunting. The plants balance the animals' power by providing medicine. Both the cosmogonic myth and the story about the origin of medicine argue not for avoidance or removal of the natural anomalies but rather for their integration into the community and for understanding of their special roles.

The final episode is the fish story referred to earlier in which the thematic concern with demographic balance is explicitly reiterated:

> Men came after the animals and plants. At first there were only a brother and a sister until he struck her with a fish

and told her to multiply. . . . In seven days a child was
born to her, and thereafter every seven days another, and
they increased very fast until there was danger that the
world could not keep them. Then it was made that a
woman should have only one child in a year, and it has
been so ever since. (240)

My Cherokee students tend to react to this episode as serious in
theme and humorous in content. As one said, "The Indians wore
out a lot of fish that way!" Some of them also see the incident
with the Great Buzzard as tongue-in-cheek on the storyteller's
part. Such reactions bring to mind Barre Toelken's observation
that the humor in Navajo trickster tales serves to punctuate
serious social issues for the Native audience.

The Cherokee cosmogonic myth thus implicitly argues for
balance and harmony as life-sustaining principles (the breaking
of the cords and consequent tilting out of balance result in the
end of the world), as ecological principles (to prevent
overextension of any species or land form), and as poetic
principles, as seen in the symmetrical design of space and in the
episodic movement between states of imbalance and states of
balance. The episodic form underscores the processes implicit in
the imagery of negotiation between and among human and
natural elements. Rather than making a sudden appearance, the
earth itself grows *gradually* from the particle of mud; the
conjurors *gradually* move the sun until it is right; entrance to the
underground world depends on the cooperation of its residents.
Particularly striking when one juxtaposes this myth with other
American narrative performances and literary works are the
integration of anomalies into the cosmic community and the
multiple creative forces (the unidentified artisan, the little Water-
beetle, the Great Buzzard, the conjurors, etc.) who work together
to balance the work of art that is the earth.

III

Similar images, motifs, and event structures widespread in
Native America help justify the assumption that parallel
arguments in narrative form were in oral tradition before
European contact. Ake Hultkrantz identifies a three-tiered
cosmos—with the world above, the ordinary surface world, and

the world below—as typical of Native agricultural societies such as the Cherokee. This general shape also occurs in Pueblo storytelling of the Southwest and appears in Leslie Marmon Silko's novel *Ceremony*. James Welch references a parallel Blackfoot cosmos in *Fools Crow*. The earth-diver motif, taking the form in the Cherokee of the little waterbeetle, has a worldwide distribution. Anna Birgitta Rooth's historical-geographic study maps approximately 300 examples of the motif in Native America.[7] Examples in other Native American storytelling events of multiple creators and of images that suggest social and ecological balance are noteworthy as points of reference in approaching American literature as a whole.

As well as the multiple creators of the cosmogony, councils of animals and plants who act in consensus appear in such Cherokee stories as the origin of medicine mentioned earlier and the acquisition of fire. Perhaps the earliest appearance of such multiple creators who work in harmony is in the sixteenth-century Quiche' Mayan *Popol Vuh*, in which a council of creators "conceive the emergence of the earth from the sea" (Tedlock, *Popol Vuh* 34) and, on their fourth attempt, produce satisfactory humans (48). Such multiple creators are often embedded in a diction of symbolic relatedness. Interrelatedness is explicit in the Cherokee story in references to Beaver's grandchild (the little Water-beetle), to the father of all the buzzards, and to the primordial brother and sister. This trope of interrelatedness that can extend across species and into the cosmos itself implies an ethical warrant for the narrative's ecologically sensitive argument and reinforces a widespread indigenous social ideal based on reciprocity and consensus.

As noted, the balancing process evoked in the image of the earth as an island floating on the water is reinforced structurally, as each episode negotiates between states of imbalance and states of balance. Tedlock has edited examples from the Zuni of similar episodic structures. The Zuni tell how the elder and younger brothers work together to exit from the four worlds underneath where "it is dark" and they "step on one another's toes." Like the primordial mythic Cherokee, overpopulation concerns these Zuni characters who climb upward to achieve "the breath of the light of day" and to seek "the Middle place"

(Tedlock, "History Myth"). Hughes translates a cosmogonic parallel from her native Big Cove Cherokee community that echoes the Zuni diction. Hughes uses the term "the center" to refer to the place in the Great Buzzard's mountains where the Cherokee settle (King and King 157). Both the Zuni concept of "the Middle place" and Hughes' image of "the center" imply frames of reference that are simultaneously geographic, ecological, and social.

Solving problems through negotiated social consensus and through adaptation and modification, rather than through total erasure and an entirely new start, is often modelled in Native American myths. Like the anomalies in the Cherokee myth, earlier creation attempts are integrated into the final world of the Mayan *Popol Vuh*. In the evolutionary Mayan cosmology, contemporary species of monkeys result from an earlier try at making humans. Similarly, the Cherokee's mythic brother and sister still take productive fishing trips, just not as often. In both works individual impulse is tempered by the needs of the cosmically defined community of individuals. Such images of adaptation join with incidents of negotiation and with the episodic narrative structure to suggest that the Cherokee conceive "the American dream" as process, rather than as a steady state to be reached. The questing for that dream, like the floating island suspended from the sky vault, swings back and forth, and realization of the desired balance requires continuous active participation across the cosmic community.

When we juxtapose the multiplicity of community, the questing for ecological balance, and the negotiating strategies modelled in this narrative with selections from our most often read American writers, we may find it easier to identify contrasts than to locate comparisons. A few of the contrasting images my students point out indicate the range of possibility. One such image is John Smith's description of New England where "Nature and liberty afford us that freely which in England we want . . . [to the effect that] if a man work but three days in seven he can get more than he can spend" and only "a very bad fisher cannot kill in one day . . . one, two, or three hundred cods" (31). This vision of America, in which the fish virtually leap into the fisher's boat, requires little labor in return for substantial individual profit (to the delight of all students regardless of ethnic heritage!), and the writer expresses little concern for the environmental impact of realizing that vision. In this ideal community, the human species and the singular point of view take precedence ("we," "a man," "a bad fisher"). The public cosmos of William Byrd II of Virginia is likewise limited. Byrd literally draws a line around his world and excludes from it the anomalies, that is, the swamp and the inhabitants of North Carolina. Jean de Crèvecoeur's easily visualized social landscape also pushes the anomalies (the backwoods families and the Indians) to the edges of the community.

On the other hand, some comparable elements do appear in our best known literary visions of community. While a singular perspective focuses Benjamin Franklin's autobiographical vision, and while the multitudes contained in that vision cannot match Walt Whitman's, Franklin nevertheless valorizes social reciprocity and a discourse of negotiation. Negotiation is also a primary problem-solving strategy for Frederick Douglass. Violence serves Douglass as a last resort in the interests of self-protection. Furthermore, Douglass accepts a wide range of people and viewpoints into his world. The communities created by later Afro-American writers tend to be similarly multifaceted. In the fictive worlds of Alice Walker and Toni Morrison, the extraordinary and the ordinary interweave as these authors create room for anomalous beings. Anomalies also figure fairly often in Southern literary works. One thinks of the humorists of the Old Southwest, of Eudora Welty, and of Flannery O'Connor. Negotiating and modifying behaviors between the extremes of these writers' fictional communities are not always present, however. As in Harriet Arnow's *The Dollmaker*, Welty's artists are finally distanced from the home communities, however richly evoked and inclusive those communities may be. In fact, the anomalies most often find places only on the fringes of community. Maxine Hong Kingston has created one of the most complex artist figures. In *The Woman Warrior*, Kingston finds that her gender makes her anomalous in China and her ethnicity makes her so in America. Social limitations make her role in each society ambiguous.

Whatever specific works we choose as course companions, the Native American discourse of harmony exemplified in the Cherokee vision of creation can stimulate class discussions of the environmental, social, and poetic premises underlying communities depicted throughout American literature. Such a juxtaposition of discourses gives access to the borderlands where the closure implied in "Do Indians really believe . . . ?" can give way to the revisionary question voiced painfully by one student, "Why could the settlers and Indians *not* communicate from the start?" The present context suggests another phrasing to this essential question, why was William Bradford unable to hear the discourse of harmony across the "hideous and desolate wilderness"? To engage our students in answering that question is to begin a critical episode in the quest to balance the world of the American literature class.

NOTES

1. Within the North Carolina Snowbird Cherokee community described by Sharlotte Neely, social interactions exhibit the Harmony Ethic's basic features of non-aggressiveness, individual non-competitiveness, personal generosity "even when people cannot afford to be generous" (36), and adaptation of consensus-based social forms to the requirements of federal bureaucracies. The Snowbird, however, practice the Harmony Ethic selectively. They have employed the adversarial legal system during conflicts with other communities. Neely sees this flexibility as evidence of the community's adaptiveness.

2. Vecsey and Venables see Native religions as expressing both the ideal of harmony with nature and the need to exploit the natural world to sustain life (23).

3. Roger Abrahams's "Introductory Remarks to a Rhetorical Theory of Folklore" offers a model for this critical stance.

4. James Fenton's discussion of the Iroquois cosmogonic myths suggests a similar reading of those lengthier materials.

5. For definitions of these terms see Propp, *Morphology of the Folktale* or Dundes, *The Morphology of North American Indian Folktales*.

6. Along with Dennis Tedlock, I read such etiological incidents as stylistic devices, the purpose of which is verisimilitude rather than representation of belief ("Pueblo Literature").

7. Alan Dundes, in one of his provocative psychoanalytic interpretations, sees this motif as a symbolic manifestation of "a cloacal theory of birth" and of male "pregnancy envy" ("Earth- Diver" 1038.).

WORKS CITED

Abrahams, Roger D. "Introductory Remarks to a Rhetorical Theory of Folklore." *Journal of American Folklore* 81 (1968): 143–158.

Anzaldúa, Gloria. *Borderlands/La Frontera: The New Mestiza*. San Francisco: Spinsters/Aunt Lute, 1987.

Arnow, Harriet. *The Dollmaker*. 1954. New York: Avon, 1971.

Benedict, Ruth. "Introduction to Zuni Mythology." 1935. *Studies on Mythology*. Ed. Robert A. Georges. Homewood: Dorsey P, 1968. 102–136.

Dundes, Alan. "Earth-Diver: Creation of the Mythopoeic Male." *American Anthropologist* 64 (1962): 1031–1051.

———. *The Morphology of North American Indian Folktales*. Folklore Fellows Communications 195. Helsinki: Suomalainen Tiedeakatemia, 1964.

Elliott, Emory, et al. *American Literature, a Prentice Hall Anthology*. Englewood Cliffs: Prentice-Hall, 1991.

Fenton, James. "This Island, The World on the Turtle's Back." *Journal of American Folklore* 75 (1962): 283–300.

Hudson, Charles. *The Southeastern Indians*. Knoxville: U of Tennessee P, 1976.

Hughes, Laura. Course on the Cherokee Language. Cullowhee, NC: Western Carolina U. 1990–91.

Hultkrantz, Ake. *The Religions of the American Indians*. Trans. Monica Setterwall. Berkeley: U of California P, 1979.

King, Duane H., and Laura H. King. "The Mythico-Religious Origin of the Cherokees." *Redemption Denied, an Appalachian Reader*. Ed. Edward Guinan. Washington: Appalachian Documentation, 1976. 157–161.

Kingston, Maxine Hong. *The Woman Warrior: Memoirs of a Girlhood Among Ghosts*. NY: Alfred A. Knopf, 1976.

Malinowski, Bronislaw. "Myth in Primitive Psychology." *Magic, Science and Religion and Other Essays*. NY: Doubleday, 1954. 93–148.

McKenna, Teresa. "Politics, Process, and Pedagogy: Walking the Thin Line of Difference in Multicultural Theory and Practice." Penn State Summer Seminar in Theory and Culture, University Park, 24 June 1993.

Mooney, James. "How the World Was Made." *Myths of the Cherokee*. Bureau of American Ethnology. 19th Annual Report. 1900. St. Clair Shores: Scholarly P, 1970. 239–240.

Neely, Sharlotte. *Snowbird Cherokees: People of Persistence*. Athens: U of Georgia P, 1991.

Propp, V. *Morphology of the Folktale*. Trans. Laurence Scott, 1958. 2nd ed. Austin: U of Texas P, 1968.

Rooth, Anna Birgitta. "The Creation Myths of the North American Indians." *Anthropos* 52 (1957): 497–508.

Silko, Leslie Marmon. *Ceremony*. NY: Viking P, 1977.

Smith, John. "From 'A Description of New England.'" *Anthology of American Literature*. Vol. I. Ed. George McMichael et al. NY: Macmillan, 1989. 24–32.

Tedlock, Dennis. "History Myth of the Coming of the A'shiwi as Narrated by Kyaklo." *Traditional Literatures of the American Indian: Texts and Interpretations*. Ed. Karl Kroeber. Lincoln: U of Nebraska P, 1981. 59–64.

——, trans. and ed. *Popol Vuh: The Definitive Edition of the Mayan Book of the Dawn of Life and the Glories of Gods and Kings*. NY: Simon and Schuster, 1985.

——. "Pueblo Literature: Style and Verisimilitude." *New Perspectives on the Pueblos*. Ed. Alfonso Ortiz. Albuquerque: U of New Mexico P, 1972. 219–242.

Toelken, J. Barre. "The `Pretty Language' of Yellowman: Genre, Mode, and Texture in Navaho Coyote Narratives." *Genre* 2 (1969): 211–235.

Vecsey, Christopher, and Robert W. Venables, eds. *American Indian Environments, Ecological Issues in Native American History*. Syracuse: Syracuse UP, 1980.

Welch, James. *Fools Crow*. NY: Penguin Books, 1987.

Master-Pieces and Mistress-Pieces
Performative Expansion
of the American Literary Canon

Michele Lise Tarter

The classroom doors flew open and in ran a group of painted bodies, screaming an unidentifiable, quite foreign language and (gently) prodding my students' arms and legs. "What is happening?" I worried to myself. "Is this a teacher's nightmare, or a dream come true?" We were all taken, quite by alarm, into captivity. Down the corridors of Hellems Hall we were led, through its ivy-covered doorway and along the University of Colorado campus "removes": a first stop at the trees in the North Quad, to gather sticks for support on our "journey"; then to Norlin Library's cul-de-sac, to experience the captors' body language and the "seeming" barriers of cross-cultural communication; next to the Sibell Wolle Art Gallery, where we were given food that looked like entrails (in actuality, dried pears from the local health food store); and finally, to the creek at the edge of the university campus, where we sat together in the power of silence and listened to the harmony of water rushing along rocks and birds speaking yet another language above us.

In this creative group project, the class and I were meant to be experiencing Mary Rowlandson's Indian captivity narrative as we were certainly bringing life to her performative text. Fifty minutes later, the class understood with more appreciation the trials beset upon Mistress Rowlandson as she was forced out of her Puritan home and taken captive by Indians in 1676; her feelings of alienation, fear and survival; and her ultimate salvation in weathering the turbulent trial of life in the great outdoors. We understood captivity, that is, through experiential learning. But why were students so "moved" by this text, I asked myself, to perform and experience it to such an extreme? What was it about this Puritan woman's narrative, written so many centuries ago, that evoked such an enthusiastic response from the class, culminating in a theatrical metanarrative?

"Master-Pieces"

Teaching a course so controversially called "Masterpieces of American Literature," I am currently involved in the university debate of canon expansion and revision in literary studies. At first, investigating the term *masterpiece* with the class, I make it a point to problematize the construction of a traditional canon composed of works written primarily by white men and then propose expanding its boundaries by including texts written across lines of gender, race, and class. My own study of women's autobiographies, journals and diaries has inspired such a re-visioning of the term and its definition, as well as a reconsideration of traditional androcentric criteria used to judge a work's excellence or value and the significance of gender in literary analysis. Therefore, in addition to teaching many texts which have been historically classified as masterpieces of American literature, I place great emphasis on women's voices, women like Mary Rowlandson, who have been silenced, marginalized, or censored in American literary history.

In "Canons to Left of Them," a review of Paul Lauter's *Canons and Contexts*, Lillian S. Robinson writes that students previously have been given "a limited and distorted view of our common cultural heritage" (18). Paula Bennett adds to this discussion in "Canons to Right of Them," her review of Lauter's *Heath Anthology*, noting that there is "another way to look at our literary inheritance, one based on inclusion, not exclusion, and that is what the *Heath* is about. It seeks to restore the voices of those who have been 'disappeared'" (15).

Expanding canonical boundaries with the unburied or "reappearing" voices of American writers has been the most important dimension of my work in research and pedagogy, for I have seen overwhelming and quite revitalizing responses of students in the classroom. Strongly affected by Katha Pollitt's article, "Canon to the Right of Me," I, too, questioned the purpose of our literary canon, as well as my role as an instructor. Pollitt considers both sides of the canonical debate and ultimately posits who finally suffers at the end of this heated controversy:

> Something is being overlooked: the state of reading, and books, and literature in our country at this time. Why, ask yourself, is everyone so hot under the collar about what to put on the required reading shelf? It is because while we have been arguing so fiercely about which books make the best medicine, the patient has been slipping deeper and deeper into a coma. (329).

Students and texts, I realized, have lost each other in our culture, and particularly in the academic realm where "superior" or hierarchical knowledge seems inaccessible to them. As the instructor of "Masterpieces of American Literature," therefore, I felt determined to work toward a re-connection, introducing students to many long-lost textual voices by adding some "personal" dimensions to their literary study. First and foremost, I have urged them to explore the realm of "difference" in literary voices. No longer adhering to the conflation of male and universal norms, my classes have explored the dynamics of storytelling and literary creation in relation to issues of gender, sexuality, race and class; ultimately, through this lens of plurivocality and in the participatory act of reading, they have realized that with respect to such differences, there, too, can be a sense of interdependence and coexistence, not only in the works they read but in their very classroom environment. The definition of masterpiece and the act of hierarchical mastery are then deconstructed with mutual respect, inclusiveness, and connection.

My teaching methodology has evolved from this philosophy, and over the past two years of teaching this course, I have begun to incorporate various ways in which students might challenge the traditional readings of American literature and find their own voices in the process of interpretation. I ask them to keep a reading journal, in which they personally respond to each textual assignment (including canonical, noncanonical, feminist and multicultural texts) and thus write consistently, albeit informally, throughout the course. This act of writing in turn prepares them for dynamic classroom discussions. Their entries, given no prescriptions, have proven to be quite fascinating and diverse: some are short, some long; some are drawn, while others are poetic responses; even one thus far has consisted of a very large word—"why?" In all of these entries, the impetus for writing is a reconsideration of canonical and noncanonical literature, and what this debate's implications and issues mean on a personal level. For more formal writing, I assign eight short papers, in which students write on a topic relevant to particular class readings in a concise, three-page essay. These expository assignments are in fact my opportunity to keep a constant dialogue with each student, as well as a means of teaching them writing and analytical skills. Finally and most outstandingly, in terms of student responses, I place great emphasis on their working together in group projects, in which four students sign up for a text, read it closely, research it thoroughly by reading historical or critical essays about the work and then present their interpretative analysis to the class. I encourage the students to be as creative as they dare, believing in the power of their oral interpretations and in the force of group dynamics.

"Mistress-Pieces"

Beginning this course with Mary Rowlandson's Indian captivity narrative, I am always surprised to see a group's creative interpretation of this Puritan woman's text. While some students have enacted a courtroom performance, whereby Mistress Rowlandson was put on trial for writing what the Puritans deemed "fiction," and others have depicted a *Twilight Zone* episode which flashed two twentieth-century women into Rowlandson's community at the time of her release from captivity, the most stimulating class experience thus far has been the movement to the "great wilderness," as the class was led around the campus in wonder, doubt, and in a state of experiential captivity. In the ensuing class discussion about the project (which is the final requirement of this assignment), students articulated their feelings about Rowlandson's narrative, directing most of their responses toward her graphically physical descriptions, conditions, and survival techniques in the wilderness. Recognizing the possibilities of Puritan censorship with this woman's story, they questioned how much she wrote and what material was erased by her editors. The final authority, they contended as a class, was the physicality of her text, her body which signified the drama and expanded the gender boundaries of her Puritan culture. That is, while her words and spiritual exegesis might have been edited, erased or even created by the male ministers surrounding Rowlandson and her spiritual autobiography, she nevertheless told *her* story of captivity and survival through the lines of her body, the physical description which only she could relay with authority:

> The portion of some is to have their Affliction by drops, now one drop and then another; but the dregs of the Cup, the wine of astonishment, like a sweeping rain that leaveth no food, did the Lord prepare to be my portion. Affliction I wanted, and Affliction I had, full measure, (I thought) pressed down and running over. (Rowlandson 65)

It was this narrative strategy, I realized, which evoked such a theatrical and quite physical group project. And the performance of such a "mistress-piece" did not end with this woman's text.

On the day the class was to analyze and discuss "The Travel Diary of Elizabeth House Trist: Philadelphia to Natchez, 1783–84" the creative project's group had left "marching orders" (on tawny, old paper) for us in the classroom. Walking in Trist's footsteps, we were to descend the hill yonder (Hellems Hall steps), go out the doorway and head north, where we encountered "Thomas Jefferson" in costume, standing by a large tent set up in the campus's North Quad. Once we were seated on the lawn, Jefferson told us that he'd asked Elizabeth House Trist to keep a record of her journey (keeping in mind his plans for the Louisiana Purchase). Out of the tent came "Betsy" with her diary, followed by Lewis and Clark with their huge book (their "manly" record, as they said, denoting the stereotypes of gender and genre in diary literature). In this performance, Betsy would first read her description of a place in the American frontier, and then Lewis and Clark would follow by reading their account of the same place, although recorded nineteen years later. As the class watched these narratives come to life through their peers' enactments, they, too, heard the differences in the writing styles: while Elizabeth Trist wrote about the land, its colors and the feelings evoked by places as well as the people and the cultural differences she encountered, Lewis and Clark's accounts, the students remarked, seemed much less poetic, less peopled, less cultural and more geometric. In this performance of body and text, students recognized how this woman's narrative, much more inclusive of others around her, had been erased for over 200 years because of the dismissal of "her-story." And, the project's group had gone to quite a lot of work to accomplish this end: they had carefully read Trist's journal; investigated her life, family and connections to Jefferson; and then read Lewis and Clark's accounts to reach some sort of comparative analysis. The performance evolved from their own research journey. As they noted, the group felt compelled to bring these gendered differences to life for the class.

Upon reading Harriet Ann Jacobs' *Incidents in the Life of a Slave Girl*, the designated group transformed the classroom into a gala New Year's Eve celebration. We were told to celebrate with hats and noisemakers, given to us as we entered the room, and then to proceed with the countdown. At the stroke of our imagined midnight, joyous shouts resonating everywhere, the group ripped down the sign reading "Happy New Year" quite violently, revealing another underneath which read "Slave Auction," thus illuminating Jacobs' recorded memories of this terrible day in slave history. A slave auction ensued, in which the group decided arbitrarily to auction all blonde-haired people in the room. Briefly forced onto an auction block and evaluated according to their appearances, these specified students admitted feeling distressed and uncomfortable, but the next scene proved to be even more unnerving. The group had constructed an actual crawl space, modelled after the one Jacobs describes living in for seven years of her life to escape slavery under the hands of Dr. Flint and yet remain on her homeland to watch her children grow through the small eyehole in the wall. A student in the class volunteered to go in this space, while a group member read Jacobs' discomforting descriptions of an extremely hot, rat- and bug-infested, claustrophobic, and nearly paralyzing existence. The student lasted only three minutes in this space and then broke out.

Finally, taken from so many more examples, the group interpreting Maxine Hong Kingston's *The Woman Warrior: Memoirs of a Girlhood Among Ghosts* had the class enter a darkened room and sit on the floor in silence. In this space, the group members then proceeded to shine flashlights on their faces as they read passages from Kingston's fictional autobiography, signifying the many "ghosts" of her life and the many voices which make up her multifaceted character in the narrative. Quite effectively, this group captured the mood and tone of this story in their shades of darkness and light, performing the ghosts as well as the plurivocality of this Chinese American woman's story.

In each of these projects, which have taken place during the last two years of teaching "Masterpieces of American Literature," students have been moved to performance specifically when interpreting women's stories. Why, I wondered theoretically, were they responding in such a way, the classroom evolving and transforming into a performance space? What gender considerations might there be in this paradigm and praxis? And finally, what critical advantages were surfacing through the inclusion of such women's narratives in the American literary canon?

Women's Writing and Performance Theory

At the onset of my theoretical investigation, I recognized that a striking similarity among these women's narratives is their very physicality. That is, the women's autobiographical texts clearly highlight the physical experiences of these women, depicting their actions, movements, and corporeal transformations. While some may argue that this interpretation resorts to the traditional Aristotelian binary framework, which sets up men in relation to the mind and spirit and women to the body, I would argue that it is not quite that simple. The body, as Adrienne Rich writes, is a "resource" for women—not a negative result of Judeo-Christian dualism but rather an integral element of wholeness and *humanity*. The feminist vision, she writes, will "come to view our physicality as a resource rather than a destiny. In order to live a fully human life, we require not only control of our bodies . . . we must touch the unity and resonance of our physicality, the corporeal ground of our intelligence" (*Of Woman Born* 62).

Looking at the emphatic bodily movements and progressions of these texts, ranging from Mary Rowlandson's captivity and survival to Trist's travel adventures to Jacobs' physical liberation and Kingston's physical ghosts, one begins to decipher the ways in which women write their bodies as the final authorized "voice" of intelligence; the movement reflects their stories of transformation, in a world where their identities have been either appropriated or silenced. We must realize that for centuries past, these female voices across racial and class lines have been controlled, censored, edited or erased, and that diary literature was once their only sphere of expression. With so many "bodyguards" around them, these women could write their narratives privately, elaborating on their "resourceful" experience as women, their performances both within and without the social construction of "woman."

In an essay titled "Performative Acts and Gender Constitution," Judith Butler posits that gender constitution and identity are due to a person's repeated, corporeal acts. She writes that the body becomes the site of possibilities and change, the locus where the historical idea of "woman" and the self-styled performance of gender possibilities meet and interact and create new identities:

> One is not simply a body, but, in some very key sense, one does one's body and, indeed, one does one's body differently from one's contemporaries and from one's embodied predecessors and successors as well. (272)

I would argue that women's autobiographical literature has always been an extended site of corporeal performance, a private body without bodyguards, a place to write, create and concomitantly preserve their female voices for future generations. As Butler writes, the elemental structures of "embodiment," of doing one's gender, are "to do, to dramatize, [and] to reproduce." Applying this performance theory to women's writing, the site of expression and of *doing* one's gender constitution and identity, it is possible to re-vision the interstices of gender, race and class in American literature. Such "mistress-pieces," I would argue—for lack of a better term—must be given an equal space in the canon in order to give students a much more complete picture of what has always been so safeguarded as literary *his*-story.

I have realized through this theoretical investigation and analysis that women's autobiographical writings inspire the dynamic of experiential learning in the classroom because they are themselves corporeal projects and sites of performance. As critical texts of American literature, they offer unlimited possibilities for revitalizing history and literary analysis, expanding definitions of "woman" and "other" in America, and ultimately inviting readers to take an active, performative part in bringing the literature to life and action once more. Looking at theoretical studies of women's autobiographies, there could be a myriad of reasons for this interpretive, dynamic response in the classroom. In particular, psychoanalytic studies of women's relational patterns and the ways in which they write in and through relationship to others as well as to themselves might inspire some fruitful lines of pedagogical inquiry (see, for example, Carol Gilligan, Nancy Chodorow, and Judith V. Jordan and Janet L. Surrey). Although the space of this essay cannot deal with these ideas thoroughly, it is certainly meant to offer some new information in relation to these innovative and quite provocative texts in the classroom.

In "Reading Ourselves: Towards a Feminist Theory of Reading," Patricinio P. Schweickart explores the activity of reading and incorporates women into this once predominantly male-centered study. Analyzing Elaine Showalter's study of "gynocritics," which focuses on women as writers, Schweickart then carries this investigation over to the study of women as readers. In considering feminist criticism about reading and its ultimate imperative, Schweickart writes:

> The point is not merely to interpret literature in various ways; the point is to *change the world*. We cannot afford to ignore the activity of reading, for it is here that literature is realized as *praxis*. Literature acts on the world by acting on its readers. (24)

This discussion ultimately recounts Adrienne Rich's experience of reading and writing about Emily Dickinson's poetry. Rich, we are told, went to Dickinson's home in Amherst, and her writing represents a subjective, personal reading of the nineteenth-century poet: "Here [in Dickinson's bedroom] I become again, an insect, vibrating at the frames of windows, clinging to the panes of glass, trying to connect" (*On Lies* 161).The text, for Rich and for feminist readers, is not an object but rather another subjectivity, an embodiment to meet, a voice to hear, an identity with which/whom to *connect*. As Schweickart notes, the whole paradigm of reading literature must shift, so that mainstream reader-response theories, preoccupied with control issues of the textual object, can re-vision the subjectivity of the author, whereby the act of reading will be "defined by the drive 'to connect,' rather than . . . the drive to get it right" (38). This re-visioning, I would suggest, is critical to our profession, as we strive to facilitate the meetings between students and the many different voices or subjectivities of our American literary heritage.

These women's narratives have offered a great deal to my classroom, representing sites of performance, of unlimited possibilities, and of connection and experiential learning. The students have found this literature to be refreshing, "untraditionally inspirational," and, most importantly, sites of resistance to hegemony and institutionalized identity. With my expansion of the canon and the inclusion of many more voices, students' awareness of and identification with literature has been enhanced. As I have witnessed in my pedagogical experiences, they have *only* learned *more* from such marginalized, multicultural, and quite corporeal projects, from their own interpretation of these unburied voices, and thus they have learned more about reading themselves.

WORKS CITED

Bennett, Paula. "Canons to Right of Them." Rev. of *The Heath Anthology*, ed. Paul Lauter. *The Women's Review of Books*, September 1991: 15–16.

Butler, Judith. "Performative Acts and Gender Constitution: An Essay in Phenomenology and Feminist Theory." *Performing Feminisms: Feminist Critical Theory and Theatre*. Ed. Sue-Ellen Case. Baltimore: Johns Hopkins UP, 1990. 270–282.

Chodorow, Nancy. *The Reproduction of Mothering: Psychoanalysis and the Sociology of Gender*. Berkeley: U of California P, 1978.

Gilligan, Carol. *In a Different Voice: Psychological Theory and Women's Development*. Cambridge: Harvard UP, 1982.

Jacobs, Harriet Ann. *Incidents in the Life of a Slave Girl: Written by Herself.* Cambridge: Harvard UP, 1987.

Jordan, Judith V., and Janet L. Surrey. "The Self-in-Relation: Empathy and the Mother-Daughter Relationship." *The Psychology of Today's Women: New Psychoanalytic Visions*. Eds. Toni Bernay and Dorothy W. Cantor. Hillsdale, NJ: Analytic P, 1986.

Kingston, Maxine Hong. *The Woman Warrior: Memoirs of a Girlhood Among Ghosts*. NY: Vintage, 1975.

Pollitt, Katha. "Canon to the Right of Me." *The Nation*, 23 September, 1991: 328–332.

Rich, Adrienne. *Of Woman Born: Motherhood as Experience and Institution*. NY: W. W. Norton, 1977.

———. *On Lies, Secrets, and Silence: Selected Prose, 1966–1978*. NY: W. W. Norton, 1979.

Robinson, Lillian S. "Canons to Left of Them." Rev. of *Canons and Contexts* , by Paul Lauter. *The Women's Review of Books*, September 1991: 18–19.

Rowlandson, Mary. "A True History of the Captivity and Restoration of Mrs. Mary Rowlandson." *Journeys in New Worlds: Early American*

Women's Narratives. Ed. William L. Andrews. Madison: The U of Wisconsin P, 1990. 27–65.

Schweickart, Patricinio P. "Reading Ourselves: Toward a Feminist Theory of Reading." *Speaking of Gender*. Ed. Elaine Showalter. NY: Routledge, 1989. 17–44.

Trist, Elizabeth House. "The Travel Diary of Elizabeth House Trist: Philadelphia to Natchez, 1783–84." *Journeys in New Worlds: Early American Women's Narratives*. Ed. William L. Andrews. Madison: U of Wisconsin P, 1990. 201–232.

Sharing Responsibility for American Lit
"A Spectacular and Dangerous World of Choice"

Anne L. Bower

For many of those who theorize about the teaching of literature, the main concern is to create a theoretically sound basis from which to teach majors and graduate students. But I believe it is equally important that our introductory literature survey courses grow out of a pedagogy that centralizes questions of how a national literature is defined and redefined, how it shapes our culture and therefore our lives, and how we, in turn, shape the literature. To this end, I have tried to create a survey course that asks students to share the responsibility for American Literature.

At the first meeting of English 290: Introduction to American Literature, thirty plus sophomores (with a smattering of students from other years) are glancing over the syllabus. I can see the brows wrinkling. I know they're wondering why we're going backward, starting with a novel written in 1987 and ending with seventeenth-century material. They must be curious also as to exactly what we'll be reading—except for the two novels specified, all the course outline reveals is that during particular weeks we'll read materials selected from different time blocks. Now I see some heads shake. That means they've either discovered that although this is a literature survey course it entails considerable writing, or it means they've reached the section explaining who will select our shorter readings: poems, short stories, essays, pieces of autobiographies, etc. In authoritative black and white they read that it will be them—the students—who select the bulk of our texts. And now they're reading that they'll also have responsibilities for leading class discussion of their selections. Oh dear. For some that is a terrifying prospect (and perhaps even cause to consider dropping the course). And then we begin talking about how American Literature is selected and sequenced in the academic world. Under objectives, the course syllabus states that "students will gain new appreciation for and knowledge of American Literature, giving thought to what the term defines—both the 'American' and the 'Literature' parts of the term." Throughout the ten-week quarter we'll return to questioning how a body of texts becomes "American Literature" and what that means.

Expanding a literary canon only begins the necessary process of investigating what teaching and learning literature is all about. On its own, as Paul Lauter explains, adding new writers to the canon doesn't really change much. Such action equals "altering the hand-me-downs, not stitching a new suit" (8). I want, using Lauter's metaphor, an introduction to American Literature that allows students to handle the stuff, coordinate the colors, see the choices of patterns, and learn to stitch new suits or dresses or overalls or evening gowns. You might say I want them to break free also of fashion's dictates and become more independent and creative in deciding what to wear when. If students continue to think of literature as selected and arranged and therefore owned by others, then the capacities for critical reading developed in the literature class are applied to capital-L literature, and seldom extend beyond the classroom. A pedagogy that allows the students and me to make many and various kinds of connections between who we are and what we read, who we are and what the authority systems under which we live have had us read in the past, can allow us to see what Gayatri Spivak calls "the idols of the mind" (31). For Spivak, an "*idolatry* of reading," with the usually concurrent "self-idolatry of the privileged reader," maintains separateness between "the verbal and the social text." As if literature were in one box and our lives in another. And I do believe that because capital-L literature has been so often presented as an "other," as a set of hallowed, difficult, "deep" texts owned by teachers and critics and scholars, students have found it not merely irrelevant but, worse, unpleasurable and intimidating.

Like Jane Tompkins, "I have come to think more and more that what really matters as far as our own beliefs and projects for change are concerned is not so much what we talk about in class as what we do" (656). "Do." So long as the instructor does the bulk of structuring, discussing, and devising assignments, students—be they reluctant readers or literature lovers—take the role of consumers. Since I'm trying to introduce the concept that American Literature is something we create, I need a classroom methodology in which the students "do" American Literature. After all, "the classroom is a microcosm of the world; it is the chance we have to practice whatever ideals we may cherish. The kind of classroom situation one creates is the acid test of what it is one really stands for" (Tompkins 656). So I must seek a pedagogy that encourages the students' creative interaction with American Literature and culture through their active participation, combining my expertise with theirs in an interplay of different voices, levels of experience, subcultures, and attitudes. Lauter, too, asks those of us discontented with our earlier courses and teaching strategies to consider "whether the very dynamics of classrooms promote or forbid change" (267).

The course I am going to describe was devised to cope not only with an expanding canon, but with particular circumstances—some difficult and some beneficial. So, although I think what follows displays a pedagogy founded on valid theoretical principles, in no way can I say it will work for everyone. Ohio State-Marion is a two-year branch of an immense state university. "Main" campus sets most of the curricular and administrative policies that guide the "extended" campuses. Thus: Introduction to American Literature, a sophomore-level survey course, was established as a *one quarter* course; no one could offer it as a multiquarter course or drastically limit the period covered in the one quarter-survey.[1] Ten weeks to introduce all of American Lit. That is a special, difficult condition. It made me desperate. As if someone said, "Here's a full orchestra, now set it up to perform in a closet." As I tried to pare down and down and down the number of selections we could read, from the earliest to the most recent texts, it became clear to me that if only I selected this sampling, then the course, by rights, should be called "Anne Bower's American Literature." Should my feminist principles favor a female-weighted or carefully gender-balanced selection? Should a sociohistoricist angle stress texts having to do with class and race conflict? Was it more valid to look at figures squelched or figures elevated by the literary scholars of various eras?

Suddenly a totally new idea (which of course means that it's old to someone else) came to me: What if I were to let the students participate in choosing our selections? Choices wouldn't range entirely free of course. We have to order our textbooks well ahead of each quarter. So I decided to order an anthology containing a good range of material from which the students could select our readings (right now we use the third shorter edition of *The Norton Anthology of American Literature*, edited by Nina Baym et al). My authority would be exerted in choosing the two novels we could read, and I would also allow myself to choose a few of our shorter selections, working to pick underrepresented genres or populations. (For instance, as it turns out, students are frequently less confident about poetry than prose; if they had complete control, some quarters would see our course nearly poetry-less.) Students would be offered instruction—in the classroom and through conferences—on how to select a text and how to present it.

What could happen with such a situation? We might have a course without Henry James. Without Emerson. Without Hemingway. Or, nearer and dearer to my own heart, without Edith Wharton or Gwendolyn Brooks or Kate Chopin. What if a daring student wanted to add a selection not in the anthology (and presumably xerox us all copies at his or her own expense)— some science fiction, or part of a mystery, or some Stephen King? Would such a course still be "Introduction to American Literature"? Could I live with it? Lauter asks, "How do we decide what to include in a course or in an anthology? Once we recognize that the answer to that question is not foreordained by God, the curriculum committee, or even the Norton anthology, a spectacular and dangerous world of choice opens before us" (101–02). But it's not just the choice, it's the choosing.

Somehow it has seemed more than right to enter this dangerous world. The people I teach at Ohio State University-Marion are mostly first-generation college students; in an average classroom about a third of them will be "nontraditional," that is, returning to higher education after three to twenty years out of the system. Their years of living, working, and reading benefit and enrich the classroom. And since our classes tend to be of manageable size (usually twenty-five to thirty-five students in an introductory literature class) and now mostly meet for periods over one hour, we can foster discussion as a classroom mode. Also, because the university provides decent teaching loads for most of us, instructors can arrange to meet with students individually or in small groups, where assignments can be negotiated and revision work practised. Almost all of these students hold part-time or full-time jobs, and many have families as well. That condition hampers our work; their time for homework, after-class discussions, research, and student-teacher conferences is seriously limited.

These students' personal backgrounds seem to make them skeptical of capital-C culture; in their varying life and work experiences they have practised a variety of reading strategies (including "reading the world," as Spivak puts it in an essay by the same name) and evolved complex attitudes towards authority. They come to post-secondary education for a range of reasons, often vocational, but often also spurred by a desire to seek new connections and values. My students' TV, music, comic books, magazines, newspapers, movies are the "textual" representations with which they are most familiar. Usually they want to expand the academy's more traditional definition of "Culture," while they also want to feel more comfortable with the academy and its standards. They seem at home with the idea that defining American Literature contributes to defining Americanness, and that these acts of definition are as important for what they tell about the process of defining as what they tell about the product defined.

Conditions at other institutions, both negative and positive, may influence the applicability of much of my methodology to others' teaching. However, I hope that the underlying principles can be adapted to a variety of situations.

No matter what our circumstances, a new pedagogy for an expanding canon of American Literature must address at least four elements: (1) the primary texts students will read and how to select them; (2) the order in which to present or sequence those texts; (3) the best ways to work with the texts; and (4) the nature of the students' own production of texts. Because my own methodology stresses student actions and choices, my survey course responds to those four prompts this way: (1) Students, using a variety of choosing techniques suggested on the syllabus, will select over half of what we read, drawing primarily on a bounteous anthology, but with the option of going outside that collection. (2) In order to a) begin with what is familiar and move then to less familiar literary styles and modes and b) get away from constricting and inadequate notions of literary periods, the course will move from the present to the past. (3) Each student will have responsibilities regarding the text he or she has selected, making the reading assignment, devising any homework that will lead to better classroom discussion, and leading that discussion. The instructor's role will shift among discussant, discussion leader, facilitator of or consultant to small group practices, and lecturer. (4) Students will have a variety of options for writing assignments, to encourage them to find alternative ways of producing texts that effectively interact with the selections of American Literature they read. Thinking about and planning each of these elements brings into play the relationships among the instructor, the students, the primary texts to be studied, the various secondary texts used by students and instructors, and the institutional setting in which the class takes place. As a result, devising a new pedagogy calls up questions of authority.

During the first few sessions of my American Lit survey, considerable discussion centers on how each student will select a particular text for inclusion in the course, how to create a useful homework assignment for it, and how to lead us in productive discussion. Since they are also reading a contemporary novel (the first quarter it was *In Country* by Bobby Ann Mason; currently, I'm using Toni Morrison's *Beloved*) and discussing it and responding to homework assignments I design, I can use ongoing classroom practices to illustrate possible approaches to a text. Those truly stymied by having to select a text can meet with me privately; a conference often helps them see possibilities they overlooked, finding ways to connect their own lives, past education, work experience, personal backgrounds, or interests in topical issues to a piece of literature. During these early meetings, and again at the course's conclusion as we reflect on our work, discussions often lead us to investigate the makeup of our anthology; students sometimes bring in others they have at home, and I bring in some from my office. Because they are working with the anthology in a way new to them, with heightened awareness of what's in and what's out, the concept of an editorial policy (and how that comes to be) becomes meaningful to them. The students thus begin to realize the constructed nature of a national literature.

By the end of the course's third week, I've sorted out students' choices, made a few selections of my own, and printed and distributed our reading list. When I say, "This is the reading list for your American Literature class," pointing out some of the inclusions and exclusions that have surprised me, students can appreciate the unique nature of "their" syllabus. The first time I taught the course this way the works selected for 1914–1945 were Gwendolyn Brooks' "The Mother," Katherine Ann Porter's "The Fig Tree," Thomas Wolfe's "The Lost Boy," William Carlos Williams' "The Widow's Lament" and "In Springtime," Faulkner's "Spotted Horses," pieces of Hart Crane's "The Bridge," Fitzgerald's "Winter Dreams," and Langston Hughes' "Dream Variations and "Song for a Dark Girl."

These are not the selections I would necessarily have made myself. It hurt to see Hurston go by the board. Wolfe was someone I, like most of my colleagues, had ignored, even denigrated. But these choices all had sound bases. The young woman who chose "The Fig Tree" did so because she wanted to read work by more women and had not yet been introduced to Porter. Another was attracted to Wolfe because someone (she couldn't remember who) had extravagantly praised Wolfe's voluminous novels. But she also picked this particular story because it dealt with childhood loss and death, both of which were central to her own emotional growth at this particular time. Then, too, she liked the repetitive language. "Spotted Horses" appealed to a student because, as someone born in the south, she loved the way Faulkner handled southern dialect and conversational style. Another appeal of the story was that she thought our study of American Literature ought to include humor. The Fitzgerald short story was picked by a student who had read *The Great Gatsby* and wanted to read more by this author. As a lover of early twentieth-century history, this young man was also fascinated by the sociohistorical background of Fitzgerald's work. Instructions on the syllabus had encouraged those different ways of connecting to a text.

When I began asking students to select texts, I underrated their integrity and interest, fearing that many would pick a text because it was short or because they had already worked with it in high school. Of course, a certain amount of that kind of "base pragmatism" (Lauter's term, though he is applying it to weaknesses in professional selection systems [102]) may still operate beneath the articulated statements of interest and connection students present to me and their classmates in introducing a text.[2] But I have consistently found that students, given time, advice, and trust—create fine rationales for their literary selections.

The second time I taught the course, when we came to this time period, the choices were somewhat different. Fitzgerald's "Winter Dreams" remained, but the man who chose it focused more on Fitzgerald's life and how that related to the story than on the story's sociohistorical context. We read Faulkner again, but a different selection, "A Rose for Emily," with the student leader asking us to look in detail at the author's use of time. We read two short William Carlos Williams poems ("The Red Wheelbarrow" and "Queen Anne's Lace") but also Wallace Stevens' "Thirteen Ways of Looking at a Blackbird." This time, Richard Wright's "The Man Who Was Almost a Man" entered the syllabus, chosen by a young man fascinated by Wright's way of exploring different kinds of violence within such a short fiction. Willa Cather's "Neighbor Rosicky" attracted a "nontraditional" student with interests in rural life and the transmission of values about the land.

On the third round of this course I find that students have for the first time included Hemingway but dropped Faulkner.

Ralph Ellison's "Battle Royal" is favored, and for the first time, Sherwood Anderson's "The Egg" is part of our list. Wolfe's "The Lost Boy" and poems by Langston Hughes and William Carlos Williams are repeats, too. And so it goes. But regardless of the particular choice, as I discover in conference with the students as they seek advice and strategies for their class leadership role, the act of choosing gives students a sense of ownership and responsibility in regard to the selected texts.

More than the creation of "relevance," as we used to call it in bygone decades, justifies the time this survey course gives to the act of choosing reading materials. Pointing out the enormous "knowledge explosion" that confronts us, Gregory Ulmer realizes that we need to focus our attention on "the relation between the student and knowledge" (Ulmer 61). Ulmer's main concern is with those who have already entered "the discipline": English majors and graduate students. But undergraduate general students also deserve epistemological insights into academia.

> As it is now, only a select few, after passing through years of replicating the known and of being socialized into discipline loyalty, are allowed to learn the actual nature of a discursive field, allowed to see its frame: the inner "mystery" of any discipline is not its order or coherence but its disorder, incoherence, and arbitrariness. (Ulmer 61–2)

The kind of classroom practice that Ulmer wants "permits the student to . . . confront simultaneously the provisional, permeable character of all knowledge, the creative 'ground' . . . of the formation of a discipline" (Ulmer 62). A pedagogy that depends upon student participation even in the very selection of texts and assignments will begin exposing to them the discipline's "frame."

However, given the many methods my students use to select texts, it is legitimate to ask what overall framework can emerge in this course. From a pedagogy created out of so many different interests and approaches will "disorder, incoherence, and arbitrariness" result as the only structure students find? Throughout *Professing Literature*, Gerald Graff reminds us that some theory (stated or unstated) always underpins the selecting and sequencing of course material, whether originating in departmental politics, ideas of progress and patriotism, or self-aggrandizing needs for status within one's discipline. "Unresolved conflict being just the sort of thing a democratic educational system should thrive on," he'd like to see such conflicts "part of the context of the average student's education [and] the average professor's professional life" (6). When we juxtapose texts largely picked by students, conflicts preselected by the instructor will not focus discussion. You cannot plan a course around race or gender or class conflicts when you don't know what texts that course will contain. Will a student-selected amalgam of reading materials therefore lack coherence, body, form? Can it be more than just a Whitman's sampler of four centuries of writing identified now as "American"?

Clearly, the question of a literature course's organization is as important as the course's basic material: what kind of "periodization" should one observe, what "themes" might link selections, which "conflicts" best focus textual and contextual differences and similarities? Gregory Jay suggests that our pedagogy should "replace the idealist paradigm with a geographical and historical one." Looking at what he terms "writing in the United States," he would have us and our students consider "writing committed within and during the colonization, establishment, and ongoing production of the US as a physical, sociopolitical, and multicultural event, including those writings that resist and critique its identification with nationalism" (264). Acting from a similar concern with the idea of literary categories, Lauter finds that "conventional definitions of periods in American literature . . . shape significantly the ways in which we think about culture, emphasizing works that fit given frameworks, obscuring those which do not" (Lauter 36–37). But also like Jay, he abhors the notion of studying literary texts in a "historical void" (37).[3]

In thinking about this question of categories—which is, after all, the question of how we sequence and frame as well as select material—my main contribution is to keep students aware that there is nothing "natural" about a course's structure; each element is constructed; some real person makes each decision. Who controls the vision of your national literature presented in an introductory survey course? To whose belief systems and agendas will it conform?

Putting together a course is fun. Usually an instructor defines particular frameworks and themes that bring into focus the issues and voices he or she most values among the concerns of diverse persons writing in the United States. And really, there's nothing wrong with a particular professor putting his or her spin on a course in American Lit, as long as that person explains how this spin was derived and lets students know that it is not the only way the literary top can hum. But I want the students to participate in the fun of constructing the course—the delight of making connections, along with the hard work of not obscuring separations. The pedagogical model evolving in my American Literature survey takes as basic that the texts produced by a large, diverse population over a period of centuries can be systematized many many ways, and that any thematic system will necessarily skew students towards thinking of the country's literature as participating in and/or growing out of a limited number of "movements," "national ideas," "influences," or "patterns." My view is that while certain concerns may *seem* uppermost at a given moment, they may actually only be of central concern to a limited number of people, probably the people who hold most power in the society at that moment. For instance, while "exploration" or "new frontiers" may seem to encompass much literature of the nineteenth century (and this was the way it was first presented to me as a college student), that category leaves out or distorts texts that primarily explore domestic relationships, present and solve mysteries, or figure an outcast's attempts to fit into an existing city society.

Fortunately, the anthology I use does not attach value-laden labels to eras. While Baym and her coeditors do supply introductory material before the selections in "Early American Literature 1620–1820" and the other time-marked groupings, time blocks alone mark off the materials. Since my course begins in the present and works backward, and since we always have too much to read anyway, I do not assign the introductory material. Rather, each time we move back into another time-marked group of texts, we stop to consider what was happening in the world of the authors writing then. Using collective brainstorming or general discussion, we place ourselves among the wars, immigrations and migrations, natural disasters, art exhibits, technologies, popular songs, educational institutions, scientific discoveries, businesses, concerts, headline news, weather, etc. that formed the world of these writers. We then can investigate our own preconceptions of a category like "American Literature between the Wars, 1914–1945." Thus, the course does not experience an "historical void," but the periodization of history and literature is somewhat "denaturalized," its framework something we build—faults, gaps, overemphases, and all.

Because the course materials are variable, different strands of significance emerge and are then picked up at various points in this course; one of my functions is to keep track of what's coming into our conversation or tapestry and point out reoccurrences or similarities if they are not being noticed. However, the novel I pick to start off our exploration of American Literature does set a particular tone. Because, for instance, of their initial exposure to *Beloved*, one of my American Lit classes often brought discussion of later texts back to issues central to their discussion of Morrison's novel: the enduring presence of racial conflict; different ways of defining freedom; "realism," the interplay of fiction and history, alternative religious/spiritual systems; and gender issues (as related to characters and authors). However, a class that started off with a novel concerning effects of the Vietnam war, Bobbie Ann Mason's *In Country*, moved along different paths. As they read other works, that group often focused on the idea of being true to one's self and one's personal values but also being loyal to one's community; personal and social freedoms; the use of art to reveal special qualities of individuals and groups, places, events.

Teaching this American Literature survey, I have found that rather than preset major themes according to one's own or another's authority, rather than predetermine for the students the big issues in American Literature, one can productively allow the students themselves to enter into relationship with formulating central issues. Periodically, I draw the students' attention to this aspect of our communal work. For instance, in a class in which we had discussions of Hawthorne's "Young Goodman Brown" (1835), a section from *Narrative of the Life of Frederick Douglass* (1845), and Poe's "The Raven" (1845), a wrapup exercise asked students to briefly write down what this group of writings tells us about America, American Literature, or literature. Each person read the written response aloud: One student thought each text struggled in some way with an idea of freedom; another found each one an expression of loneliness or confusion; one asserted that all three selections propounded a message—that is, she generalized that all literature provides a site of instruction; and still another focused on the variety of forms used by different American writers. One student concluded that American Literature was American because it showed such a variety of different cultures and experiences; another expressed the idea that there is no one "American" experience; another that these were more different than similar, proving that really the main thing they shared was merely the nationality of the authors. Such an exercise forced us all to acknowledge that there is no one way to summarize the relationship of these three selections.

My experience has been that the students themselves, although often wanting to oversynthesize material, will align and realign the works read in American Literature, discovering for themselves paradigms with which to structure a sense of their national literature.[4] Gregory Jay believes this should not be left to chance; he "advocate[s] courses in which the materials are chosen for the ways in which they *actively interfere* with each other's experiences, languages, and values and for their power to expand the horizon of the student's cultural literacy to encompass peoples he or she has scarcely acknowledged as real" (274, emphases his). Chance actually operates pretty well: the odd juxtapositions that occur from students selecting texts provide unforetold opportunities for cross-textual disruption.

At least a week before the student's selected text will be discussed, that student meets with me in conference. He or she has read the text (and usually the introductory information supplied by the anthology editors) and comes to my office with some ideas. Some students have already identified a question, problem, or technique in this text which they wish the class to work with. Thus, a student who had selected Stephen Crane's "The Blue Hotel" knew right away that he wanted to assign the class two questions to answer. These were questions that jumped off the page for him, one about form and style, the other about content: (1) What is the function of repetition in the story? (2) Is this a story about American attitudes towards immigrants? In the conference he and I went over the story, first looking at the different kinds of repetition and then at whether or not the story ironized or underscored stereotypes about immigrants. I gave the student a bit of historical information about immigration patterns and conflicts. When it came time for his text, the student asked his classmates to read out some of their answers to his two questions; it turned out that collectively we had quite a bit to say on both questions. Then the student-leader moved the discussion to the relationship between the story's form and content.

Other students only come up with a discussion starter/focus after considerable probing. A young woman who wanted us to read Bryant's "The Prairies" at first seemed to think it important that we know more about the history and ecology of American prairies. She and I went across the hall to the Prairie Office (Ohio State–Marion nurtures a small prairie on the campus) to learn more; she borrowed a video; I wondered if she would end up taking us onto the prairie acreage. Instead, she decided to use a creative approach. Her homework assignment was that we each write a paragraph imagining what we could see and feel, were we standing in the middle of a pre-1800 prairie. Many of the resulting descriptions and reactions formed sharp contrasts, both to Bryant's own progressivist, manifest-destiny attitude and to each other's assumptions about the prairies.

In spite of our conferences, not all students produce stimulating assignments nor can all of them spark effective discussions. At times, comments from discussion leaders and participants can be superficial, poorly thought out, naive, or repetitive. However, more of the time, both the assignments and the discussions excite and actively involve most of those in the classroom. Other teachers who share classroom leadership with their students agree. By having her students take on much more responsibility for presenting material, Tompkins has discovered a livelier, more engaged classroom in which she can listen but still contribute intensely to the group's discussion (657). "It's true that in some cases the students don't deal with the material as well as I could, but that is exactly why they need to do it" (657), she decides. Tompkins is referring to graduate students, students who plan to profess literature. For them it is essential to "polish" their analytic and presentational skills (657). I contend that all students—whether future engineers or second-grade teachers, doctors or stock brokers, personnel officers, textile designers, or literature professors—will derive benefits from increasing their analytic and presentational skills. At the same time, by taking such an active role in the literature classroom, they will have new ways of seeing their own relationship to their national culture.

The literature survey classes designed on the main campus of my institution do not require much writing, partly because the sections are often very large. However, one of the advantages of teaching at a regional campus is that the smaller class size allows the instructors time to read more student work. Frequent and varied writing assignments allow students to increase their analytic and synthetic thinking skills, their expressiveness, their verbal facility, and their "textual author-ity," to use Sharon Crowley's term. Since few of the students in a literature survey class will become literature majors, it makes little sense to train them in strictly literary research. Rather, in their brief homework assignments, short papers, examinations, and course project I offer them a number of options to encourage exploration of different ways of producing texts.

In one section of the American Lit survey I assigned three mini-papers (two to three typed, double-spaced pages), shaping options for each assignment which allowed the students to engage different aspects of their own aesthetic, ethical, historical, and analytic processes. For instance, for the first mini-paper, four possibilities existed:

1. In our discussion of *In Country* we may have missed an issue that really matters to you. State the issue clearly and then discuss why you think it is central to the novel, why this issue matters to you, and what happened to

our discussion because we left it out or only touched it lightly.

2. Write a poem modeled on any in the section of our text called "American Poetry Since 1945" and explain why you chose this particular poem. Discuss as well what happened to you when you wrote your poem—how did it add to your ideas about the poem in the text?

3. Choose a poem from the "American Poetry Since 1945" section—one that we haven't discussed in class—and explain carefully what the poem means to you and how you achieve this meaning.

4. Other? If you have a different topic in mind that would work for a two–page paper concerning recent literature, ask me about it. You need my approval; I want to be sure that you aren't attempting too much and that your topic is on target for this section of the course.

Quite a few students chose #4, particularly those who enjoyed (or felt most confident with) research projects. They might explore historical, biographical, or other background to a text or investigate critical responses to it. Having a variety of approaches is no "trick" to make students feel good because they have a choice. Rather, it is a clear demonstration that all of these kinds of writing equally validate the student as writer and as thinker-about-texts.

In the same way, when it comes time to create a major project, the students must take considerable responsibility for choosing their own topics. The options suggested attempt to echo the variety of approaches we have used in discussing texts and to continue our multileveled conversation about what American Literature is and does. In a handout, I suggest that "the project can incorporate research, creative writing, personal experience, information from other courses or from activities outside the university." I give examples of possible topics that might involve them in writing additional sections of plays or fiction, creating musical accompaniment or illustrations for a text, performing research on an artistic technique or historical context, writing lesson plans for a story, or arguing for inclusion in our anthology of someone not yet between Norton covers. Students must submit a detailed proposal for my approval; I return these at a conference in which we discuss ways to improve the project.

These kinds of projects yield two wonderful results. First of all, students can write about things that really matter to them, and can often create texts that have lasting value to them. Secondly, the papers, in their variety and sense of engagement, are mostly pleasurable to read and often highly informative. Some examples: A few prospective teachers have written well-thought-out, detailed lesson plans for short stories or poems, including reading assignments, discussion questions, writing assignments, and quizzes. When they move into student teaching as juniors, they will have one "unit" already planned. A recent student, for instance, designed plans for teaching Booker T. Washington's *Up From Slavery* along with Harriet Jacobs' *Incidents in the Life of a Slave Girl*. In the "creative" vein, one student wrote an additional chapter for *In Country*. As a Vietnam veteran, he wanted the novel to tell us more about Emmett's future. His carefully crafted chapter did a surprisingly good job of mimicking Mason's style. Another quarter, a student-writer attempted an extension of *Beloved*, seeking a realistic way towards a "happier" ending. A prospective geography major who wanted a research-type project, mapped the troop movements in Hemingway's *Farewell to Arms*. Another student, a lover of musical theatre, presented a paper arguing that *West Side Story* legitimized musicals as literature. Others have argued for the inclusion in our anthology of particular science fiction writers, believing that genre to have not only great entertainment value, but rich ways of exploring human conflict and changing environments. In each case, because the student's textual production is connected to personal, career, or academic activities already valued, the project/paper extends his or her sense of owning the literature and sense of legitimacy as a critical reader.

In spite of giving students such control of the survey course, I am not willing to cede all my classroom authority. I pick the two novels we'll work with and determine the anthology we use. I create many of their assignments and grade their work. I often stand while they sit; I write on the board (public space), they in their own notebooks (private space). Does such exertion of professorial authority trivialize their participation in creating the course? No. We are *sharing* the responsibility. Students are interested readers and writers, mostly lacking depth of experience and expertise; they need a leader-mentor-facilitator with proven expertise. The classroom becomes a studio or laboratory space where women and men can practice the acts of selecting, sequencing, discussing, and writing about literature—the acts of making their literature. One of my pedagogical goals is that students see themselves as makers of their culture, not just passive consumers (which to me is a sort of victim stance). Another of my goals is that the classroom not replicate hierarchical power structures. As Jane Tompkins sums it up: "What we do in the classroom is our politics. No matter what we may say about Third World this or feminist that, our actions and our interactions with our students week in week out prove what we are for and what we are against in the long run" (660). If I believe that American Literature, or "Writing in the United States" as Jay terms it, truly belongs to and is created by all of us, then my classroom methodology must reflect and enact that standard as much as possible.

In "Deconstruction and Pedagogy," Vincent B. Leitch discusses Roland Barthes' ideas about authority in the classroom as related to deconstructive practice. Barthes explained in a lecture at the Collège de France, when he assumed the Chair of Literary Semiology there, that the discourse of one's teaching transmitted and enacted one's relationship to institutional power and that therefore pedagogical "method can really bear only on the means of loosening, baffling, or at the very least, of lightening this power." He had found that the best way to affect such a "lightening" within the scene of teaching was "digression, or ... *excursion*" (quoted in Leitch 50, emphasis Barthes'). By sharing the leadership role with my students—their individual voices at times leading, all of us joining in chorus or counterpart sometimes, my voice central at moments—I can "lighten" the power of stereotyped concepts of American Literature, of literary study, of the professorate, and of academe. Taking myself out of the spotlight means the students receive greater illumination.

NOTES

1. Happily, members of the English Department at Ohio State (including extended campus faculty) voted that, as of winter quarter 1993, the American Literature survey will extend over two quarters.

2. And my own pragmatism—that dreadful moment when I realized I could not cut this wealth of literary material down to a ten-week course. What of that? The opening of, or attempted opening of, the canon is a theoretical response to our late twentieth-century cultural condition: "Theory is what is generated when some aspect of literature, its nature, its history, its place in society, its conditions of production and reception, its meaning in general, or the meanings of particular works, ceases to be given and becomes a question to be argued in a generalized way" (Graff 252). But theory also includes teaching, which is part of literature's "production and reception," for by selecting and sequencing what is taught as literature, colleges and universities contribute to the "production" of literature by establishing the contexts and methods for reading, talking, and writing about literature. Literature departments and teachers determine much of students' reception of that literature. I agree with Graff that one's awareness of conflicts or controversies within one's field does not have to be repressed before teaching takes place; rather, these tensions can usefully enter into the classroom discussion (260–61).

3. Jay suggests a chronological study that would begin with "native-American expressive traditions and include those narratives produced by the first European explorers and colonizers, Spanish and French as well as English" (269). In using a historical base, he would have us work "in terms of how various cultural groups and their forms have interacted during the nation's ongoing construction" (271). Or one might look at the ways texts have been used in the United States and "the value writings have had for their subjects" (271). Jay also says he'd like to use "a list of problematics whose analysis would put texts from different cultures within the US [sic] into dialogue with one another" (277).

4. As a two-year regional campus we have few or no foreign students, which is why I can so readily name American Literature as the students' national literature. Whether or not their particular kind of Americanness seems to them well represented by what we read is, of course, a topic of value.

WORKS CITED

Baym, Nina et al., eds. *The Norton Anthology of American Literature*. 3rd ed., shorter. NY: Norton, 1989.

Crowley, Sharon. "writing and Writing." *Writing and Reading Differently: Deconstruction and the Teaching of Composition and Literature*. Eds. G. Douglas Atkins and Michael L. Johnson. Lawrence: UP of Kansas, 1985. 93–100.

Graff, Gerald. *Professing Literature: An Institutional History*. Chicago: U of Chicago P, 1987.

Jay, Gregory S. "The End of 'American' Literature: Toward a Multicultural Practice." *College English* 53 (March 1991): 264–81.

Lauter, Paul. *Canons and Contexts*. NY: Oxford UP, 1991.

Leitch, Vincent B. "Deconstruction and Pedagogy." *Theory in the Classroom*. Ed. Cary Nelson. Urbana: U of Illinois P, 1986. 45–56.

Spivak, Gayatri Chakravorty. "Reading the World: Literary Studies in the 1980s." *Writing and Reading Differently: Deconstruction and the Teaching of Composition and Literature*. Eds. G. Douglas Atkins and Michael L. Johnson. Lawrence: UP of Kansas, 1985. 27–37.

Tompkins, Jane. "Pedagogy of the Distressed." *College English* 52 (October 1990): 653–60.

Ulmer, Gregory L. "Textshop for Post(e)pedagogy." *Writing and Reading Differently: Deconstruction and the Teaching of Composition and Literature*. Eds. G. Douglas Atkins and Michael L. Johnson. Lawrence: UP of Kansas, 1985. 38–64.

SECTION THREE

The Teacher as Text:
Rethinking Authority in the Classroom

Making the World Safe for Democracy and the Classroom Safe for Slavery
Teaching America to Americans

Peter Caccavari

When I first thought about what had happened in my American literature survey course at the Douglass campus of Rutgers University in the fall of 1990, I felt confident that I had the answers. It seemed to me that in a course about the United States and democratic society—with an emphasis on slavery, freedom, and the experiences of African Americans—my students had been unable to transform a democratic content into a democratic pedagogy. I was struck by the irony of students studying slavery and its effects while insisting on a sort of master-slave relationship in the classroom where I would provide them with information which they could passively absorb. I wanted to look into how this irony could escape them and why they would want such a learning situation despite the works they had been reading.

My first impulse was to blame the students, to see this problem as a weakness of theirs, not in their character but in their socialization through the education process. For a long time I did not consider that by seeing them as demanding enslavement in the classroom I was foreclosing the possibility of seeing *any* democratic assertion on their part. I assumed that I knew what enslavement and freedom looked like, that, like common sense, they would be apparent to everyone who had eyes to see. But Thomas Paine had to write *Common Sense* precisely because it was *not* readily perceived by all and had to be proposed and argued. I began to question some of my own assumptions about how to interpret my students' responses and my own classroom practice. Although I continue to maintain that my students were asking for a passivity that is counterproductive to learning and contrary to the principles to which they purport to subscribe as citizens of a democratic nation, I have come to recognize some of their resistances as genuinely democratic and my own role as more suspect than it appeared before.

On the first day of my American literature class, I have my students do a short writing assignment where they give their own working definitions of what "literature" is and what "American literature" is. Let me offer some examples of the responses from my Rutgers class:[1] "Literature is a long text that tells a story. It can be fiction or truth. It seems that they are written for entertainment and to strike the emotion and imagination of the reader." "But whatever literature is present, there is always a purpose for it." "Literature is a form of writing which often has a moral to it." "[Literature is] anything written down and compacted to form sentences that tell you something." "Literature is something that withstands the test of time and enables each generation to obtain something within its meaning."

These statements show an awareness of the relevant issues. Literature involves entertainment and instruction (little do they realize their knowledge of Horace). For some, literature deals more with the realm of the emotional than the rational (poems versus manuals), but for others it is the medium which is the defining criterion (both poems and manuals are literature; this statement coming with no awareness of poststructuralism). Or, literature is the result of longevity; as a result of literary Darwinism, Shakespeare becomes Literature while Danielle Steel will become extinct (or at best, literature with a lower-case "l"). Finally, in a phrasing with import for understanding "American" literature, one student thinks that literature encodes cultural identity ("enables each generation to obtain something within its meaning").

Drawing from their experience of reading and making provisional attempts at theorizing that reading (not unlike Aristotle's methodology in the *Poetics*), these students show themselves to be rather sophisticated. When they come to defining "American literature," though, the critical apparatus shows some inadequacies, as seen in the following responses: "American literature is written by American authors during the post-colonial era." "American literature is writing by American authors, which some people think differs from works of literature by authors in other countries. American literature may often focus on particular aspects of America and its history or American people." "American Literature, I assume, is literature that is perhaps born from the American culture. It represents the attitude and tone of American society and is distinguishable from other Literatures because of the heritage and culture of one nation." "American literature is representative of the type of literature prevalent in the American society. I personally find it interesting because I *am* an American and it is certainly more interesting than some English literature I've been exposed to."

In the latter set of definitions, there is still some sophistication in the analysis, to be sure. Colonial American literature is not American literature because a society must be a nation to have a national literature. American literature is qualitatively different from other national literatures. This difference arises from different traditions, histories, and cultures. Because literature reflects the society which produces it, American society must produce an American literature. (This student may find fellow travelers in some New Historicists.) Finally, being American means that the reader has an *a priori* relationship to the literature which enables her or him to understand it better or feel connected with it more than a non-American (or, I suppose, an un-American).

But what these definitions ignore or accept as given is that "American" is not what needs definition. Americans will "naturally" be more interested in American literature. American literature is that written by Americans. But will all American women "naturally" be interested in *Moby Dick* or *The Awakening*? Are T. S. Eliot's or Phillis Wheatley's poems, or Henry James's or Paule Marshall's novels "American literature"? What needs definition for these students is the relationship between America and literature. Even this relationship between America and literature is mystified. American literature is "born from the American culture," "represents the attitude and tone of American society," "is representative of the type of literature prevalent in American society." What, however, is the nature of this birth, of this representation?

As a way of concretizing these issues and others, I then show the students a fascinating essay written by Henry Neumann for the U.S. Bureau of Education in 1918. The essay is entitled, "Teaching American Ideals Through Literature." Preceding the essay is a "Letter of Transmittal" from the bureau's commissioner, P. P. Claxton, contextualizing Neumann's agenda. Referring to World War I, which was then three months from ending, Commissioner Claxton wrote:

> The great struggle in which we are now engaged for the maintenance of our American ideals of freedom and democracy among ourselves and for the possibility of their extension throughout the world makes this a most opportune time for setting forth these ideals in an orderly way and for calling to the attention of teachers and others who have the direction of the reading of large numbers of people the books in which they are most adequately expressed and suggesting methods of using them.

Not only have students generally not considered at length what literature is, what American literature is, or even what an American is, but they have not considered what the purpose of teaching American literature is. They assume that the purpose of teaching American literature is to reveal the purpose of American literature itself. The process is transparent, revealing only the object. Moreover, the students usually feel that teaching and learning also share this relationship of transparency and objectification; the teacher offers the student Woolf's "nugget of pure truth" wrapped up and placed on the mantelpiece "for ever." Lectures and courses are themselves "letters of transmittal," a handing over of knowledge from one person to another.

Now this sort of self-referentiality and analysis of the power structures within the classroom seems old hat to many of us who teach. However, it is not old hat for our students. In fact, it is their very understandings of America and literature that *prevent* them from recognizing their own intellectual enslavement. Claxton suggests why this is the case. American ideals of freedom and democracy require "maintenance" both "among ourselves" and extended "throughout the world," which was the purpose of the then-current war (as well as our most recent one). As Claxton points out, the classroom is a precise analog of this local and geopolitical process. American ideals must be set forth in an "orderly" way, and students' readings must be under the "direction" of teachers who are most knowledgeable in "using" American literature. At the very beginning of his essay, Neumann reiterates Claxton's points: "Properly directed, there can be no more serviceable vehicle than American literature" (5). American literature and the access to it requires "direction," and the value of American literature lies in its "serviceability." The purposes for teaching American literature are identifiable and act something like a law: "What conceptions should a study of American poetry and prose enforce?" (9). Ten conceptions follow, each requiring a teacher to "enforce" it.

Within this police-state/policeman-of-the-world ideology is the liberal gesture of tolerance. The sixth conception of American ideals is that "a true democracy requires respect for differences" (14), the eighth is that "The ideal of freedom requires changes in social arrangements" (17), and the ninth is that "our democracy will profit from understanding other countries" (19). Neumann makes some genuinely inclusive attempts, calling racial, religious, or sectional prejudice "un-American" (16). He assails the United States' previous diplomatic "isolation" (19). He applauds Edmund Burke's ideas about the American Revolution, whose "arguments against the use of force still hold good against the policy of conquest" (20). But earlier, Neumann praises America's sons who "volunteered their lives to free Cuba" (5) and, citing as exemplary of "these worthier expressions of the American spirit" which "reach far back in our history," quotes from Bliss Perry's *The American Mind*:

> There will always be something fine in the thought of that
> narrow seaboard fringe of faith in the classics, widening
> slowly as the wilderness gave way, making its road up the
> rivers, across the mountains, into the great interior basin,
> and after the Civil War finding an enduring home in the
> magnificent State universities of the West. (Neumann 5–6,
> Perry 39)

Once again, despite the half-hearted appeals to tolerance, the connection between the policy of conquest as a tool of national diplomacy and domestic education could not be made any clearer. Along with the pioneers, the "classics" conquered the wilderness and spread civilization. The frontier having run out, World War I provided the forum for extension of American intellectual and political culture abroad.

I then set my students to work on books that I think bring up these questions of America, American literature, Americans, teachers, and students. I start off with Whitman (as a poet who claims to be the poet of America and Americans and whom Neumann uses for his expansionist purposes), Dickinson (as a very different contemporary of Whitman), Jean Toomer (as what "black" is, what an African American is), and then Zora Neale Hurston and her collection of African American folktales and voodoo, *Mules and Men*. I use *Mules and Men* as a way of questioning the students' conceptions of literature, both in terms of genre (literature is poetry and fiction, not folktales or voodoo) and medium (literature is written, not oral). It also raises questions about American literature. The idea that "Americans" have an *a priori* relationship with American literature becomes difficult in light of the alienation most white (and also many black) students experience in reading these tales.

Slavery was a frequent topic in discussions of *Mules and Men* and supplementary readings of Charles Chesnutt's story "The Gophered Grapevine," one of Joel Chandler Harris's Brer Rabbit stories, and Alice Walker's "In Search of Our Mothers' Gardens."[2] What interests me is the students' demonstration of Christopher L. Miller's understanding of the act of reading: "The interpretive tie between reader and text is also a bond of enslavement" (284). Putting it another way, Robert Scholes calls reading "a submission to textual authority" (39). The students bring about this enslavement, this submission, and in an act of

Orwellian bravura call it freedom. Using a distinction made by Houston Baker, Jr., I would argue that they are "possessed" by the text (as a slave is possessed by a master) instead of "POSSESSED" by the text (as in the spirit work of voodoo) (391). An example of this former kind of possession includes thinking Walker's mother was a slave, even though the students know that slavery didn't exist in the United States in the 1920's. This also happens with the framing narrative structure in *Mules and Men*. The tales of slavery sometimes make students think that Hurston and her fellow "liars" are themselves slaves.

Some may contend that these students are simply misreading. They are certainly misreading, but not, I think, simply. Another example should demonstrate this. Often, the white students will use the language of the texts to refer to African Americans in general in class discussion or assignments when they know that such language does not correspond to their normal usage. This usually manifests itself as white students referring to "negroes" when, in everyday conversation outside of the class, they would usually say "blacks." This tendency has even been so drastic as to come out as a white student using "nigger" in class to refer to blacks in general. My first assumption was that this was a racist outburst. Although that may be true, it may very well not be. If "negro" is not your usual term but you use it because the text uses it, then might not "nigger" (which appears frequently in *Mules and Men*) in this specific instance be merely a difference in degree, not in kind?

In a more recent class at Xavier University, I had this experience affirmed. In writing journals, students (most of whom were continuing students and anywhere from their late twenties into their forties or older) again reproduced the language of the text even when it was not their own language. We had read Chesnutt's *The Conjure Woman*, and three students used "nigger" without quotation marks or any other indication that the words were not their usual terminology when referring to blacks in the story generally. I am convinced that they would never have said this when referring generically to African Americans in other contexts. The most interesting case was a very bright, very progressive middle-aged woman who began using "nigger" generically in her journal but, after a while, wrote: "I find using the word nigger unsettling—I will use slave." After that she did consistently use "slave," except when "nigger" seemed to her to be a specifying term in the text. For instance, she used "free nigger" twice to denote a free man of color (a term not used in the stories) and "a cross-eyed nigger" once to refer to the kind of person it takes to make a lucky rabbit's foot, according to the story. Again, neither of these appeared in quotation marks, but both came directly from the text. Clearly she saw them as either a technical term (in the first case) and an identifying epithet (in the second case). This woman was particularly concerned in class discussion with issues of gender and race, which would seem to indicate that her motivation was not racist but textual.

This enslavement to the text, this possession, is an institutionalization of Neumann's America. The text is "directing" and "enforcing" the students. The act of reading is intimately tied to their understanding of the act of learning. To counteract this tendency, I thought that I would make discussion and not lecture the method of teaching and learning in the course at Rutgers. What I did not realize was that not only did my technique not liberate the students, but it created an authoritarian vacuum which they then supplied with "the text." I finally began to understand this when I read my course evaluations at the end of the semester. Around midterm I had taken questions from students and answered them in a handout to the entire class. To the question, "Why don't we have more of a lecture-type class in order to spur discussion?" I responded:

> Lectures don't spur discussion; they bludgeon you into silence. Too often students want instructors to do all of the intellectual work for them. Lecturing invites, if not demands, passivity. I'm not sure that such a way of knowing is worth much. Not only do you not learn much that way, but I don't either. And a class where I don't learn something is a waste of my time. I am always open, however, for new ways to spur discussion & would welcome/encourage all suggestions.

By the end of the semester, the evaluations reflected an interesting twist on my midterm comments. Student after student said that I was knowledgeable about my subject but should have lectured more. The words "structure" and "waste of time" appeared a number of times, and students suggested that the lack of the former resulted in the latter. The two ideas were succinctly combined in a single comment: "Some type of lecture, even if it only lasted for 15 minutes, is necessary to stimulate discussion and cut down on all the 'dead air' time that existed in this class." One student went so far as to say that I should be "a little more autocratic instead of all the time being one of us." Democracy, as they noted, is a messy and inefficient process. Another student remarked: "Our energies were not focused on what was most necessary. We spent too much class time listening to complaints that I personally am not interested in. I feel that valuable time was lost on more than one occasion." However, the same student said that my best quality was that I did not lecture. I had seen structure as silence and lecture as a waste of time and had told the class so. But numerous students saw the dynamics differently and contested my interpretation of them. Were they resisting enslavement by critiquing the course, or were they demanding their own enslavement by reverting to the passivity (and comfort) of lecture?

After studying slavery and its texts, after learning about democratic ideals and their multiplicity, many of my students wanted nothing more (and nothing less) than to be slaves, to be univocal "Americans." Four of the six books we read were by African Americans. That was "too narrow" for a course on American literature, they said. They wanted pluralism, just not too much of it. They wanted freedom (the freedom to object to my syllabus), just not too much of it. Like Neumann and his teachers (and of course students have learned most of this from their teachers), the liberal gesture of tolerance is a symptom of a contradictory desire for control and homogeneity. Whitman's opening for *Leaves of Grass*, "I celebrate myself,/And what I assume you shall assume,/For every atom belonging to me as good belongs to you," perfectly expresses the wishes of many of my students to submit to another while completely believing that submission to be the full expression of their individuality, as well as their common nationality and humanity.

Kathleen Diffley has noted a similar aspect of Whitman and poses an alternative relationship between self and community in Frederick Douglass's *Narrative of the Life of an American Slave* that might be instructive to students:

> Instead of the "I" that Whitman celebrates, something beyond it emerges when Douglass talks about slavery. "I" becomes "others," the one becomes many, and the many act together: both to resist the dominant law of slavery that is enforced upon them and to nurture the "I" that will tell their story. If Whitman's is a singular American vision (and twice over for being both recognizable and absorptive), then Douglass offers a communal American alternative, a story of identity shaped and constituted by the group. (4)

Diffley's interpretation of Douglass's *Narrative* is relevant to how students read. If they can free themselves of the absorptive "I" of a text, which they take to be their own "I," and make the one many, then they can find space both for themselves and the text in their readings. Furthermore, they can do so not only for themselves as individuals, merely replacing an absorptive "I" with an isolated "I," but they can see themselves as a community of differing interpreters with a common purpose (interpretation itself). From this viewpoint, perhaps the student who objected to spending too much class time listening to individual complaints that were not personally interesting could see such "complaints" as ones in which his or her interest might not be personal but democratic and communal. In addition, with such texts as Douglass's, students can see that narrative resistance is as important as political resistance, and that in fact the two are related. Judith Fetterley's "resisting reader" can be a goal to strive for, while still seeing that such reading, such resistance, does not go on in isolation but within a variety of communities, within a social context.

All these things can be pointed out to students, but then as teachers we naively expect our students to *believe* them. Not that they cannot understand such things. Not that they choose not to understand them. Rather, it is something like the problem of therapy: a client can be shown the problem, but until he or she is ready to act on it, no change can take place.

Ellen Cantarow has written about this difficulty, noting how it reflects teachers' idealism and forgetfulness. She speaks of her experience as a teaching assistant at Harvard in 1968:

> I suppose that in the back of our minds there was some obscure notion that one of our students would stride forth into Walter Bate's lecture hall and, arms akimbo, call from the aisle, "Bullshit! What a lay-on! Now, you listen to us! What *we* want is ..." Imagine how we felt when one evening, near the close of the semester, a student, astonished that we should suggest that he raise questions in a lecture course we were discussing, said, "But why should we ask questions? The professor asks our question for us!" Thus did some of our fledglings cower in the nest, mouths agape, waiting for the next bit of intellectual grub.
>
> Of course, in such expectations we were ignoring all our knowledge about the way political maturation takes place. We expected that what it had taken us years of long reflection and active work in the movement to understand, our students might comprehend through one semester of discussion in a classroom. (89)

Cantarow, like Diffley, shows the connection between narrative resistance (here the narrative of the lecture) and political resistance. But she also reminds us that students do not develop new patterns of thinking and acting overnight, just as we did not. It is not enough that some information is *true*; it must also be *usable*. This is not even a matter of making material "relevant." The knowledge that Cantarow hoped the student would understand was extremely relevant. The problem was not that he did not see this (he did not) but that he had no way to use this relevance. It is like being given a hard drive and being told that a computer is a very useful device when you do not have a computer. Yes, a computer is a useful device, and a hard drive makes it even more so, but a hard drive by itself is not even as useful as a typewriter. All the pieces must be in place, and it takes time to assemble them all (let alone learn how to use the assembly once it is complete).

I want to follow Cantarow's example and take seriously the comments of my dissenting students and reflect critically on my own pedagogy. Students can ask for structure without asking for totalitarianism, and I recognize this. Warren Rosenberg talks about the reaction of one of his American literature students to Harriet Jacobs's *Incidents in the Life of a Slave Girl*. The student, whom Rosenberg calls "extremely bright," asked, echoing my own students' concern for time management and Frederick Tayloresque efficiency: "Professor, why are you wasting our time?" Rather than see that moment as an example of student ignorance or arrogance and an opportunity for ridicule, Rosenberg instead took the student seriously and reflected on his course. The book and the reactions it provoked "forced me to modify how I teach," he says, resulting in a very different theory and pedagogy. This is an important example to teachers. What is needed is a compromise, a structured collegiality wherein students and teachers share information, creating guidelines and even archeologies of knowledge that are collaboratively arrived at, though most likely without consensus.

On the other hand, we must avoid an idealized understanding of collegiality and collaboration. Criticizing Northrop Frye's *Anatomy of Criticism*, Barbara Bailey Kessel and Katherine Ellis separately take issue with his contention that liberal education is meant "to make one capable of conceiving society as free, classless, and urbane." Despite his belief that such an education creates "the emancipated and humane community of culture," both Kessel and Ellis contend that such education has in fact been used to maintain class distinctions.[3] By aspiring to the homogenizing universal and invoking a liberal irony, according to Kessel, Frye reinforces the status quo. The manifestation of this attitude in the academy can be such that, if the professor "takes his irony far enough, he simply finds all convictions naive and rather amusing" (185). More recently Wayne C. Booth has criticized certain kinds of pluralism as a newer version of humanism and liberal irony:

> Any effort to be a pluralist in the classroom can be nothing more than a pretense, a pretense that is likely to produce not good solid tubs that will *contain* at least *something*, but leaky vessels containing nothing and thus doing nothing for the world—unless we count blurring distinctions and defending power elites, status quos, and textual canons. (469–70)

Therefore, both liberal irony and pluralism can reinforce current inequalities through a passive inclusivity. Although today we would all like to think that we know better, with what enslaving rather than liberating agendas (both known and unknown) are we captivating our students?

An approach which encourages collaboration and has greater structure than my free-form discussions is one offered by Peter Hawkes. He uses small group work to facilitate collaborative textual interpretation and to provide "experience in democratic decision making, a process whose tensions allow students a 'way in' to their national literature." According to Hawkes, "Only two things are necessary for collaborative learning—a group and a task" (140). His method has the advantage over mine of a tangible structure (groups and specific tasks) while still relating democracy to classroom collaboration. Hawkes requires that groups arrive at a consensus in their tasks, while noting in their reports to the entire class any dissent. In this way Hawkes attempts to make his classroom practice relate to the texts studied. He believes that American literature, as well as collaborative learning, "concerns the problems of becoming an independent self within a democratic society" (142). (Diffley has shown more abstractly the problems of the independent self and democratic society in the writings of Whitman and Douglass.) Hawkes provides students a method that is not tyrannical (or at least not any more tyrannical than majority rule) for enacting these problems rather than simply telling students about such problems. Such enactment, I would suspect, has a better chance of producing changes in patterns of thinking and behavior than either lecture or even class discussion.

I find Hawkes's approach provocative and promising. I imagine it can accomplish a good deal. It has the advantage over Neumann's plan for post-World War I literature classrooms and Frye's "emancipated and humane communities of culture" of not idealizing democracy for the benefit of certain groups but practicing it by all and thereby drawing attention to its difficulties and contradictions. Like the truism about writing fiction, Hawkes's method *shows* rather than *tells*, and so is more effective. Such practices would help create the kind of students which Cantarow wanted to come out of her classes.

As hopeful as Hawkes's practice is, and as positive as the goals of collegiality and collaboration are, we should be alert to their shortcomings as well. We need to be aware of our blind spots which hide our ideological inconsistencies. This does not mean we have to throw out all pedagogies as ideologically tainted. It only means that we must recognize their limitations and do what we can to overcome them, or at least acknowledge them. Economist Mary Beckman criticizes collaborative learning for its "hidden curriculum," much as Kessel and Ellis critique Frye and the New Criticism and as I have critiqued Neumann. Despite gestures toward inclusion, Beckman argues, grades retain a hierarchy of power, reinforcing such a hierarchy in the workplace which, she says, is also becoming increasing collaborative (130). Even in Hawkes's democratic experiment, presumably he still gives grades, a kind of academic taxation without representation. Like Booth, Beckman thinks that the pluralism of collaboration reaffirms authority, only disguised as a kinder, gentler one: "However, the classroom openness to a plurality of perspectives may give students the false impression that the instructor's evaluation of the student may be mild or even nonexistent. The teacher may, in fact, have rather stiff but unrevealed requirements" (131). Beckman comes to the conclusion that "I do not believe that the result of collaborative learning is the furtherance of democracy. But I do believe that collaboration prepares students in the latest techniques of capitalism" (132). She notes that workers are suspicious of collaboration as a tactic by companies to get more work out of them without real power sharing. Requirements become vaguer and evaluation becomes more mysterious and sometimes sterner (130).

Students' comments in my course evaluations reflected such suspicions. While I think that Hawkes's practice avoids some of this, it does not entirely do so. My students had a complex rationale underlying their desire for the safety of lecture and the text. They had real reasons for why they wanted such a classroom, and if I hope to be an effective teacher, I dismiss those reasons at my peril (and theirs). While I may disagree with many of those reasons and assert the validity of an alternative pedagogy, their concerns must be seen as more than ignorance or self-interest. As teachers we are not beyond the pale of ignorance and self-interest either. We must not, as my student did, feel disinterested in the "complaints" of our students, for resistance and passivity are not always readily distinguishable. Booth reminds us that "even the most highly educated, most brilliant mind will see only fragments of what might have been seen. At this point pluralism becomes the best possible teacher of the humility that is the prerequisite of all further learning. And the earlier a student can learn *that*, the better" (478). This kind of humility is not a passive submission to a text or mind but an active engagement with it, understanding that knowledge is fundamentally social. "Humility" has connotations of debasement and subservience, but it is related to a Latin word meaning "ground" or "earth." Such a context shows how all knowledge is "grounded," situated in a particular perspective as a result of placement, and how such knowledge is useless unless teachers and students can bring it "down to earth." And the earlier students *and* teachers learn *that*, the better.

NOTES

1. Some demographics may be in order here. Douglass College is a liberal arts women's college within Rutgers University. Agricultural students from Cook College, as well as the fine arts majors from the Mason Gross School, both of which are also colleges within the university, generally take their English classes at Douglass. My class included sophomores, juniors, and seniors, and approximately two-thirds of the students were neither majoring nor minoring in English.

2. I have recently taught Chesnutt's *The Conjure Woman*, from which "The Gophered Grapevine" comes, in its entirety at Xavier University, a small, Jesuit liberal arts school in Cincinnati. Earlier in this essay I asked if all American women are "naturally" interested in either *Moby Dick* or *The Awakening*. Teaching *The Conjure Woman* shed some light on this question while raising other questions. A number of white students enjoyed the stories because of Julius's trickster qualities and the resulting irony, whereas a number of the black students disliked the

book because of Julius's lack of formal education, because of the reminders of slavery, and because of the frequent use of the term "nigger." Black students will not necessarily feel any intrinsic connections between works by black writers, nor will white students necessarily feel that works by black writers are alien to them. Barbara Bailey Kessel writes that "oppression is not amusing or ironic to those who are actually oppressed. It is an aesthetic mode most appropriate to the ruling class" (184). This may explain in part the response I got in class, but it does not explain everything. Henry Louis Gates, Jr. has shown that "Signifyin(g)" by African Americans is a kind of irony that is different from the irony practiced by the dominant culture which Kessel describes. Furthermore, in this past class most of those who liked the book were women.

   3. Frye 347; Kessel 178–79 and 184; Ellis 164–70.

WORKS CITED

Baker, Houston A., Jr. "Caliban's Triple Play." *"Race," Writing, and Difference.* Ed. Henry Louis Gates, Jr. Chicago: U of Chicago P, 1986. 381–395.

Beckman, Mary. "Collaborative Learning: Preparation for the Workplace *and* Democracy? *College Teaching* 38 (1990): 128–33.

Booth, Wayne C. "Pluralism in the Classroom." *Critical Inquiry* 12 (1986): 468–79.

Cantarow, Ellen. "Why Teach Literature? An Account of How I Came to Ask That Question." *The Politics of Literature: Dissenting Essays on the Teaching of English.* Eds. Louis Kampf and Paul Lauter. NY: Pantheon, 1972. 57–100.

Diffley, Kathleen. "Reconstructing the American Canon: E Pluribus Unum?" *The Journal of the Midwest Modern Language Association* 21.2 (1988): 1–15.

Ellis, Katherine. "Arnold's Other Axiom." *The Politics of Literature: Dissenting Essays on the Teaching of English.* Eds. Louis Kampf and Paul Lauter. NY: Pantheon, 1972. 160–73.

Fetterley, Judith. *The Resisting Reader: A Feminist Approach to American Fiction.* Bloomington: Indiana UP, 1978.

Frye, Northrop. *Anatomy of Criticism: Four Essays*. NY: Atheneum, 1966.

Gates, Henry Louis, Jr., ed. *"Race," Writing, and Difference*. Chicago: U of Chicago P, 1986.

―――. *The Signifying Monkey: A Theory of African-American Literary Criticism*. NY: Oxford UP, 1988.

Hawkes, Peter. "Collaborative Learning and American Literature." *College Teaching* 39 (1991): 140–44.

Kessel, Barbara Bailey. "Free, Classless, and Urbane?" *The Politics of Literature: Dissenting Essays on the Teaching of English*. Ed. Louis Kampf and Paul Lauter. NY: Pantheon, 1972. 177–93.

Miller, Christopher L. "Theories of Africans: The Question of Literary Anthropology." *"Race," Writing, and Difference*. Ed. Henry Louis Gates, Jr. Chicago: U of Chicago P, 1986. 281–300.

Neumann, Henry. "Teaching American Ideals Through Literature." Department of the Interior, Bureau of Education Bulletin. No. 32, 1918. 3–21.

Perry, Bliss. *The American Mind*. Boston: Houghton Mifflin Company, 1912.

Rosenberg, Warren. "'Professor, Why Are You Wasting Our Time?': Teaching Jacobs's *Incidents in the Life of a Slave Girl*." *Conversations: Contemporary Critical Theory and the Teaching of Literature*. Ed. Charles Moran and Elizabeth F. Penfield. Urbana: National Council of Teachers of English, 1990. 132–48.

Scholes, Robert. *Textual Power: Literary Theory and the Teaching of English*. New Haven: Yale UP, 1985.

Envisioning Freedom
Jazz, Film, Writing
and the Reconstruction of American Thought

Melba Joyce Boyd

Gabriel García Márquez's novel *One Hundred Years of Solitude* contains a satirical passage that parallels the current dilemma in American culture. The town of Maconda is stricken by the plague of insomnia. "In that state of hallucinated lucidity, not only did they see the images of their own dreams, but some say the images dreamed by others" (46).

> It was Aureliano who conceived the formula that was to protect them against loss of memory for several months. He discovered it by chance. An expert insomniac, having been one of the first, he had learned the art of silverwork to perfection. One day he was looking for the small anvil that he used for laminating metals and he could not remember its name. His father told him: "Stake." Aureliano wrote the name on a piece of paper that he pasted to the base of the small anvil: stake. In that way he was sure of not forgetting it in the future. It did not occur to him that this was the first manifestation of loss of memory, because the object had a difficult name to remember. But a few days later he discovered that he had trouble remembering almost every object in the laboratory. Then he marked them with their inscription in order to identify them. When his father told him about his alarm at having forgotten even the most impressive happenings of his childhood, Aureliano explained his

261

method to him, and José Arcadio Buendia put it into practice all through the house and later on imposed it on the whole village. With an inked brush he marked everything with its name: table, chair, clock, door, wall, bed, pan. He went to the corral and marked the animals and plants: cow, goat, pig, hen, cassava, cladium, banana. Little by little, studying the infinite possibilities of a loss of memory, he realized that the day might come when things would be recognized by their inscriptions but that no one would remember their use. Then he was more explicit. The sign that hung on the neck of the cow was an exemplary proof of the way in which the inhabitants of Macondo were prepared to fight against loss of memory: This is the cow. She must be milked every morning so that she will produce milk, and the milk must be boiled in order to be mixed with coffee to make coffee and milk. Thus they went on living in a reality that was slipping away, momentarily captured by words, but which would escape irremediably when they forgot the values of the written letters. (Márquez 48–9)

Loss of memory was a more serious condition than Aureliano's literacy plan could counter. Likewise, the travesty of illiteracy in urban schools cannot be solved with functional systems of memorization because the horrendous reality that enshrouds Afroamerican students is not addressed in classroom literature or in the purpose of learning. Estranged from our historical and cultural memory as a people, we are trapped in an illusion—a convex television image of ourselves constructed by somebody else's imagination. Meanwhile, students are taught definitions and syntax, "keys to memorize objects and feelings," but after an extended period of insomnia, many cannot remember the value of life or letters (Márquez 48–9).

> I stand at your door I guess
> I'll wait a moment more, Your hall light
> comes on, Now my turn to fire upon,
> But I wheel away, Defer my plight for
> another day, to dream of your face, But
> a video screen takes its place. (Ham)

To a large extent the video consciousness of young Americans is the result of living in a visual culture. But more importantly, their loss of memory is the consequence of the destructive impact of popular culture on their imaginations. Because the basis of thought is imagery, visual culture provides the illusion of immediate gratification. To students living in an insensitive, oppressive bureaucracy that pretends to be a democracy, television offers a quick fix and a venue for escape from a depressive reality.

Without conscious interaction to mediate popular media experiences, simplistic thought and superficial values are ingrained into the imagination and affect behavior. Because they do not read, their perceptual depth and their aesthetic understanding are limited. Too many Americans receive the visual experience with myopic passivity. They are visually illiterate and verbally blind.

To some extent the dynamics of "call and response" and improvisation in Afroamerican cultural tradition provide creative analytical systems that edit the viewing of the dominant culture in a critical manner.[1] The film *Hollywood Shuffle* contains a sequence, "Real Brothers at the Movies," wherein two "blood brothers" sneak into the movies to critique them and likewise, Siskel and Ebert. With hard realism, they dismiss unbelievable and poorly produced films as "bullshit." This satire reflects the unsolicited perspective that a visit to a movie theatre in a black community would reveal, where the audience talks to the characters in the film and inadvertently to the director.

This interactive relationship with the medium usually contains an analysis that is clear and clever. Otherwise, some member of the audience will verbally embarrass the critic. One must be articulate and creative with words when soliciting attention. Likewise, the current popularity of rap music—with its complex syntax, coded vocabulary and thematic focus on the "word" (truth)—reiterates the verbal propensity of Afroamericans.

But the point of this essay is not to convince the reader that Afroamericans are analytical thinkers or that oral cultures are verbally rich. Rather, the issue here is that education has failed and tradition has faded. Furthermore, it is not enough to teach students higher-level thinking skills and then proclaim that this is the distinction of a university education. Rather, what is needed is vision, the capacity to see beyond the immediate situation and to reconstruct the American thought that values a free and just way of life.

American cultural vision has been hypnotized by the method and the madness of television. For even our best cultural security defense system seems to have failed us. Deep in the inner passages of our intuitive thoughts, despair and illusion confuse us within and distance us from our souls. Without our feeling-thoughts, we abandon sensitivity and humanity and pursue materialism and fame. In our present state of amnesia— lost in the breakdown of corrupt systems, bankrupt in bargain warehouses and abandoned used car lots—ignorance is bliss, and wisdom is folly.

Jazz and the Reconsruction of American Thought

Some years ago, the jazz composer and musician Anthony Braxton gave a lecture demonstration on his "modular notation" compositional theory at the University of Michigan in Ann Arbor. Braxton explained:

> The creative musician in this context utilizes an increased operating arena as both interpreter and improviser. For [modular notation] does not function as a "lead" or generating factor (in which one would play a theme and then commence to improvise) but instead was conceived with regards to the total infra-structure of the music. What this means is that the performer's responsibility takes on a different role from that of the classical or improvising tradition (as it is viewed in this cycle). The interpretation of this composition would thus involve executing the fixed elements of the piece in both a traditional and extended sense; that being: reading and interpreting both conventional notation (in five clefs) to alternative fixed elements (i.e., modules) wherein the performer has the option of reading a figure forward or backward in the sequence of her/his choice.[2]

Synergism lifted the energy of music beyond the boundaries of known quantities any single composer could inscribe but that

Braxton, through his creative vision, anticipated. "At the heart of this work is my desire to create a composition that in 'transformation' can function as a 'ritual' activity (when the composite astral and vibrational precepts are established for rebuilding culture for the next cycle)" (Braxton *For Trio*).

As a musician, I understood this theoretical construction and extended thinking and writing that is useful and historically grounded, modular notation would identify thematic parallels in a structurally infinite context. In the instance of Afroamerican people, the investigation of our Native American and labor struggles would reveal the multicultural complexity of our racial essence and our cultural ingenuity. Likewise, such cross-cultural realizations with other communities would contribute to a collective consciousness, whereby visionary exchanges can occur and enhance humanity.

But the initial content for study should be based on an American history that considers the quest for freedom and justice as a way to restore memory and to generate a humanistic vision for the future. Because of the complexity of our multiculturalism, classroom content must be initially introduced to students that reflects the particular experience of the students. Subsequently, this memory is interfaced with other cultural experiences in cross-cultural exchanges that reveal parallels in the past and present pursuits of laborers and oppressed communities to aspire for their inalienable rights.

Standard American English provides a language for all Americans, and students must master this system for broader cultural interactions. But at the same time, language and language acquisition can stimulate middle-class arrogance. Therefore it is essential that some of the content contains literature that engages the dialect. When students maintain a connection with their indigenous tongue in the classroom, it enhances their self-worth and a sense of appreciation for their communities. Persons who are bi-dialectic are less likely to disconnect themselves from the perspective of their origin. Furthermore, certain elements of insight and, therefore, vision are embedded in the imagery of the indigenous language. Repression of the dialect will inhibit creative and intellectual expansion. It is possible to code-switch accordingly, which will

afford them intellectual and cultural mobility within and outside
of the community.

As this country moves into the twenty-first century,
democracy is still an unrealized dream for almost half of its
citizens. Teachers must teach students to read and write
literature in a manner that discerns the social and cultural
dynamics that enforce systemic repression. The ignorance
and/or the denial of social and economic oppression in the
United States are the primary forces which plague the society
and the environment. Knowingly and unknowingly, to act
without a moral consciousness facilitates oppression. Alice
Walker explains:

> Many of us are afraid to abandon the way of the Wasichu
> because we have become addicted to his way of death. The
> Wasichu has promised us too many good things, and has
> actually delivered several forms of death. But "progress,"
> once claimed by the present chief of the Wasichus to be
> their "most important product," has meant hunger, misery
> enslavement, unemployment, and worse to millions of
> people on the globe. The many time-saving devices we
> have become addicted to because of our "progress" have
> freed us to watch endless reruns of commercials, sitcoms,
> and murders.
>
> Our thoughts must be on how to restore to the Earth its
> dignity as a living being; how to stop raping and
> plundering it as a matter of course. We must begin to
> develop the consciousness that everything has equal rights
> because existence itself is equal. In other words, we are all
> here: trees, people, snakes, alike." (Walker 148)

Too many Americans of European descent have forgotten the
reasons their ancestors fled the repression and tyranny of kings
and queens and landlords and governments and religions.
Because they do not know human history and have been
overcome by illusion, the politics of greed have circumvented
their political and moral courage. At the same time history
reminds us of the legacy of the Underground Railroad and of the
multiracial struggles of working-class people. There is a history
of collaborative liberation movements comprising those aspiring

to preserve the integrity of humanity, and the value of that history is the essence upon which a new vision must be rebuilt.

With regard to Afroamericans, the internalization of "Wasichu" thought not only enforces our own repression but, in some instances, our own genocide. Because, like the Native Americans, we are a colonized people, and it is essential that we understand the nature and the reality of our socioeconomic circumstances and resist psychological enslavement to the structure and systems that manipulate us and these circumstances.

The study of Native American culture is also crucial to the health of the future Americans and the "Reconstruction of American Thought." Likewise, encountering the legacy of Chicanos and other Latinos reveals the historical ignorance of our contemporary history, which has relegated indigenous people to the status of illegal aliens. Or the continued alienation of Asian Americans, who connected the East to the West with the railroad and yet are regarded with disdain and intimidation— the irony being that those who make these determinations were the aliens who invaded the land and set the borders, to divide the identities and the histories of the people already here.

The upper class dictates a value system that has to be confronted, and in the Third World literatures of the United States this confrontation is, for the most part, an aesthetic function. For this reason, and because of the limitations of my studies and of the length of this essay, the literature and films suggested are from the Afroamerican perspective. However, this course of study is one suggested beginning that should be complemented and extended with other materials and related with reference between the various movements of experience and those relayed in the Afroamerican context.

It is important, therefore, to use modular notation in the formulation of an American matrix from which students can move into their historical relationships with Native Americans, with Latinos, with Asian Americans and with Euroamericans from an equitable vantage point, ignoring the arbitrary boundaries of race, gender and class to free our collective memory and to transform our dreams.

The dream of freedom enjoins the amalgamation of cultural paths into a future. This future can be envisioned through the imagination of jazz, an American cultural expression which engages the energy of multidimensional layers of experience and projects us beyond our cultural contradictions and narrow predilections. Jazz offers a confirmation of the madness and a new organization for the complexity of that madness. It is the yearning of the spirit to decode and adjust the assault of repression while reconstructing renewed vision.

The Films

I discovered a unique film of Polish origin that influenced both the ideological perspective and the conceptual properties of this pedagogy. *Cages*, an animated film by Miroslaw Kijowicz, simplifies the complex dynamics of hierarchical social structures and demonstrates how they affect relationships and human behavior. Understanding this structure is an important lesson in survival because the systems that operate within this format facilitate oppression. *Cages* was created before the social revolution of 1990, while Poland was still governed by an oppressive totalitarian regime. Hence, the thinking in the film reflects structural similarities to progressive Afroamerican thought, which also evolved as a consequence of oppressive social circumstances.

Additionally, jazz constitutes the sound tract, which indicates a cultural kinship with Afroamericans; but more importantly, jazz functions as the creative and intellectual imagination of the film's perspective. The film contains no dialogue or narration, which allows endless verbal associations on the part of the viewer with the film's visual vocabulary and syntax. This is a critical structural and thematic dimension of the composition and of this pedagogy. *Cages* serves as the blueprint for visual literacy and for social, political and creative analysis. This film could be used as the vortex of and the introduction to any cultural studies course.

The subsequent film selection is based on experiences derived from the historical and/or cultural memory of

Afroamericans. Each provides a unique function in terms of conceptual content and context. They are arranged in a manner that facilitates a holistic, cyclical vision of history. The settings are any time in the twentieth century in the United States, which provides a contextual range that interfaces with the nineteenth century and can extend into the twenty-first century.

The Brother From Another Planet —written, directed and edited by John Sayles—is a tightly meshed satirical presentation of the Afroamerican dilemma and the legacy of liberation. The main character is an alien who has escaped slavery from a more technologically advanced society than Earth; and yet, in fundamental ways, the two planets are parallel. The film demonstrates how the historical dynamics of slavery still affect our contemporary economic situation and how this will extend into the future if significant changes do not occur. It also presents a timeless reality within an endless universe. The setting of the film provides a cyclical view of history and a thematic format that demonstrates the patterns of oppression and the symbols of resistance. Moreover, the film focuses on the deadly force and the source of drug trafficking. This is an essential subject that must be addressed in classrooms. [3]

Violence is a critical issue in American culture and in *Almos' a Man*, a short story by Richard Wright directed into film by Stan Lathan. The story provides an excellent introduction to a major American writer and to the subject of violence. Wright's insight into this cultural paradox is especially keen. The major symbol in the story is the "gun." Wright's focus on this object provides an exercise in contextual analysis, as the audience's understanding of the theme is dependent upon their perception of that object relative to the broader setting of racial and economic oppression and its adverse affects on a desperate young man with a narrow notion of manhood.[4]

What we think we see is largely influenced by what we have been conditioned to see. The conflict between our intuitive notions and our socialized beliefs often renders a frustrated imagination that resigns itself to the dictates of rumors that distort the truth. Memory and language are easily confused by subjectivity, by social conditioning and by intellectual manipulation. *The Sky Is Gray*, a short story by Ernest Gaines and a film also directed by Stan Lathan, provides a literary and a visual challenge to discern the ambiguity of imagery and language, and the contradiction between illusion and reality.

The story exposes the limitations of existential thought and the danger in ignoring the spiritual power of language. The imagery evolves around the contradiction between democratic principles and oppression as reflected in the life/struggle of a black woman trying to salvage her family despite racism, sexism and second-class citizenship. This film is especially important because it demonstrates the ambiguous position of the black woman, whose sexuality is devalued because of her strength and whose strength is resented because of her sexuality. It also dispels the negative myths about female-headed household.

The controversial novel and film *The Color Purple* contain the depth and honesty to generate passion and enthusiasm for reading. [5] The teaching of the film/novel experience requires a text that can capture and maintain the interest of students, and this novel was one of the most widely read in the Afroamerican community since *Native Son*. The issue of domestic violence is especially important for this study because it reflects how internalized oppression and the perception of manhood and womanhood is made manifest in the Afroamerican experience. At the same time, Alice Walker offers an alternative vision for new humanhood, which absolutely has to be considered for future generations.

Jazz, Film and Writing with Cyclical Vision

Acknowledgement of the visual cultural reality of young Americans indicates the relevancy of imagery in thinking and, conversely, in teaching. Like jazz, I have interrelated theoretical principles of perception and psycholinguistics and applied them to a structural analysis of film and literature. Jazz is the underlying current of my imagination, and it infuses my imagery and the syntax for my ideas. More specifically, I connected Braxton's composition theory to a system for reading and writing. In response to a film and literary text, the fixed elements of the experience are incorporated in the written interaction, which is free to move in any temporal or spatial direction relative to thematic impetus in the text. The dynamics of the experience are analyzed during class discussion— singularly and collectively—in a cyclical historical context. The writing evolves that discussion towards a resolution that extends the theme into the future. The writing, like the music, should be a visionary experience.

Modular notation critiques binary thought systems while it instills a perspective that resists literal definitions, superficial descriptions, and linear symbolic associations. In order to achieve this aim, diagrams operate like the modular notation system to determine abstract associations contained in the text, without sacrificing individual responses in writing. In order to get beyond black and white, male and female, and into the broader and deeper meanings of humanity and equality, words as concepts must examined in contextual as well as in cultural terms. Otherwise, racial, gender and class divisions will persist as perceptual and actual barriers inside imaginations and between and within communities. Therefore, the discussion of language is very much concerned with the repressive dynamics inherent in connotative usage that subliminally reinforce the conceptual underpinnings of discrimination.

Like jazz, cyclical vision pivots on the intersections of associative imagery, thereby engaging meaning in a contextual manner. In order to more fully experience the creative world of the text, students are encouraged to temporarily suspend subjective judgment and to focus on the parameters of the imagery as reflected through the point of view of the camera.

Understanding the literary limitations of the students, film becomes a most effective mechanism for "alternative vision" because the experience is perceived through the eyes and ears. [6] Even though the historical and cultural knowledge of the students is usually limited to their suspension in time and space, certain emotions and behaviors are consistent. The universality of the themes will bridge the distance. By first seeing a novel abstraction, words can be supplied in new arrangements to explain the difference between what they perceive and what has been shown.

The film compositional experience progressed through time and space until it reaches the climax, and then it resolves the conflict of actions as it gravitates towards the center of meaning. In order to understand the ending, a holistic, interrelated sense of knowing must be achieved. A nonsequential evaluation of plot sequences focused on the central point of conflict as expressed in the climax directs the abstract perception of the experience to a higher level of seeing. This is determined by the active growth of symbolic gesture as an organic composition, moving from the inside out, oscillating in a forward and backward motion toward the resolution of meaning.

If a student believes the story is about y then she must first consider the contextual restrictions of the text. She must substantiate her position through textual references, distinguishing her feelings (values) from the point of view and contextual reality of the creative composition. Because the discussion format begins with holistic perception, intuitive thought is encouraged, but this thought should consider the intuitive thought patterns of the characters observed within the contextual limitations of their world. Therefore, the student engages the point of view of the characters and the analysis effectively engages broader and deeper perceptions. In order to achieve a balanced visual perception, students must understand not only their subjective response to the creative composition, but also how the elements of a creative composition are objectively organized to evoke subjective responses.

Holistic perception of film and literature includes a continuous, analytical process of response and reflection. Cyclical vision entails associative planes of symbolic meaning pivoting on the ambiguity of imagery. The ability to transcend linear, sequential logic and literal definitions is related to the cognitive functions of the right brain hemisphere, which is developed through creative activities. Therefore, the tendency to perceive on the literal level is directly related to repressive conditioning in the classroom, which discourages creative manipulation of language and ideas.

Cyclical vision demands a balanced coordination between the left and the right hemispheres of the brain. Complex films

and writing activate the right brain hemisphere, while verbal
discussion and analysis activate and develop the left brain
hemisphere. Diagrams are used as frameworks for analysis and
as a foundation for creative and analytical associations.
Ultimately, thinking has to expand beyond the boundaries of
any community in order to acquire and to interact with thought,
information, and experiences that fundamentally impact upon
the community in critical ways.

The parameters of setting, temporal and spatial, identify
the historical and cultural perceptions the subjects engage
relative to themselves, each other and outside forces, seen and
unseen. Reflection on the experience is relative to the point of
view of the perceived experience. It is a planet, another world
one can enter:

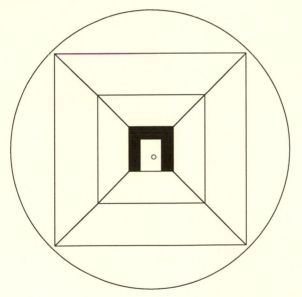

As in modular notation, this structure engages the retroactive,
interactive as well as the progressive momentum of the plot.
Therefore, in theory, this figure is actually rotating, like a planet.
If the story could be presented as a hologram, the complexity of
the cellular construction would be three-dimensional. But
beyond the physical plane, abstract dimensions extend into the

implications and ramification of the imagery and cannot be understood if the action is not realized in a holistic, interrelated context. Activity can be isolated and associated in a variety of ways, released from the linear perception of time and space through the imagination.

During the discussion of the film, the compositional elements are enlisted in the following categories:

Colors   Shapes   Sounds   Textures   Lighting   Positions

Those categories outlined are then associated analytically with each other and within the contextual world of the film—actions define meaning. The compositional elements are considered in terms of the action, upon which symbolic connections are based.[7]

Colors:	Shapes		Shapes:	Sounds
Colors:	Sounds		Shapes:	Textures
Colors:	Textures		Shapes:	Positions
Colors:	Actions		Sounds:	Textures
Colors:	Positions		Sounds:	Positions
	Sounds:	Actions		
	Textures:	Actions		
	Textures:	Positions		
	Actions:	Positions		

For example, in the film and the story *The Sky Is Gray*, the color red highlights the underlying theme.

red > birds > captured > caged > pets > love

James wants to keep birds as pets because he likes them. His mother forces him to kill them for food. Hence, the significance of the color red changes when they are killed, therefore the meaning changes with action:

red > birds > captured > killed > sacrifice > blood > life > food.

In another instance, the color red is associated with coats. James thinks about his mother's old, drab, black coat. He wishes that he could buy her a bright, red one. In the film, the little girl that James is attracted to wears a red coat. There is sometimes a difference in the appearance of color in the film and in the story, but in both instances the thematic perspective is the same. Hence:

(film) red > coat > protection > girl > love

(story) red > coat > protection > mother > love

The imagery is processed through cognitive operations like a montage, juxtaposed and expanded into symbolic patterns via verbal interaction.[8] Patterns and parallels are determined by the character's or characters' actions and interactions relative to time and space. The question to be reflected is: How and why does the experience of one character affect another? The ambiguity of imagery and the relativity of perspectives establish the foundation for grounded abstraction. These determinations are then analyzed in terms of "dynamic symmetry."

Dynamic Symmetry

Dynamic symmetry entails the identification of patterns and parallels in other times and spaces related to the theme of film. This process extends the abstract analysis of the film text beyond the parameters of the screen and requires flexibility in thought and perspective. The abstract associations derived from the dimensions of the film text are now viewed thematically. This level of seeing is extended into the broader historical context. The sum of the parts equals more than the whole. These resolutions conversely lead to conclusions about the past and resolutions about the future.

Anthony Braxton explains, "The use of improvisation in 'Modular Notation' is regulated by color and shape." When the mother and son are invited to eat in the warmth of Helena's kitchen, the tablecloth in the film is red gingham.

red > tablecloth > warmth > food > life > love

The associations converge at the end of the story wherein Helena and her husband invite James and his mother, Octavia, for lunch, which literally brings them out of the cold. The convergence of the abstract meaning of the red imagery is reflected in the imagery of the birds and the coat.

An analysis of setting is key to understanding the title and the theme as well. The color grey must be analyzed in terms of the physical and the social forces that affect the characters:

Grey > day > cold > sleet > clouds > above > earth

Grey > society > white > over > black

male > over > female

rich > over > poor

In the film, the characters are dressed in black and white to reflect the ambiguity of language, as the value of the color changes according to the character's behavior. This behavior is also considered relative to the setting, which anticipates a certain code of conduct in a repressive, segregated society, and yet, there is a range in behavior. In the film we find:

white characters:

nurse > white uniform > cold > mean > arrogant > racist

Helena > black shawl > white hair > kind > human

black characters:

preacher > black suit > white collar > ignorant > blind > confused > afraid > angry

student > black suit > white shirt > intelligent > cynical > despair > lost

Octavia > grey coat > strong > consistent > clear > faith > love > truth

Symbolic Connection: Symbolic Connection = Parallel

Symbolic Connection: Symbolic Connection = Parallel

Symbolic Interaction: Symbolic Interaction = Pattern

Symbolic Interaction: Symbolic Interaction = Pattern

Parallels and Patterns = Thematic Conclusions and Resolutions

Even though students are initially requested to confine their concentration to the cinematic text, individual knowledge and experience (or the lack of it) will influence the ingestion of imagery. The point is to emphatically stress the difference between the text and historically relevant data that can be incorporated as an extension of one's analysis. The underlying or preceding historical data are to be perceived as intersecting with the cyclical sphere of the film from another space, possibly inside and beside the textual imagery. It is to be understood as associations stimulated by the film as the reference for order or disorder, progression or regression, in an attempt to transcend contradiction. Likewise, historical projections that can be made should not be confused with textual parameters but, rather, should be identified as temporal/spatial dimensions that extend the experience of the future relative to the text, which is the student's present:

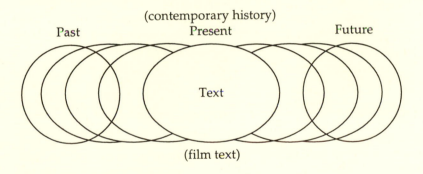

(film text)

These distinctions are made during the analysis in order to avoid errors in judgment and to aid interconnections. Patterns and parallels can be sighted (and cited) not only as extensions of the imagery in the textual experience, but also in historical and cultural spaces that may be distinctive, and yet universally parallel with the one being analyzed. The visual perception of other planetary spheres operating outside the cyclical sphere of the film experience is associated relative to their temporal/spatial perspective and how and where the two experiences intersect.

Depending on the flexibility of the learned and determined information of the student, the range for comparative analysis is infinite, and so are the possibilities for creative thinking. Introduction of secondary literature—whether creative, historical, or sociological—can reinforce and expand the associative energy of the imagery. This theoretical paradigm is integrated into the discussion of selected films. The foundation of this pedagogical argument is the advantage of the visual over the verbal to introduce complex concepts and verbal correlatives.

The collection of all points and each dimensional plane, acting and interacting, define and expand the ramification of meaning for the future. The image inside the image, or the metaphorical level of seeing, extends the theme of the film experience to interface with other worlds and possibilities. This imaginative level of seeing requires an intellectual and a creative risk that approaches synergism.

Concluding

There are many excellent documentary films on the black American experience now available on videocassette for classroom use. In addition to these, some commercial films are also useful; for example, *Boyz from the Hood* and *Juice* could be shown to extend the imagery of *Almos' a Man*. *Native Son*, the film, provides an excellent demonstration of conceptual use of the themes of black and white in its adaptation of the novel. When considering the film selection, consider the spirit of the work, just as Alice Walker realized that the nature of the director Steven Spielberg was aligned with her spiritual concerns: "'In ancient times, people believed that you thought with your heart,' Alice Walker said. 'They didn't really know about the brain. In more modern time, people say you think with your brain. Only there are a few of us who still actually think with our hearts'" (Dworkin 68–70).

Film and literature can derive meaning from suffering, provide focus for clarity, and jazz thought does emanate vision for the recovery of memory and in a reconstruction for the future. It entails rigorous training and requires diligent practice, but at the right moment students will take flight on the power of free imaginations.

NOTES

1. "Call and response" is a West African language pattern that has been retained in the cultural patterns of Afroamericans in the United States. The lead voice in song, poetry, speeches, etc., addresses the audience or involves the audience in anticipation of a refrain for affirmation.

2. Also refer to Graham Lock, *Forces in Motion: The Music and Thoughts of Anthony Braxton*.

3. For a more detailed analysis of this film see Melba Joyce Boyd, "But Not the Blackness of Space: Icon from the Underground."

4. For a related discussion on Richard Wright's use of black-and-white in literature and the adaptation into the film *Native Son*, see Melba Joyce Boyd, "Teaching Richard Wright's *Native Son* to Urban Students."

5. For a discussion of the politics around the film's controversy and an analysis of gender construction in the film, see Melba Joyce Boyd, "The Salt in the Sugar: The Hot Reception of the Novel/Film, *The Color Purple*."

6. "Alternative vision" is the capacity to realize another perspective into reality(ies) that extend into the future.

7. In *Visual Thinking*, Rudolph Arnheim explains: "In vision and hearing, shapes, colors, movement, and sounds are susceptible to definite and highly complex organization in space and time. The two senses are therefore the media par excellence for the exercise of intelligence" (13).

Conversely, Robert Richardson's *Literature and Film* explains the interdisciplinary relationship of the two mediums of expression:

Because language is by nature an image or symbol-making
process, literature has always been able to make effective,
conscious use of it. . . . Film too, in so far as it thinks of its
material as presentations of images of reality and not as
slices of life or actual reality, has an equally wide range of
possibilities for conscious use of imagery. (17)

8. The psycholinguist Allan Paivio determined in *Imagery and
Verbal Processes* that "the mind is a storehouse of images of concrete
objects and events. Language builds upon this foundation and remains
interlocked with it" (473).

Likewise, the psychologist Jean Piaget proposes that "images are
essential for representing and effectively thinking about concrete
features of the perceptual world" (quoted in Paivio 18).

Works Cited

Arnheim, Rudolph. *Visual Thinking*. Berkeley: U of California P, 1969.

Boyd, Melba Joyce. "But Not the Blackness of Space: Icon from the
Underground." *Journal of the Fantastic in Arts*. 2.2 (1989): 95–107.

———. "Teaching Richard Wright's *Native Son* to Urban Students."
Teaching Richard Wright. Ed. James Miller. NY: Modern Language
Association, 1994. Forthcoming.

———. "The Salt in the Sugar: The Hot Reception of the Novel/Film, *The
Color Purple*." *Protest, Rebellion, and Dissent Within the Black
Community*. Ed. Berndt Ostendorf and Maria Diedrich. Tübingen,
Germany: Gunter Narr Verlag P, 1991: 115–127.

Braxton, Anthony. Jacket notes. *For Trio*. Arista, AB 4181, 1978.

Dworkin, Susan. "The Strange and Wonderful Story of the Movie *The
Color Purple*." *MS* December 1985: 68–70.

Ham, Greg. "Helpless Automaton." *Business As Usual*, by Men at Work.
CBS, 1982.

Lock, Graham. *Forces in Motion: The Music and Thoughts of Anthony
Braxton*. NY: De Capo P, 1988.

Márquez, Gabriel Garciá. *One Hundred Years of Solitude*. NY: Avon
Books, 1970.

Paivio, Allan. *Imagery and Verbal Processes*. NY: Holt, Rinehart and Winston, 1971.

Richardson, Robert. *Literature and Film*. Bloomington: Indiana UP, 1969.

Walker, Alice. *Living by the Word*. NY: Harcourt, Brace Jovanovich, 1988.

Authors, Authority, and the Graduate Student Teacher
Against Canonical Pedagogy

William J. Savage, Jr.

Graduate student teachers work in an institutional middle ground, in a vaguely defined and shifting space between undergraduates and faculty. In a rigidly hierarchical institution, we occupy more than one position: in relation to our professors, we are students, while in relation to undergraduates, we are teachers. (For administrators, of course, we are cheap labor.) We are engaged in obtaining the credentials which would grant us a measure of authority to teach literature to college students. Yet at the same time we are already called upon to teach literature, usually by leading discussion groups in conjunction with large lecture courses, but occasionally on our own. This neither-here-nor-there institutional position would seem to severely limit the pedagogical opportunities available to graduate student teachers interested in noncanonical material and methods, but in fact our status allows us—albeit on a small level—to work against canonical teaching methods.

To begin, I should discuss the context out of which I argue, the terminology I will be using, and the institutional framework out of which many of my assertions and most of my teaching experience come. Graduate students at Northwestern, like grad students in most universities, teach freshman composition and lead discussion groups in conjunction with large lecture classes; we also sometimes design and teach freshman seminars on topics of our own choice. I will be concentrating both on experience gleaned from such freshman seminars and on discussion sections, although I believe that many of my assertions about teaching noncanonical American literature and teaching with noncanonical methods in such settings would apply to nontraditional methods of teaching composition as well.

As for terminology, the word canon is one of the most contested terms in literary studies. I do not subscribe to the idea that the canon of American or English literature is or was an all-powerful monolith, utterly dominating literary education. After all, I managed to get a B.A. in English without ever reading *Paradise Lost, Moby Dick, The Scarlet Letter,* or countless other examples of allegedly required reading. As even some of its defenders admit, the traditional canon has—and always has had—constantly shifting borders, as various authors and texts move in and out of fashion, or are read in different ways or for different reasons. But neither do I subscribe to the view that since the canon was not a monolith, it never really existed and therefore need not be undermined. Instead, I would argue that we need to think not of *the canon* but of *canonicity,* of the myriad ways in which texts and authors—and importantly, pedagogical methodologies—can have a measure of literary status and authority granted them in some social situation or another. Two writers who have tried to shift the discussion from the canon to canonicity are Alastair Fowler and Wendell V. Harris, and I wish to look briefly at how they define different sorts of canonicity in order to make clear how I will be using the term.

Fowler distinguishes six different sorts of canon: potential, accessible, selective, critical, official, and personal. The potential canon includes all literature; the accessible consists of whatever is available to readers at a given time; specific lists of authors and texts, as in course syllabi or anthologies, comprise selective canons; those works widely written about by critics at a given time constitute the critical; the official canon is a vaguely defined combination of the accessible, selective, and critical canons; and the personal, finally, is the canon of a given individual (97–99). These categories, as Harris points out, "rest on no systematic taxonomic principle and therefore overlap" (112). Harris adds several other shades of meaning to this roster of definitions of "canon," including the pedagogical, the diachronic, and the nonce. The pedagogical is that selective canon commonly taught in high school and college, "shorter than the official canon" and "unlikely to correspond exactly to the critical." The diachronic canon consists of those authors who stand the proverbial test of time, combined with "contemporary authors who have high visibility." Finally, the nonce canon is the "rapidly changing periphery" of writers who are taken seriously in the wider literary culture and who eventually, perhaps, enter the diachronic (113).

These distinctions prove useful because they demonstrate the different ways in which a text can have some sort of canonical authority or weight, some claim on being "literary." A text need not be Melville or Twain to have canonical authority in one sense or another, and which individual texts fit into various canons at a given time shifts continually. The varieties of canonicity most relevant to the experience of undergraduates (and the graduate students teaching them) are the pedagogical canon and the various select canons they have encountered in literature classes, and when I discuss "the canon" expected by undergraduates it is the pedagogical canon I refer to. Relatively few of the undergrads taught by graduate students will have extensive experience with literary criticism and theory and its attendant critical canon; instead, their idea of which authors have canonical authority will be informed by their experience at the high school level, where they probably read *The Great Gatsby*, *Billy Budd*, *A Farewell To Arms*, *The Scarlet Letter*, *The Red Badge of Courage*, and other "classic"—and easily teachable—works of American literature.

Beyond the varied levels of canonicity attributed to different texts, students will be all too familiar with some canonical critical methodologies. Certain New Critical methods of reading have become canonical in the sense that they have been widely accepted, accepted to the point of being thought of as natural, permanent, and beyond question. This canonization of method has led students to develop a sense of what they believe literary studies to be, a sense of how teachers expect students to read whatever they encounter in an English class. Students usually will believe that we read literature closely and deeply to find its hidden meanings. This expectation comes from the New Critical emphasis on doing whatever interpretive work it takes to find unity in a given text. As Gerald Graff has pointed out, students often see literary studies as the process by which we seek out problems in texts only to argue them away. This is a result of their high school training, where "their interpretations had been predetermined by an assumption . . . that when you encounter an apparent anomaly in a literary work—especially if it is a canonized one—it's not a real anomaly" (76). In other words, most undergraduates have been trained in the dominant New Critical literary culture, trained to find unity at all costs, because the primary value one could ascribe to a literary work is organic unity, and why would we be reading a text in an English class if it weren't valuable?

In order to begin discussing these issues and their impact on the graduate student teacher, I want to further complicate the idea of canonicity with two ideas: what I call the "topic canon," and the idea of canonical pedagogical methodology. As many writers have pointed out, the argument over the canon is more than just a question of which authors should be taught. Many arguments seem to came down to this issue, but more important is the conflict over the context in which these writers or texts should be taught, i.e., the conflict over which *topics* we consider sufficiently literary to be discussed under the rubric of English departments. Just as we have generally accepted canonical and noncanonical authors and texts, so we have canonical and noncanonical topics for English courses. This distinction comes down to more than its representation in the popular debate over the canon, where it is portrayed by the right and by uninformed journalists as an apocalyptic conflict between traditional Western humanistic objectivity and the dangerous politicization of literary studies by Marxists, feminists, Freudians, and deconstructionists. While an ideological conflict over the canon and multiculturalism certainly is taking place (and given the mass media coverage of the PC controversy, many undergraduates are aware of it, if only vaguely), many teachers on both sides of argument over the topic canon have at least one thing in common: their canonical pedagogical methodology.

The canonical method for teaching (especially for teaching introductory classes), shared by the traditionalists and various canon-busters alike, is the lecture course, with its attendant graduate student discussion leaders. I am not claiming that all universities have huge lecture courses at the core of their curriculum; many schools, especially smaller ones, do not. But such courses are widely thought to be an efficient (read cost-effective) way to teach, and they are more common than not, and even courses with small enrollments can still be centered on lectures. (As an undergraduate, I never took an English class with more than thirty-five students, yet lectures were often the primary method used.) Given this dependence on the lecture, we can see how graduate student teachers occupy an institutional position roughly analogous to noncanonical literature. Canonical texts and professors lecturing have institutionally sanctioned authority; noncanonical texts and graduate student teachers leading discussions lack that authority. I do not want to push this comparison too far, but it holds in at least one way: undergraduates know that graduate students do not have as much authority as professors, and so perhaps are more likely to resist our attempts to teach noncanonical materials or in noncanonical ways.

At its root, the distinction between canonical and noncanonical methodology is a matter of how we—professors, grad students, undergrads, university administrators, the culture as a whole—conceive of the authority of the teacher in the classroom. Do we think of the teacher as the sole repository of literary knowledge and the arbiter of the value assigned to whatever text is being taught, which he or she then imparts to the student? This is the pedagogical model most lecture courses—whatever their content, canonical or not—are implicitly based on. The lecturer, often a tenured professor, speaks; the students write down what he or she says, try to memorize it, and repeat it in papers and blue-book exams. Learning is believed to be the accumulation of correct interpretations or of the correct grounds for arguing about interpretations, be those interpretations traditional or on the cutting edge of theory.

Graduate student teachers enter the picture in an important way in that our noncanonical institutional status offers a tremendous opportunity for effecting change in how pedagogical authority is implemented, albeit on a small level. Potentially more revolutionary than alterations in the roster of acceptable texts to be read or theories to be applied to texts (the opening up of the textual and the topic canons) would be a reevaluation of how pedagogical authority is understood, institutionalized, and acted upon. Graduate student teachers can oppose the canonical teaching method by thinking of teaching literature as a cooperative venture, where teacher and student both bring something to the process and both contribute to the construction of meaning and value. Graduate students, who generally do not lecture to large groups of students, have the opportunity to explore this method early in their teaching careers, when the institutional structure in which we teach allows or requires us to work with small groups of students and when our pedagogical habits have not yet fossilized.

My experience as a graduate student teacher in discussion sections, basic composition, and freshman seminars has led me to theorize about and attempt to implement such a noncanonical way of teaching, a method which does not place all authority in the teacher. Based on discussion sections and workshop-oriented methods for teaching composition, its goal is not to impart a single method for reading or a set of authoritative interpretations to students, but instead concentrates on creating an attitude of open-mindedness about literature and literary questions. Teaching literature, noncanonical or canonical, should be about imparting the idea that everyone should be open to questions. Our goal, above and beyond providing information about the nuts and bolts of literary studies, should be to make students open to the experiences of others (and Others) as embodied in literature, open to questioning the way our culture constructs differences like "reading serious literature" and "reading for entertainment," open to looking at their own lives with what they learn from literary studies. This directly conflicts with the canonical New Critical method—be the material taught as part of the traditional canon or not—because being open to questions implies admitting that problems really exist, that teachers do not always have the answers, and that sometimes there are no pat five-page-paper answers to literary questions.

Many arguments in favor of the traditional canon implicitly oppose such openness. The idea that what everyone should read in a university setting consists of a set group of texts—the Great Books—is based on a gesture of limitation, of cutting off possible interpretive behavior or even argument about what is worth interpreting. Mortimer Adler puts this position most clearly with a comment made upon publication of the revised edition of the Great Books by Encyclopedia Britannica in 1990. He claims that the debate over literary value and canonicity is "utter nonsense. Rubbish, rubbish, rubbish. . . . This is the canon, and it's not revisable" (Blades 14). Apparently the irony of claiming that the canon cannot be revised upon the publication of his own revision of the canon escapes Adler, but this assertion also makes it clear that closure rather than openness is at the heart of many arguments in support of the traditional canon.

At the same time, we should not be so naive as to believe the argument that simply reading noncanonical literature in and of itself—whatever the pedagogical method of the teacher—will cause students to be open-minded, or to believe or behave in a particular way. Literary education is not so simple. The fact that the canon has been challenged at all shows that "just reading" a certain body of texts will not cause all readers to take certain intellectual or ideological positions. The right's fear that teaching noncanonical texts will create a legion of radical Marxist feminist deconstructionists wreaking havoc on the intellectual and moral life of the Republic is absurd. If literary education worked that simply and directly, if reading certain texts in certain ways directly caused readers to hold particular values, then we would all be good New Critics, happily espousing the canonical values we hold due to having properly read Melville and company. What makes the idea of teaching open-mindedness intriguing and valuable is the fact that while reading particular texts does not cause particular values to be held or acted upon, learning to read open-mindedly might very well do so. Open-mindedness is a widely applicable value, one which students might take out of the classroom with them and act upon long after they have forgotten whatever they might have learned about the symbolic structure of *The Scarlet Letter* or the domestic sentiment of redemptive maternal love in *Uncle Tom's Cabin*.

Given this goal of creating openness, how can graduate student teachers make use of our mixed institutional status in order to reach students and effect change? My own experience and interviews with other graduate students have suggested to me that we basically have two pedagogical gestures available to us: whether in discussion sections or our own classes, we can assert our quasi-professorial authority as experts-in-training (at the very least, more knowledgeable and better read than undergrads); or we can attempt to establish a rapport with students, attempt to make learning and teaching a cooperative venture, a group of students together navigating through the complicated landscape of literature and criticism.

This can, but doesn't necessarily have to, involve distancing ourselves from the professoriate, constructing ourselves as outsiders, opposed in some ways to the interpretations and arguments made by professors. One faculty member, recently hired at Northwestern, laments the fact that he can no longer use just this method. He points out to me that undergrads generally expect certain sorts of things from graduate students and different sorts of things from professors; now that he has attained professorial authority, he can no longer make the "This is what the professors all say, this is what I think, and what do you think?" gesture. Students expect him to work from a certain authoritative position, one which differs from the "I'm just a grad student in the same boat as you all" stance he based his teaching style on. Of course, these gestures will have very different results and implications depending on whether graduate student teachers are teaching on our own or in conjunction with a lecture course; but the second is clearly most important for the creation of an open discussion of literary value and meaning among our students.

However, we must remember that we have little control over the students we end up teaching. Whether we teach at an elite research university, a community college, a liberal arts college, or an urban commuter school, English courses are often part of a core curriculum, and many students will be taking our classes only to fulfill distribution requirements. Such students will often resist whatever we teach, be it canonical or not, not because of our material or our method but because they resent being forced to study literature at all. On the other hand, the educational expectations brought by students to English classes do vary between types of schools, often on the basis of class identification. But we should be careful to avoid falling into the classic (and classist) stereotype that students at ivy-covered elite universities, being so darn smart, will respond enthusiastically to cutting-edge work, while students in benighted backwater schools will want to stick with the old-fashioned canon in order to amass the cultural capital which comes with higher education. Many students at more expensive or elite schools expect to read the same books their parents did, and may resent reading noncanonical authors, while students at regional or commuter schools will often enjoy noncanonical material, at least in part because of the different ways the noncanonical interests in class, race, and gender figure in their lives outside of the university.

But we do have, given the pool of students available to us, some control over who we teach and how we teach them, and we can strive to create an open-minded attitude in our students. First, seemingly mundane matters of course title and description are crucial in relation to the sorts of students who will end up sitting in our classrooms. In the freshman seminars I have taught, I have always assigned a mixture of canonical and noncanonical novels. The main title I gave my course (the subtitle changed every term), "Huck Finn and American Fictions," reflects this blend. I found that I often encountered opposition to teaching noncanonical novels alongside *Huck Finn*, *The Great Gatsby*, *The Grapes of Wrath*, and other standards from the pedagogical canon, texts my first-year students had often encountered in high school. One reason for this was the fact that my course title did not signal to students that they should expect to be reading noncanonical fiction: *Huck* in many ways represents the canon of American literature, and many of my students expected to get the standards. When they also got *The Awakening*, *The Big Sleep*, *Love Medicine*, *Paco's Story*, *Sula*, and *The Man With the Golden Arm*, they resisted, feeling, perhaps, that they had been sold a bill of goods and were not being taught

American fiction at all, but instead a bunch of Bill Savage's favorite books.

Getting my students to take these novels seriously was problematic for me, since I did not want to use the first gesture available to the graduate student teacher and claim professorial authority by standing behind a lectern and saying, "Shut up, take these books seriously, and get it right on the exam or else." So I have had to come up with other ways to cause my students to engage the material, to read open-mindedly. First, I have had to practice my theory and be open to my students' objections. Instead of proceeding from the assumption that anyone with half a brain in their head would agree that the books in question were worth reading (an assumption which informs many professors' attitudes towards their material, canonical or not), I have had to actively try to convince my students that noncanonical texts were worth reading. I would begin by being open about their concerns, their resistance. Yes, I would admit, you've never heard of some of these novels, and might never see some of them in another English course. They are outside the usual pale of literary studies, noncanonical. Now, given that, let's look at how they differ (or if they differ) from the texts you've read and are expected to read again here. And, by the way, aren't you glad that we're not reading *Moby Dick*? Then, before discussing each of the noncanonical novels, I would give a very brief—five minutes or so—spiel on why I thought the book was worth reading in a course their parents were paying lots of money for. Of course, I didn't always succeed in convincing the entire class that these noncanonical novels deserved their attention, but many students would react to this gesture of openness enthusiastically, especially in conjunction with the course's organization, which I discuss below.

The importance of course titles and descriptions became clear to me when I talked about these issues with other graduate students at Northwestern. My friends reported that when their course title and description clearly indicated that they were teaching noncanonical material and in noncanonical ways, their students were very receptive to the material and their methods. When some of the same books were taught in a course which was not overtly marked as noncanonical, and which had a mixed bag of canonical and noncanonical material, they encountered resistance similar to what I had run into. This indicates that many undergrads—at least at Northwestern, but I suspect anywhere—will be somewhat aware of the canon debate when choosing an elective English course. Students who want to read more than the high school standards will choose those courses which teachers have marked as noncanonical, while students who want more of the safe stuff they already know will opt for the canonical course. How well a class would react to the noncanonical material or methods brought to the course by the graduate student instructor would be at least in part based on the self-selection of receptive (or nonreceptive) students into the course due to its title and description.

This form of self-selection has a very real danger in relation to the project of creating open-mindedness, however. If students always choose courses which match their presuppositions and personal inclinations, it can result in the preaching-to-the-converted situation many of us are familiar with from conferences, where most of the deconstructionists will be in one room dismantling the Western tradition, and the Western traditionalists will be muttering about the impending end of the world next door, and precious little dialogue between the groups takes place. While it is pleasant—and can be very productive—to teach a class without conflict over basic issues, it is crucial for all teachers to try to reach those students who disagree with them, to attempt to get even the most resistant students to open up to the possibilities of noncanonical material, and to be willing and able to honestly engage the objections these students have rather than simply dismissing them as wrong, misguided, or the inevitable result of false consciousness. We should remember that one motive for canon-busting arose from the disdain many traditional professors showed towards graduate students asking why certain books and certain types of texts were not being taken seriously and read in the university. Teachers of noncanonical material should not repeat this blunder by dismissing out of hand the concerns of students with canonical attitudes. Perhaps the greatest skill a teacher can have is convincing the most resistant student in the class that what is being taught is worth teaching, and we will always have resistant students in our classes.

But given that we have only some control over who ends up taking our courses, what can we do to teach openly? Once whatever students we end up with take their seats in the classroom, we can begin to teach openly by organizing our courses in noncanonical ways. First and foremost, the class should be centered around discussion: I never gave fifty-minute lectures more than twice in a ten-week term. I organized my course around a theme (personal identity one quarter, mobility another, sense of place another) and explicated my ideas about this theme during the first class. So, in one sense, I set the agenda for the course in that initial lecture, and then relied on the subsequent discussion to create open-mindedness. I counted on a format of discussion to empower my students, to lead them to believe that what they were interested in was actually interesting and that open-mindedness was itself a goal.

But we should not kid ourselves into thinking that discussion in and of itself causes open-mindedness. I have taken graduate seminars which were ostensibly centered on discussion and student reports, and—looking at the syllabus—I thought the class would be very open, full of intellectual possibilities, but the professor had a list of points to be made each week come what may, and firmly steered the discussion to those points, creating a lecture thinly disguised as discussion. This must be avoided, as we need to find ways to empower students to set the agenda, to lead the class towards their own interests.

After that first meeting, my students would sign up to write a paper on a book which interested them (or, more realistically perhaps, on a book which was scheduled at a convenient time). Students would meet with me before writing their paper, and the paper would be read to the class and would form the basis for the discussion. I would not see the paper until a few hours before class time, and never came to class with anything more than a few questions or comments prepared. Of course, this method directly opposes how we have been trained to think about teaching; but I do not believe this is a bad thing. As Jane Tompkins points out in "Pedagogy of the Distressed," too often teaching has become a sort of performance, where the focus was not on the student but on the professor and how "smart," "knowledgeable," and "well-prepared for class" she was (654). Tompkins came to realize that traditional, canonical teaching methods resulted in her "putting on a performance whose true goal was not to help the students learn but to perform before them in such a way that they would have a good opinion of me" (654). Such a performance would naturally be most possible in the canonical lecture course, where the virtuoso teacher stands in front of the class like a singer on a stage and performs for fifty minutes, but is more difficult to manage in a discussion-based classroom where you are seated in a circle along with the students and where, crucially, the course is organized around students reading their own work to each other.

This organization took the class out of my hands and put it into theirs. In personal conferences I required before the papers were written, I could make suggestions, I could cajole, I could prod and push; but my students could, and did, go back to their dorm rooms and write about what interested them. Sometimes this method worked and we had stimulating, interesting discussions which seemed to end far too soon; other times it did not, and I would have to fly by the seat of my pants and guide the discussion in a very overt way in order to avoid spending most of the class fidgeting and getting nowhere. But in either case, the focus of classroom discussion was not on finding *the answer* to questions raised by papers or by student comments, but on seriously discussing interesting questions, questions which might not lead to any firm answer. I repeatedly stressed that an intriguing question, one which opens up more possibilities than can be discussed in fifty minutes, is more important than a boring answer, and my students generally responded enthusiastically. This noncanonical method made me less important and my students more important. Each time I have taught this way, my students have became accustomed to responding more to each other's ideas rather than spouting what they thought I wanted to hear, and after a very short period of time a large number of them felt perfectly willing to disagree with points I would try to make. To some degree, I had succeeded in teaching open-mindedness or, at the very least, in creating an open-minded classroom.

A brief example might make clear how this can work. When I assigned Nelson Algren's *The Man With the Golden Arm* in the course which dealt with the theme of social and physical mobility, I was primarily interested in the way Algren's lumpen-proletariat characters were trapped in their very small world on Chicago's West Side, in contrast to Huck's freedom of movement, or even the initially hopeful migration of the Joads. The vast majority of the novel takes place in a single small neighborhood and the only physical manifestation or symbol of the idea of mobility was the Loop-bound el, which of course just goes in circles around the characters and ends up right were it began. But, this particular quarter, the students who wrote papers on the novel were interested in how Algren portrays his female characters as either crushing burdens to their men or as potential sexual saviors, in an ironic twist on the old Virgin/Whore dualism, and on Algren's use of metaphor. These two topics, one feminist and noncanonical and the other rather staid and traditional, were valid enough, and we never did talk much about what interested me.

But so what?

The discussions and the papers were engaged with the material, were conducted seriously, and resulted in more questions than answers: that we did not talk about what interested me did not mean that the class failed to be open to the material. Quite the opposite: if nothing else, the performance of these students meant that the class was open to things that I was not originally open to myself, that they were showing me things about the text, that I was learning while I was teaching. Perhaps most rewardingly, the class managed to see Algren's problematic treatment of women as just that—a problem which could not be dismissed in the usual way canonical New Critical methodology argues away "apparent" contradictions in the quest for unity.

Up until this point, I have been dealing with situations where graduate student teachers design and teach their own courses. But obviously, the pedagogical situation is different when we teach in conjunction with lecture courses: then we will be in the situation of leading discussions about texts we had no input in choosing and, after lectures, we had as little to do with. How can graduate student teachers make use of our middle-ground status in order to teach with noncanonical methods in discussion sections?

First, while the select canon for that class is out of our control, what we do in discussion sections, what we do in the overcrowded and overheated classroom we are assigned by the powers that be, is not. Of course, a professor interested in teaching noncanonical material may make the similarly interested graduate student teacher's job easy. But even in this situation, we need to be open and to avoid the temptation to lecture in discussion, to display how smart and cutting-edge (or traditional) we are. Even if the professor gives good lectures, no fifty-minute hour can possibly cover everything which would be said about a text, and so discussion sections become the vital place where we can empower our students to see their own readings as important, to think of their experience of a text as something which has value.

Of course, it is just as likely—if not more likely—that a graduate student interested in noncanonical texts or teaching methods will be TA-ing for a professor who hasn't updated his lecture notes since 1958, who will declaim about Fitzgerald's doomed romanticism, Hemingway's heros and their codes, the profound exploration of the dark side of the human psyche we see in Poe (and Melville and Hawthorne and . . .), the inherent Americanness of Huck lighting out for the territories, and so on. It is when leading discussion groups in conjunction with such lectures that we can most make use of our neither-here-nor-there status to try to teach students to read with open minds, at least in part because some students may be bored silly by the material (much of which they probably heard in high school) and be anxious for something more. It is no accident that one such traditionalist professor at Northwestern makes a point of telling his students that attendance at discussion sections is not mandatory. Well aware that many of his TAs will attempt to undercut or actively oppose his canonical readings, this professor simply tries to foreclose discussion by encouraging undergrads to stay away from the evil influence of graduate student teachers. Openness being a threat, he clearly believes that a closed, one-way discourse is the only way he can safely present his canonical interpretations.

But graduate students leading discussion sections in which they present readings or interpretations which oppose material given in lecture face some important difficulties, not the least of which is that many undergrads will be more interested in what is going to be on the final exam than in discussion: after all, the professor lecturing up there in front of a couple of hundred people is, as far as the students are concerned, in charge. This practical consideration should not be dismissed out of hand, but we should also resist the temptation to point out that often as not, we, not the professor, will be grading the finals. This could very well lead to students treating graduate instructors the same way they would a prof, that is, by parroting their positions instead of being open-minded about the issues being discussed.

But we can sometimes overcome this form of resistance in discussion sections and we can help students read openly, simply by presenting another point of view and by challenging the openness of the professor and his or her methods. One fellow graduate student taught in a course where he had to lead discussions after straight canonical lectures. He situated his oppositional readings by putting a challenge to the professor's openness, arguing to his students "that the professor represents a point of view which tends to make unavailable any number of alternative texts or readings of texts." Another graduate student told me her method for opening discussions which oppose professorial readings: "If I disagree with the professor, I will make explicit the grounds of the disagreement," she writes. In other words, her strategy would begin with a gesture of openness: making explicit her own position, before arguing against the professor. A third colleague told me that such a gesture of openness and honesty is absolutely vital to her teaching: "Initial honesty about one's liminal teaching status is much more of a help than a hindrance. Whatever authority is sacrificed (which is of a morally questionable kind anyway) is made up for in increased student engagement with the teacher, the texts, and with other students in the classroom." This engagement is crucial to teaching open-mindedness, and should begin with an openness on the part of the graduate student teacher. And it is something we can do in discussion sections as easily as in our own classrooms.

But we must remember that our students must bring something to the class for it to succeed. One of my informants writes that the extent to which she succeeded or failed to make her students open to noncanonical material depended as much on them as on her. She writes that "students who accept my alternative readings usually do so because they felt the professor's reading was impoverished, because they disagreed with the professor's reading or because [it] was not meaningful to them." In other words, students who found the professor's reading rich and meaningful and who agreed with it would probably not listen to alternative readings in the first place. We can only do so much, and what our students bring to the class— life experience; knowledge; ideas about race, gender, and class; attitudes about literature; expectations about canonicity—will be as important as whatever we bring to class when we teach. And whether we have resistant or enthusiastic students (or, more likely, some mixture), we should avoid the temptation to do it all, to carry the class on our backs. As Tompkins argues, we need to "trust the student. . . . The point is for the student to became engaged, take responsibility, feel their own power and ability" (659). Such engagement is often exactly the opposite of what canonical pedagogical methods expect: how much responsibility, engagement, power, or ability does it require to take notes and repeat canonical or noncanonical mantras on a final exam?

Neither changing the traditional canon nor creating new canons will effect the real social change most opponents of the canon strive for. We must change the culture of the university, and at the heart of that project is our pedagogy, our classroom techniques. If the canon debate is, as Katha Pollitt claims, "really an argument about what books to cram dawn the resistant throats of a resentful captive populace of students" (210), then it matters little which books we teach; it matters how we teach the books we teach, how we treat students, how we conceive of our own authority. If we can teach in a more democratic and open-minded, less authoritarian way, perhaps students will be somewhat less resentful.

To cite Tompkins again, "what really matters as far as our own beliefs and projects for change are concerned is not so much what we talk about in class as what we do" (656). My initial reaction to Tompkins' argument against performance-based teaching was that it is easy for someone teaching graduate seminars at an elite institution to make such claims: the tenured can pretty much do as they will. But further thought led me to realize that our status near the bottom of the university hierarchy allows us a similar freedom. Graduate student teachers are—in many ways and in many institutions—beneath notice, and this status actually makes us freer than many professors to teach in noncanonical ways. Teaching our own small courses and leading discussion sections might be the last chance we get for a while to teach open-mindedness to small groups of students without the pressure to do loads of publishing or to teach to large lecture courses to divert us. Perhaps in doing so we can cause change by helping to make our students open to what literature can teach them about the world, politics, and themselves. The neither-here-nor-there institutional position occupied by graduate students might allow us to effect, on some small level, such change.

WORKS CITED

Algren, Nelson. *The Man With the Golden Arm.* NY: Four Walls Eight Windows, 1990.

Blades, John. "Expanded 'Great Books' Sure to Open Great Debate." *Chicago Tribune,* 25 October 1990, final ed., section 5: 1+.

Fowler, Alastair. "Genre and the Literary Canon." *New Literary History* 11 (1979): 97–119.

Graff, Gerald. "The University and the Prevention of Culture." *Criticism in the University.* Ed. Reginald Gibbons and Gerald Graff. Evanston: Northwestern UP, 1985. 62–82.

Harris, Wendell V. "Canonicity." *PMLA* 106.1 (1991): 110–121.

Pollitt, Katha. "Why Do We Read?" *Debating P. C.: The Controversy over Political Correctness on College Campuses*. Ed. Paul Berman. NY: Laurel, 1992. 201–211.

Tompkins, Jane. "Pedagogy of the Distressed." *College English* 52 (1990): 653–660.

The Dream of Authority

Jane Tompkins

You're in front of class on the first day of school and for some reason you are totally unprepared. (How did this happen?) You grab for words, fake a smile, tell an anecdote, anything to hold their attention, but the strangers in the rows in front of you aren't having any. They start to shuffle and murmur, they look out the window. Then, chairs scrape back and you realize it's actually happened. They are walking out on you! You have gotten what you deserved.

This dream in one form or another is dreamed by thousands of teachers before the beginning of the fall semester. It is so common that most people I know discount it—everybody has that dream, they say, as if to dismiss the subject. My purpose today is to suggest that the dream—or rather, what it stands for—is not at all discountable but is a subject of investigation that leads to the heart of what we are talking about today. For the dream is about a failure of authority, and the fear of guilt—shame—humiliation that attends such failure. The question of authority and our relation to it that the dream raises lies at the heart of what it means to be politically responsible in the classroom.

I am studying for my Ph.D. exams. I'm about to take them and am in a state of high anxiety. Suddenly I realize that I haven't studied at all. I've been doing some vague research on topics that interest me but they aren't the right ones. It occurs to

me that I've never even cracked the surveys of English literature
I'd relied on in graduate school, fat paperbacks in purple and
lavender, containing all the things one needed to know. Why
haven't I touched these books? I have 25 minutes before the
exam. Maybe I can cram at the last minute, I've always been a
quick study. But I don't even do that. Instead, I get myself a cup
of coffee, find a good place to read, go back for my jacket, and so
on, until there's no time left.

I realize then, they're going to fail me. (This is all taking
place at Duke where I teach, and it comes to me that the exam is
the chance the older faculty have been waiting for: to show me
up for what I really am.) It's a ten-hour written exam with an
oral component. I've learned from a colleague I consider more
learned than myself that the exam has short-answer questions
like "Who were the Fugitives?" (Do I know who the Fugitives
were? I'm not sure.)

Then comes the familiar moment of recognition: I already
have a Ph.D. It's from Yale—how much better could it be? I
decide in a frenzy of rebellion that I won't take this exam, I will
not subject myself to the humiliation of failure. I'm walking up
the stairs now toward the exam room; there's no time left. What
will I do?

Not long ago, I read in a self-help book that if you try to
uncover the assumptions behind your dreams, you'll be able to
get hold of the belief system that gives rise to them. By changing
the beliefs, the thinking goes, you can change your experience.

In the first dream I had to believe that there was no reason
for students to pay attention to me, no grounds on which I could
command their respect. I felt that I had nothing to offer them,
and took their rejection as warranted. In my eyes and in theirs, I
was completely lacking in authority.

In the second dream, I appear as a student in an institution
where I am a full professor. (I have been a full professor for nine
years, an instructor or professor of some sort for twenty-two.) I
am almost fifty, dreaming of being in the position of a twenty-
four-year-old. I don't believe in my authority in this dream
either. Here, as before, I am a fraud, someone who's supposed to

know things she doesn't actually know. On top of that, when given the chance to acquire some knowledge at the last minute, I make myself comfortable instead.

But this dream has a new twist. I remember, in the nick of time, that I do have the proper credentials after all. I decide to stand up for myself, to insist that people accept me as I am. The institution may have decided that I need to renew my license but it occurs to me that I can refuse.

I once read that the last moment of a dream can furnish a clue to its therapeutic meaning. For, the author asserted, dreams are to be used for problem solving in one's waking life. If so, the second dream implied that I should bet on myself, risk affirming that I was already all right. In the dream, this seemed an extremely daring course of action, and it's not clear whether I will pursue it or not.

Dream interpretation may seem an unlikely basis for addressing so weighty and public an issue as the political responsibilities of the teacher. But the question of authority which the dreams raise lies at the heart of what it means to be politically responsible in the classroom. The way one deals with one's authority as a teacher acts as a model for the functioning of authority in the society at large.

I have recently become uncomfortable with my role as an authority figure in the classroom. This discomfort stems from a lifetime of accumulated encounters with authority within the academic institution, the earliest being the most crucial for me now. I believe that in our childhood experience of authority in school and at home lies the clue to our current politics, as practiced and professed. As a person of power, one who both exercises and makes statements about power, I no longer wish to be ruled by the shadows of forgotten authorities.

Before going any further, let me remind you—not that you need reminding—of a few of the ways in which we compensate for a lack of authority in the classroom: relentless self-questioning, slavish deference to students' opinions, never taking a stand or making an unambiguous point; being militantly overprepared, having everything nailed down in advance, allowing no deviations from the plan (with its safeguards and fallbacks), laying down detailed rules of procedure. Then there's the love-me-love-my-teaching convention, which involves lots of disarming self-revelation, jokes, criticizing school authorities, flattering students, accepting late papers, late attendance, nonperformance of every kind. I often mix this strategy with the high-and-outside-pitch routine requiring me to make everything I say as complicated, high-level, and idiosyncratic as possible lest the students think I'm not as smart as they are. The combination really confuses them, especially if you pile on the work, grade hard, and tell them that all you care about is their individual development.

It's easy, though, to caricature the devices we stoop to, easy to laugh at and criticize ourselves. Teaching is hard. If we alternately one-up, intimidate, and sandbag the students, it's because we are threatened and feel afraid. But of what? After all, we are the teachers. We make the assignments, judge the work, give the grades; in every measurable sense the power lies all with us. Still, teachers have nightmares before the beginning of the fall semester, get nervous before class, indulge in agonized postmortems. Can such behavior be written off as common performance anxiety, or does it have some particular cause within the institution itself? Why is teaching terrifying?

Terror is like a ball that bounces back and forth between two walls of a small room. Once you throw it hard at one wall, it rebounds to the other and then back against the first and so on until it loses momentum and gravity pulls it to the floor. With terror, though, I'm not sure what stops the ball, or whether in some instances it doesn't pick up speed and bounce harder. The walls in this metaphor are teachers and students, and the ball is the fear they pass back and forth.

The image of authority is embodied for me in teachers. Mrs. Colgan in 1B, standing tense and straight in a dress of black spots that hangs on her figure. Her lips are pursed, her hair is in a hairnet, her black eyes snap with intensity, and her whole thin being radiates the righteous authority she exercises over us; it is mixed with wrath. She is scolding, holding a small book in front of her flat, draped chest. But Mrs. Colgan has to exert all the energy she has to maintain this stance; it isn't easy. Most of the time she spoke to us in a soft, gentle voice; she liked to be soft and gentle with the children. Only when something went wrong, when someone really stepped out of line, did she become into her steely, pursed-lip self. That was when you noticed her parchment skin and cold wire-rimmed glasses. She succeeded in imposing her authority but it wasn't her preference; she had to force herself. Because I saw this, I was afraid of Mrs. Colgan but not terrified of her. I saw in her the two faces of authority: the desire to gently lead, to be kind and affectionate, to love, and the necessity to instill fear, the desperation of having to beat back the enemy by whatever means.

It is the second image that tends to remain, that must be lodged in some form in most people's memories. The teacher, the one who stands in front, who stands while others sit, the one whom you must obey, the one who exacts obedience first of all. For obedience is the basis for everything else that happens in school; unless the children obey, nothing can be taught. At least that is what I learned. Obedience first. Or rather, fear first, —fear of authority, yielding obedience, then everything else.

There was a boy in one of my classes, I think in the second and third grade, who stood in my mind as the symbol for the need of authority two, the kind I hated. His name was Stanley Koslowski—or something close to that—Stanley, and then a Polish last name, like Stanley Kowalski in *A Streetcar Named Desire*, or like my husband, whose name is also Stanley (can these likenesses be purely accidental?) He was always bad. Nothing teachers could do or say ever shut Stanley up permanently. He could be temporarily quelled, but sooner or later he always came back for more. I was terrified of being spoken to and about the way the teachers spoke to and about Stanley Koslowski, for he brought out the worst in them: shouting, name-calling, intimidation, humiliation, punishment. Every form of sarcasm and ridicule they could command, every threat, every device of shaming. If there had been stocks in P.S. 98, Stanley Koslowski would have been in them. (This talk would be different if he were writing it, too. The view of authority not at all the same. You have to correct for the bias of the good girl—class monitor, teacher's pet—the pathology of fear so strong that I never, until once in the fifth grade, deliberately dared risking the teacher's rebuke.)

Stanley, though, like Mrs. Colgan had two sides. He was terrible, we were told, he was the universal troublemaker without whom everything would have been fine. And surely he caused us hours of listening to yelling, and hours of leftover bad feeling spilling over from the teacher onto us, and oozing out from us into the corners of the room. But he was cute, and his energy was exciting. He was an appealing figure in a rough-and-tumble sort of way. At times I thought he was being victimized. Why make so much fuss over one poor boy who couldn't help himself? You had to sympathize. I mean, we were supposed to sit all day, hands folded on our desks, legs crossed (if you were a girl), silent, staring forward in our rows, our lessons so mind-bogglingly boring that even our brains had no exercise to speak of. Everything was rules. Looking back on it now, it seems that much of the time, in school, the only interest or action lay in the power struggle between the teachers, whose reign of terror enforced the rules, and the students, whose uncontrollable energy contested them.

So Stanley Koslowski had his reasons, and certainly Mrs. Colgan had hers. They were neither of them bad, but each forced the other into an intolerable position and they did what they could to get out of it. Meanwhile, as a totally cowed bystander, I grew up with a head full of contradictory fears and desires where authority was concerned.

Some of the fears came from other teachers who were much worse than Mrs. Colgan. The very sight of Mrs. Garrity in the halls with her brown suit and her red face made red by perennial anger struck terror in me (I can still feel it)—though usually one heard her first, screaming horribly and interminably at some unlucky person. It seemed to me entirely an accident that that person had not yet been me. And there was Mrs. Seebach, of the enormous bosom and enormous behind, who bellowed at us in gym class, seized by demoniac rage over a student's failure properly to execute grand right and left. The rages these teachers were capable of have rarely been matched in my experience of human beings since.

There were other authorities as well, more august. Mr. Rothman, the new principal, and (holy of holies) Mr. Zimmerman, Superintendent of Schools—presences so terrible no one dared, not even the Stanley Koslowskis, to so much as breathe naturally as we stood in rigid rows for their inspection.

I have one last image from those days which is relevant here, of a boy in third grade—his name was Stephen Kirschner—a pretty blond child with sky blue eyes and a soft-as-doeskin nature. He is standing at attention next to his seat, being dressed down by the teacher for some slight. The teacher is Rose Higgins, the kindest one of all—she called us her darlings—but she is making him miserable. He stands there, stiffly, hands at his sides, taking it and trying not to cry. Why do this to Stephen Kirschner of all people? Didn't she know he was innocent? As he stood there, he was the very picture of innocence, yet the lash, metaphorically, fell on him just the same, and as it did, it fell on me, too, for strange as it may seem, I did not distinguish between myself and the unhappy culprit. For I knew, if I knew anything in that terrifying world, that it could have been me.

After all this, I became a teacher. You would think that with experiences like these so vivid in my mind, I would have avoided school like the plague, but no. I *joined*. The teachers I consciously modelled myself on were not of course the ones I've been describing but teachers I had later in junior high and high school, Miss Edmundson, Mrs. Torrance, Mrs. Hay—who never used the metaphoric whip, but inspired, encouraged, and praised. Still, the older models remain, the deeper stratum lies underneath, its breath of ancient terror haunting me. Mrs. Seebach still pulls the strings when, threatened with the spectre of being shown up as ignorant or lazy, I clutch and start to perform my competence so that there will be no mistake.

What have all these images got to do with the focus of this essay? Well, nothing, as "the political responsibilities of the teacher" are currently understood. When most people in our profession hear such a phrase, they usually think of the following issues: the debate over the canon, Marxism, feminism, gay and lesbian rights, racism—political issues at the center of our subject matter, of what we teach but which, *as currently conceived and discussed*, are light-years away from the issues I have just been discussing. The point is that there must be a connection to our experience of power in school as young children and what we say we believe about power and the way we wield it now as adults. How can such experiences not affect one's own behavior and thus the behavior of one's students and so on down the line? Perhaps the political responsibilities of teachers lie first of all in their *way of being*, and not in any doctrine they espouse or in any texts they do or do not teach.

I do not know how the political lessons we received as children at the hands of our teachers get translated into the political beliefs of later life. There is certainly no simple correlation between authoritarian training, on the one hand, and authoritarian politics and authoritarian teaching on the other. I suspect that my own early and repeated exposure to authorities who terrified me absolutely has left me with a legacy of alternate rebellion against and servile submission to the authority figures in my life. This is the area where the work of discovery and reconstruction must be done: the space between imprinted past experience, the politics of childhood, and current behavior and belief.

Right now it seems to me our idea of what politics is in the classroom is too externally conceived and lacks a sense of history. We think in terms of curricula and structures and procedures that will guarantee equal opportunity for all. But what is the relation between "equal opportunity" and experiences of power in the third grade, where one learned that power grows out of the barrel chest of someone ineluctably in authority over us, ours not to reason why? The pedagogy that produces oppression starts early, and it is not necessarily linked to factors of race, class, or gender. It is situated in traditions of child-rearing like those Alice Miller describes in *For Your Own Good*. "Child-rearing" she writes "is basically directed not toward the *child's* welfare but toward satisfying the parents' need for power and revenge" (243). This need, in turn, is created by abuse suffered and forgotten, with the aid of splitting off and repression. "Now, it is precisely those events that have never been come to terms with that must seek an outlet in the repetition compulsion," says Miller. "The jubilation characteristic of those who declare war is the expression of the revived hope of finally being able to avenge earlier debasement, and presumably also of relief at finally being permitted to hate and shout."

I do not know what earlier debasements the teachers at P.S. 98 were avenging when they screamed. But their hatred and shouting are still echoing in my mind and I'm sure I cannot be the only one. I do not know what role exactly those teachers have played in my behavior as a teacher, but where else do one's defensiveness and strategies of counterattack, one's late summer dreams of failed authority come from if not from past encounters like these? The childhood experience of authority controls, without our knowing it, the way we exercise or fail to exercise power in the classroom as adults. These models, the models of authority and power we exhibit in the classrooms every day, are as important a factor in the formation of a politically responsible citizenry as any other. Perhaps more important than any other, except the way we exercise authority at home.

Teaching political responsibility begins at home, psychologically speaking; it begins with a frank assessment of one's own encounters with power at an early age, and the attempt to trace the connections between that past and one's present patterns of action and thought. Because, it seems to me, until you understand what made you, personally, what you are when it comes to exercising power, you cannot be a reliable example for others, say what you will about democracy and equal opportunity for all.

WORKS CITED

Miller, Alice. *For Your Own Good: Hidden Cruelty in Child-Rearing and the Roots of Violence*. Trans. Hildegarde and Hunter Hannun. NY: Farrar, Straus, Giroux, 1983.

Afterword

Paul Lauter

In many ways, these essays represent a renewal of the concerns of educational reformers of the 1960s. They share, for example, a serious interest in pedagogy and its relation to politics, and they are deeply involved with issues of process and authority, as well as with content. This may seem obvious, but I find it very heartening to see so many creative young teachers devoting their energies to these matters. For the fact is that in literary study over the past decade and more, teaching has not enjoyed much status—in professional meetings and most journals, in public acknowledgement, or in remuneration. To be sure, the Modern Language Association has for some years had divisions on teaching—including one on "Teaching as a Profession"—though these have not always concerned themselves with classroom practice. A few journals, like *Radical Teacher* and *College English*, have persisted in maintaining a classroom focus. And an occasional book has tried to translate theoretical paradigms into teaching practice.[1] But "theory" has been the name of the professional game, and its practitioners have seldom focused on the classroom.[2]

More recently, however, the dominance of theory as the center of literary study has been challenged by what has come to be called "multiculturalism," a.k.a. "canon revision." This focus on *what* one teaches has, for reasons these essays explore, led to a necessary renewal of concern for how one teaches. And this interest in pedagogy now seems to me extending from the "new" texts brought back into view by feminist and multiculturalist teachers to many traditional writers. The 1993 American Literature Association conference, for example, included for the first time an unusually large number of sessions devoted to issues in teaching Thoreau, Emerson, *Huckleberry Finn,* and other canonical stalwarts. I take that as a straw in the same wind inspiring these essays. Their underlying assumption is not that teaching is what one must do in order to qualify for the professional rewards derived from theoretical dexterity, but that teaching is at the center of our collective enterprise.

One useful role for me in this book, therefore, is to reinvoke those earlier debates of a quarter-century ago. My objective is not to enshrine the sixties—though that might serve as a healthy corrective to the now current distortions of the history of those years. Rather, I want to observe which issues of teaching were addressed and how, and with what success, and thus, perhaps, to illuminate the changing priorities and understandings in the current wave of educational reform. I also wish to provide a kind of historical bridge back to those earlier efforts. For there is a good deal of truth in the notion that one either learns from the past or repeats it, and if the current wave of educational reform has a generalizable limitation, it lies in a kind of historical amnesia. To be sure, most of the essayists in this volume are aware that debates about literary canons and the practices of multiculturalism were generated by the movements for social change of the sixties. Yet they show little direct interest in how those movements tried to develop transformative pedagogies. One finds few, if any, references to earlier writers like Herbert Kohl, Paul Goodman, John Holt, Edgar Z. Friedenberg; to the sixties' elaboration of ideas about student-centered teaching; or indeed, to the efforts in the seventies to move "Beyond Student-Centered Teaching"—to use the title of a pamphlet of that time by Brent Harold.

That is not surprising, for as Americans we are all trained—in school and out—to believe that "history is bunk"; "I am," writes Emerson, "an endless experimenter with no past at my back." This specific case, however, also reflects the isolation of college teachers from developments in earlier grades. Reformers like Kohl, Holt, and Jonathan Kozol did, finally, focus their work in the public schools. But university academics are taught—alongside balancing canapes and cocktails, and the correct citations of Derrida and Foucault—a systematic indifference for whatever it is that goes down in Schools of Education. The effect, of course, has largely been to separate creative college teachers from the often quite useful work proceeding in some schools—on, for example, student-response pedagogies and cooperative learning practices.[3] I do not mean these comments to be critical of the contributors to this volume, but I do think a new generation of reformers can learn from the successes and limitations of a previous generation of innovators.

Overall, these essays display a striking congruence of methodological interests. A number take for granted or develop ideas involving the comparative study of texts which derive from somewhat differing cultural traditions.[4] Others also focus on the need not only to historicize texts, to understand the "work" differing forms of textuality do in particular moments, but to enable students to take possession of that history for themselves rather than experiencing it (with a yawn) as a professorial lay-on. Indeed, these essays display an uncommon awareness of how different are students' needs in the markedly dissimilar institutions that are called "colleges" and, perhaps more important, how difficult it is to begin from such needs when we have so systematically been taught to pursue our own cultural ideas, liberal or conservative, even in the teeth of student fear and resistance. Indeed, these writers understand the classroom not as a neutral site for the detached discussion of presumptively liberating cultural study but as a conflicted arena in which differing personal and political agendas contest for space, in which issues of power are never absent, and in which even the subject matter—that is, what gets defined as "literature" or "culture"—is no innocent choice. Many of these essays have drawn from theoretical discussions within the profession a sophisticated understanding of classroom dynamics, of the operations of gender, race, class, and other "subject positions" in the processes by which we engage students. Moreover, almost all of these writers see their work as part of a broader, and what has to be called "political," project involving the ends, and therefore the means, of education.

In these and other respects, the essays gathered here represent a challenge to the continuing power of formalist pedagogical strategies. Formalism, and especially the close-reading tactics associated with the New Criticism, was set in place gradually over two or three decades. And, as I have written elsewhere, a formalist "pedagogical canon" persists today despite the great changes in the textual canon which inform particularly American literature curricula.[5] By "pedagogical canon" I do not mean specific, revered texts like Cleanth Brooks' and R. P. Warren's *Understanding Poetry*, though I do not underestimate the continued, if now more indirect, influence of those works. Rather, I refer to distinct formalist practices, like *explication de texte* and structural literary analysis, which continue to dominate numerous classrooms, especially in secondary schools. There, I think, many students learn that poetry is a puzzle, the solution to which is retained (for dramatic display at the appropriate moment) by the more experienced (and powerful) reader designated as "teacher." The students' task, therefore, is to guess the secret held by the teacher, as it were, behind her back—or, what is more likely, to keep silent long enough for the teacher to reveal it for consumption and the subsequent reproduction necessary for the students to pass across this hurdle and on to the next. I am, of course, drawing a cartoon, but we deny the continuing power of the formalist pedagogical canon at our peril.

That continuing power is rooted, I would argue, in modernist ideas of literary value, which have dominated the institutional life of our profession. These modernist ideas were born in conflict: in fact, Eliot, Pound, and their New Critical progeny maintained a cultural struggle on many fronts. In the first instance—and through the 1950s—these writers deployed "criticism" against older forms of historical and scholarly practice which took literature as the occasion for learning rather than *as* the learning. In this context, critics, New and not so new, presented themselves as a progressive force against the backward tendencies of genteel philologists, whose preferences might have been more eclectic as well as more tradition-bound. In addition, New Critics set themselves against the disposition of left-leaning and African American commentators to place the social or even political functions of writing at the center of their concern. The triumph of criticism, and especially its cold-war formulations of correct strategies for encountering literary texts,[6] set the terms on which English and related fields would develop during the vast expansion of collegiate study after World War II and especially during the 1960s. To say this more briefly, the translation of high modernism into pedagogical practice has been at the core of the profession called "English" at every educational level. The sixties' innovations as well as the current battles over what and how we teach are, in this sense, continuing efforts to emancipate ourselves—implicitly the profession, and thus students—from that historically constructed idea of the hermeneutical role of the critic-teacher in reproducing and valuating culture, and therefore from the politics embedded in that idea.

In many ways this account of professional history—all too briefly sketched—is familiar. But it may allow us to situate the educational innovations of the 1960s and 1970s more fully. In the first instance, these movements for change challenged the existing professional consensus on canonical grounds. They asked, "Where are the blacks?" "Where are the women?" in curricula, textbooks, bookstores, and libraries. And they prodded some of us already active in the profession—and of course, a larger number coming into it—to produce answers in the form of new editions of lost or forgotten works, as well as more inclusive anthologies and syllabi. Obviously, it was easier to effect change in these textual domains: the dominant canons *were* narrow. Moreover, an expanded canon served the interests of an expanding professoriat as well as benefitting colleges and universities anxious to maintain enrollment by recruiting new constituencies. Besides, weakly multicultural curricula *seemed* less threatening than moves, like serious affirmative action, that might endanger existing arrangements of academic power. Finally, those of us most deeply invested in changing canons continued to use terms like "literary" (as in "literary canon" or "American literary history"), which at some level sustained the separation of the kinds of writing traditionally taught in "English" from "popular culture," films, or the other forms of "textuality" increasingly of interest to those engaged in what

was coming to be called "cultural studies" or poststructural
theorists who saw the world as constituted by "texts." So we
canon-revisers undoubtedly seemed less a challenge to the
central disciplinary structuring of the academy.

On the other hand, those of us fostering canon change saw
it as a process—"two steps forward, one step back"—that would
in time bring about serious transformations of curricula,
anthologies, and the texts critics study, and thus ideas of cultural
value. Such changes have happened in significant measure, as
the revaluations of writers like Harriet Beecher Stowe, Fanny
Fern, and Charles Chesnutt illustrate, and as the reassessment of
the importance of discontinuous texts like letters and journals
suggests. In fact, as Joyce Warren has pointed out, first-
generation-to-college and immigrant students are often more
directly moved by the familiar human experiences in works like
Fern's *Ruth Hall* or Alice Cary's "Uncle Christopher's" than by
the grand but remote experiences chronicled in works like *Moby-
Dick* or "The Fall of the House of Usher." As a result, the
evaluative principles which underwrote formalist canons have,
one by one, come under increasing scrutiny: e.g., the centrality of
"organic form," the "intentional fallacy," the presumed
marginality of endemic racism and anti-Semitism, and most
recently, the strictures against and even the understanding of
"sentimentality." I mention these issues in particular because
they resonate with familiar, and often effectively suppressed,
classroom comments like "Did he mean that?" or "Aw, that's just
a tearjerker." In short, the project of canon revision, initiated in
the sixties, has necessarily involved a continuing reexamination
of literary values (however old-fashioned that phrase may
sound), not only at the level of theory but in actual classroom
practice.

At some level, the reigning assumption in the earlier
debates over the content of "the" canon (and therefore, it was
assumed, of curricula) was that reading noncanonical work was
implicitly liberatory, even if studying canonical work (like
Melville) was not *necessarily* retrogressive. A number of
commentators have, over the years, questioned the naivety of
this assumption, noting that many texts omitted from the canon
expressed anything but progressive views and that, in any case,

what students derived from a literary work did not necessarily (some argued "likely") reflect its values (Stavney provides a summary of this debate). These essays reformulate the debate in at least two ways. A number of them (e.g., Christopher, Goebel, Boyd, Roche Rico and Mano) insist that reading certain noncanonical texts in *particular* educational settings can offer *some* students—especially those from constituencies marginalized by university cultural norms—access to alternative values. At the least (Stavney, Goebel, Jay), using canonical and noncanonical texts in courses and thus placing them in "conversation" facilitates meaningful classroom dialogue. Such conversations can also generate revisionist perceptions of historical cultural constructions like "modernism" (Stavney) or "American" (Jay). Underlying this argument is a more systematic perception than was available in the sixties of the importance to what students of differing backgrounds expect and can derive from courses of "subject position" (an issue to which I will turn below). The writers in this book are also more careful to define the particular collegiate contexts about which they are writing (e.g., Bower), an especially important corrective of generalizations about "the university" at a time in which postsecondary institutions are increasingly differentiated as to constituency and functions.

The second discussion about canon to which these essays significantly contribute involves a more fundamental shift in the subject matter of "English" classrooms. As a number of these essays note (e.g., Cutter, Bower), the traditional New Critical classroom focused on the careful explication of structure and form *within* discrete literary works. What we expected our students to learn, most of all, was close reading, some conception of how literary works were artistically constructed, and a sense of what constituted the differences in writers' styles. By contrast, the structures which interest most of the teachers in this book are those which produce and reproduce literary value or significance and cultural meaning. This move does *not*, I want to emphasize, imply discarding the skills of close reading. Rather it involves the application of those (among other) skills to "reading" a syllabus or anthology (Bower), the classroom itself (Cutter), and even the discrepancies in pedagogical authority among those differently situated in a university (Savage). This shift seems to me at least as critical to the fierce debate between literary traditionalists and canon revisers as the issue of the very content of a canon. From the point of view of traditionalists, this change of focus turns the "literature" classroom into some form of "sociological" study and may even deny students the pleasure of appreciating the artistry of classic works. From the perspective of revisionists, the new emphasis not only helps students to grasp the dynamics by which cultural formations—like a canon, a course, a discipline, a university, what is demarcated and valued as "literature" or "American" (e.g., Danielson, Jay)—are historically constructed, but it also enables them to experience the "fun" (Bower) of becoming players (rather than merely consumers) in this significant cultural work. Furthermore, such learnings aid—as the conjunction of literary and critical legal studies suggests—people in "reading" the variety of "texts" which constitute their everyday lives. Finally, I think, these essays offer more pedagogically satisfying, if less uniform, ways of helping students to understand why particular texts emerge as "classic" or "canonical" than older explanations based on "aesthetic" criteria, on untheorized preferences in taste, and ultimately on an instructor's raw power to enforce these.

The second project of sixties reformers concerned not the ostensible subject matter of a course but what was then called the "hidden curricula" of classrooms, the "noise," or *process*. These, critics argued, were designed more to reenforce existing authority structures, and to force students to internalize them, than to transmit knowledge or promote learning. For example, commenting on procedures which effectively demanded that children wave their hands in response to a question, Jules Henry wrote:

> In a society where competition for the basic cultural goods is a pivot of action, people cannot be taught to love one another, for those who do cannot compete with one another, except in play. It thus becomes necessary for the school, without appearing to do so, to teach children how to hate, without appearing to do so, for our culture cannot

> tolerate the idea that babes should hate each other. How
> does the school accomplish this ambiguity? Obviously
> through competition itself.[7]

In the sixties, various methods were devised to disrupt the
political agendas which underwrote school curricula and
organizational procedures. In experiments like the Freedom
Schools developed during the Mississippi summer project of
1964, teachers were urged to seat their students in a circle,
encourage the use of first names, and make explicit the
connections between what went on in the schools and the
political movement that had engendered them.[8] Such moves,
organizers believed, would help students challenge school
authority and thus the whole structure of racist power that
oppressed them.

Whatever the Freedom School *students* took away from
their brief encounters with liberatory education, many of the
teachers learned to question their own authority in the classroom
and over texts, the content of their own studies, as well as the
social functions of the educational institutions through which
they themselves had passed. And, as activist students became
faculty, and as "movement" ideas became institutionalized in
academic programs like Black Studies and Women's Studies,
many of the innovations pioneered in experiments like the
Freedom Schools came to be adopted in college classrooms.
Indeed, in the late sixties and early seventies, matters of process
may be said to have obsessed educational reformers and, in
many respects, the social movements altogether.[9]

It soon became clear, however, that changing seating
arrangements, validating all student responses to texts,
democratizing classroom procedures, or otherwise attempting to
transfer more authority from teacher to learner ran hard against
institutional power relationships and, often, student
expectations. Initially, educational reformers understood the
problem as student "resistance" to our efforts to "liberate" them,
a kind of "false consciousness" that simply needed to be
overcome. In time, however, it came to seem that the "false
consciousness," if it existed, might reside more in the heads of
instructors who tried to ignore the quite uneven relationships of
power inherent in any situation in which one party organizes

and judges and the others are expected to respond and be judged. A teacher could, for example, devise a variety of grading procedures (e.g., contracts, group processes) but it remained clear—certainly to students—that the *power* to determine procedure and ultimately therefore final product (grade) necessarily remained with the instructor, as surely as it did with a traffic court judge.

Furthermore, by deploying a professional discourse over which their training had given them some command, instructors could, without necessarily being aware of it, magnify power differences between themselves and their students. Indeed, it is hard not to see the use of some theoretical jargon as a form of intellectual domination—though teachers I respect have insisted that once students get used to the terminology, they can find poststructuralist language helpful and even liberating. However that might be, the operation of power differentials in the classroom has proven itself to be far more complex, and intractable, than many of us imagined a quarter-century ago. As Peter Caccavari notes, even if one could remove the instructor's authority, students would turn to texts to satisfy their need for the comfort and direction of hierarchy.

The problematic of classroom process was, over time, further complicated by the emergence of difference—in gender, race, class, and sexuality—as pivotal to the dynamics that mark faculty-student interactions. I think it is fair to say that few of the earlier reformers recognized the centrality of what today we refer to as "subject position" in the organization of power in schools and colleges. Particularly when the subject matter involves multiculturalism or gender, questions of subject position become critical to any honest dialogue. These problems of power, discourse, subject position, so deeply woven into the fabric of institutionalized learning, undo the naive assumptions that some of us made about "building socialism in one classroom," to use a joking phrase of that earlier time. Still, sixties reformers, like today's innovators, rooted their efforts to contend with these problems in the fundamental perception that education, far from being insulated from power relationships, is always already constituted *by* them.

In many ways these essays can be seen as attempts to address the continuing problem of classroom (and canonical) authority (Tompkins). For, as Martha Cutter points out, if we do not examine the ends of education and what we want students to learn, "our own teaching practices will replicate the very structures of authority and domination which the canon presents." What we want above all else, I think these essays suggest, remains finding the means to enable students to develop an earned and meaningful authority over the subject matter of a course and, more broadly, over their lives. But how? And how, in particular, does a teacher steer between the reemergence, in ever new forms, of professorial domination, on the one hand, and abject submission to changing (and often consumption-driven) student imperatives, on the other?

Postmodern theorists like Lyotard have insisted that no narrative is, or will be, available to replace the now discredited master narratives of the modern world. Likewise, these essays can be read as suggesting that no master pedagogy can or should be constructed to replace the analytic procedures associated with the New Criticism. Indeed, many of these essays insist, correctly I think, upon the need to devise teaching strategies in relationship to the peculiar local characteristics of an institution or particular student body. Still, it seems to me that one can distinguish certain common pedagogical foci in these essays, however differently implemented or even described.

First, in many of the classrooms portrayed here students learn that knowledge is "produced" by producing it. Whether that means involving students in constructing accounts of domesticity, free love, and related nineteenth-century issues (Danielson) or involving them in constructing a course syllabus (Bower), the lesson taught resides as much in the process as in the product. Other teachers have made subject position the initial focus of class discussion; still others, the classroom discourse itself. Of course, what counts as "process" has shifted significantly from the sixties: the issue is not, so to speak, classroom "manner" but epistemology. In all of these cases, I think, the implicit lesson, the not-so-hidden curriculum, is that "what" one learns—subject—and "how" one learns—process— are not separable categories; that knowledge in literary study is not an object, a pearl one pries from resistant verse, but is an intellectual construction situated in a particular historical moment, in a specific cultural space.

The forms of knowledge produced through this self-scrutinizing pedagogy will, I think, be less stable, probably more contentious, less subject to professorial closure than traditional ideas of what constitutes learning. I want to say this carefully, because nothing in today's colleges seems to have enraged traditionalists more than the idea of the contingency of knowledge. I am not arguing, and the writers of these essays do not argue, that "everything is relative" and we should pack up our brains because "there is no truth" but only politics, opinion, and self-interest. If *no* account of a text is absolute, in the sense of exhausting its possible meanings and power, *some* accounts are, in fact, better than others. They are more useful in a particular situation, explain more, open more, engage readers more fully. If *no* syllabus perfectly and perpetually represents ante bellum American literary production, for example, *some* syllabi will be more effective toward that end than others; but even these will change as students, conditions, and the functions of an institution or a course change.

Or, to shift the discussion slightly, if *no* single person in a classroom, including the instructor, monopolizes knowledge, it does not follow that *all* persons in a classroom can or should contribute to the processes of learning in the same ways, in the same degree, or at the same level. The roles of teachers, teaching assistants, graduate students, undergraduates differ and are not equal, though they overlap and change. If a teacher does nothing else, for example, she or he chooses starting points, as important in a classroom as in a poem or a work of fiction.[10] And good teachers perform a variety of other roles: organizing, leading, establishing boundaries, lending ego. The point here is that the teachers in this volume seem to me less hung up than sixties radicals on trying to shed forms of authority with which institutional arrangements inevitably invest them, and more concerned to focus on other forms of authority which students can, in fact, develop. These are, I think, forms of authority based not on romanticized ideas about student power, but the acknowledgement of the value of differing experiences and differing ways of knowing to the construction of knowledge in any group.

In fact, at the very center of the classroom activities discussed in this book is, I think, an insistence that knowledge-production is precisely a *group* process, within which individuals play distinctive roles, rather than a matter simply of individual ingenuity wherein the group plays a largely unprofitable—if not altogether destructive—role. Herein, at least to me, lies the idealism and perhaps heroism of these writers. For if, as I think is the case, societies develop educational systems (whatever other functions they may serve) to reproduce core social values, then surely a challenge to America's endemic individualism within the structures of American educational institutions is a visionary, and desperately needed, enterprise.

NOTES

1. See, for example, Margo Culley and Catharine Portuges, Susan Gabriel and Isaiah Smithson.

2. Notable exceptions include Cary Nelson, as well as some of the work of Stanley Aronowitz, Henry Giroux, and others interested in "critical pedagogy."

3 See, for example, on student-response pedagogy, the work of Richard Beach and, on cooperative learning, Robert E. Slavin.

4. A recent comment by Martha Banta helps illustrate the wide acceptance of this idea: "Granted that there are pockets around the nation where some institutions of higher education have not yet heard of the need to be comparativists, or cannot accept this need, or have what they consider 'better things' to think about" (330). Needless to say, I find this consensus peculiarly gratifying; cf. Paul Lauter, "The Literatures of America—A Comparative Discipline" *Canons and Contexts.*, 48–96.

5. See "Mr. Eliot Meet Miss Lowell and, ah, Mr. Brown." William Savage's essay makes a similar point.

6. See, in particular, William H. Epstein.

7. The quotation and discussion of fostering competition is in one of the better-known articles during the 1960s, Jules Henry, "Golden Rule Days: American Schoolrooms," *Culture Against Man*, 293–5. I cannot refrain from adding here, as an instance of the outrage with which many sixties activists greeted the discovery of the underlying functions of educational institutions, a passage of which I was coauthor in 1969 or 1970. We were arguing that schools had not "failed," as was commonly asserted, but were all too successful:

> If schools have been "successful," the task of educational reformers is far different from their conceptions. For remedying the system does not involve the simple tonics of money or the reeducation of teachers that turns them into "facilitator" or "change agent." It involves, rather, changing the fundamental tasks which this society demands of its schools. So long as these remain the separation of people and the perpetuation of privilege, the cultivation of social stupidity, the inculcation of conformity and competitiveness, and the dissociation of feelings and ideas from the performance of technical functions, tinkering will not do. The educational system is, finally, a reflection of the values of the society itself. And a society devoted to war and profit will always create schools equally dedicated to those goals. (Lauter and Howe 248)

8. See *Radical Teacher* #40 (1991), which reprints the Freedom School curriculum and a number of essays about them; and Paul Lauter and Florence Howe, "Freedom Summer—Mississippi, 1964," *The Conspiracy of the Young*, 27–53.

9. See, for example, the often reprinted pamphlet by "Joreen" [Jo Freeman], "The Tyranny of Structurelessness."

10. Or in a work of criticism. To begin an account of nineteenth-century American letters with Emerson, as F. O. Matthiessen does in *American Renaissance* (1941), produces quite different results from those fashioned by starting with Nat Turner's "Confession" (as transcribed by Thomas Grey), as Eric Sundquist does in *To Wake the Nations* (1993). The same practical argument can be made about syllabi with respect not only to texts but process.

WORKS CITED

Banta, Martha. "Why Use Anthologies? or One Small Candle Alight in a Naughty World." *American Literature* 65 (1993): 30–34.

Beach, Richard. *A Teacher's Guide to Reader-Response Theories.* Urbana: NCTE, 1993.

———— and James Marshall. *Teaching Literature in the Secondary School.* San Diego: Harcourt, 1990.

Culley, Margo and Catharine Portuges, eds. *Gendered Subjects: The Dynamics of Feminist Teaching.* London: Routledge, 1985.

Epstein, William H. "Counter-Intelligence: Cold-War Criticism and Eighteenth-Century Studies." *ELH* 57 (1990): 63–99.

Gabriel, Susan and Isaiah Smithson, eds. *Gender in the Classroom: Power and Pedagogy.* Urbana: U of Illinois P, 1990.

Henry, Jules. *Culture Against Man.* NY: Random House, 1963.

Joreen [Jo Freeman]. "The Tyranny of Structurelessness." Pamphlet.

Lauter, Paul. *Canons and Contexts.* NY: Oxford UP, 1991.

————. "Mr. Eliot Meet Miss Lowell and, ah, Mr. Brown." *Critical Theory: Curriculum, Pedagogy, Politics.* Ed. James Slevin and Arthur Young. Urbana: NCTE, 1994.

———— and Florence Howe. *The Conspiracy of the Young.* NY and Cleveland: World, 1970.

Matthiessen, F. O. *American Renaissance.* NY: Oxford UP, 1941.

Nelson, Cary, ed. *Theory in the Classroom.* Urbana: U of Illinois P, 1986.

Slavin, Robert E. *Cooperative Learning: Theory, Research, and Practice.* Englewood Cliffs, NJ: Prentice-Hall, 1990.

Slevin, James and Arthur Young, eds. *Critical Theory: Curriculum, Pedagogy, Politics.* Urbana: NCTE, 1994.

Sundquist, Eric. *To Wake the Nations.* Cambridge: Harvard UP, 1993.

Contributors

John Alberti received his Ph.D. in American Literature from the University of California, Los Angeles. He is an assistant professor at Northern Kentucky University, where he teaches American literature, literary theory, and writing. In addition to editing this collection, he has published on Melville, James, and the intersection of social class and pedagogy. He is currently working on issues related to multicultural pedagogy, particularly in relation to regional, working-class universities.

Cornel Bonca is assistant professor of English and comparative literature at California State University, Fullerton. His essays and reviews have appeared in *Review of Contemporary Fiction*, *Saul Bellow Review*, *American Book Review*, and elsewhere.

Anne L. Bower teaches literature (American, African-American, fiction) and writing courses at Ohio State University—Marion. Her scholarship engages the pedagogical challenges of responding adequately to changing definitions of literature, changing student populations, and changing teaching contexts—academic, historical, political, etc. She also enjoys exploring "nonliterary" texts and is currently editing an essay collection about the discourse of community (or fund-raising) cookbooks.

Melba Joyce Boyd is a poet and an associate professor in the department of Africana studies at Wayne State University. She has published four books of poetry, including *Song for Maya* and *The Inventory of Black Roses*, and a bio-critical study, *Discarded Legacy: Politics and Poetics in the Life of Frances E.W. Harper (1825–1911)* (Wayne State UP, 1994). She has published numerous essays on poetry and poets and is currently completing a biography and a documentary on Dudley Randall, the founder of Broadside Press.

Peter Caccavari recently received his Ph.D. from Rutgers University and is currently an independent scholar. His dissertation, "Reconstructions of Race and Culture in America: Violence and Knowledge in Works by Albion Tourgée, Charles Chesnutt, and Thomas Dixon, Jr.," looks at education and other forms of knowledge production in light of race relations during the last half of the nineteenth century in the United States. He is now at work on a study connecting Populism and the African-American women's club movement as competing and complementary grass-roots efforts at mass education in an age of social and political reform.

Renny Christopher comes from a family that has worked in blue-collar trades since the immigrant generations in the late nineteenth century. She is the first in her family to go to college, ultimately earning a Ph.D. in American literature from the University of California, Santa Cruz. She has taught at University of California, Santa Cruz, Cabrillo Community College, and San Jose State University. Her book *The Viet Nam War/The American War* is forthcoming from the University of Massachusetts Press.

Martha J. Cutter received her Ph.D. in English and American literature from Brown University, where she first developed her "canon, anticanon" approach to the American literature survey. She has taught at Swarthmore College, the University of Connecticut, and the University of Oregon and is currently an assistant professor of English at Kent State University.

Sue Danielson is an assistant professor at Portland State University whose research focuses on nineteenth-century American literature with particular attention to the intersection of social and literary movements during the antebellum period.

Bruce A. Goebel is an assistant professor of English education at Montana State University. He is currently coediting a collection of essays titled "Teaching the New Canon: Students, Teachers, and Texts in the Cross-Cultural Classroom" and is conducting research on censorship in higher education.

Jeanne Holland is assistant professor of English at the University of Wyoming where she teaches in the American studies and women's studies programs. She has published on captivity narratives, early American women's poetry, Emily Dickinson, and Gertrude Stein. Currently she is completing a book on Emily Dickinson's late manuscripts.

Gregory S. Jay is professor of English and comparative literature at the University of Wisconsin—Milwaukee. He is the author of *America the Scrivener: Deconstruction and the Subject of Literary History* and with Gerald Graff is currently working on a book tentatively entitled "Teaching as a Democratic Activity."

Paul Lauter is Allan K. and Gwendolyn Miles Smith professor of literature at Trinity College. He is the general editor of *The Heath Anthology of American Literature* and is currently serving as president of the American Studies Association. His books include *Canon and Contexts* and *Reconstructing American Literature*. He is now at work writing about the rise and fall of academic cultural authority.

Sandra Mano earned her doctorate in rhetoric, language and literature at the University of Southern California. She is currently lecturer and coordinator of TA training at University of California, Los Angeles. A coeditor of *American Mosaic: Multicultural Reading in Context*, she has also written extensively on multiethnic pedagogy.

Irene Moser, throughout her graduate study of folklore, myth, and literature, has remained interested in the imaginative expressive behavior of the Native peoples of the Southeastern United States. She has taught writing and literature at Western Carolina University at Cullowhee and at Cherokee, where she also studied the Cherokee language. She now teaches American literature and interdisciplinary studies at the College of West Virginia in Beckley. Her current research focuses on the works of contemporary writers with Native American heritages.

Barbara Roche Rico earned her bachelors degree and doctorate at Yale University. She has taught literature and writing at Stanford University, University of California, Los Angeles, and Loyola Marymount University, where she is currently associate professor and director of freshman English. In addition to coediting *American Mosaic: Multicultural Reading in*

Context, she has written on issues related to marginality in both Renaissance and modern texts.

William J. Savage, Jr. recently completed his Ph.D. at Northwestern University under the direction of Gerald Graff.

Anne Stavney is a Ph.D. candidate at the University of Washington. She is finishing a dissertation on Harlem as a geographical and discursive site of the black and white literary imagination. She has published on American drama and on constructions of race in American literature. Her essay here is part of a larger project focusing on the pedagogical implications of canon revision in American literature.

Michele Lise Tarter is a visiting assistant professor at the University of Puget Sound, where she teaches colonial and nineteenth-century American literature. She has published an article on Quaker women's prophesyings, titled "Nursing the New Wor(l)d," in *Women and Language* and has an essay on early American women's prophesyings forthcoming in *The Oxford Companion to Women's Writing in the United States.* She is currently working on a book on colonial American Quaker women's autobiographies.

Jane Tompkins is professor of English at Duke University. She has written on reader-response criticism, nineteenth-century American fiction, popular Western novels and movies, and, most recently, the dynamics of classroom teaching. She is currently writing a book on her life as a student and a teacher called "A Life in School."

Index